THE
OF
DOG

THE BOOK OF
DOG

A SATIRE

D.J. MOLLES

Copyright © 2023 by D.J. Molles Books LLC

All rights reserved.

No part of this publication may be reproduced, distributed, or transmitted in any form or by any means, including photocopying, recording, or other electronic or mechanical methods, without the prior written permission of the publisher, except as permitted by U.S. copyright law.

For permission requests, contact djmollesbooks@gmail.com.

The story, all names, characters, and incidents portrayed in this production are fictitious. No identification with actual persons (living or deceased), places, buildings, and products is intended or should be inferred.

Book Cover by Tara Molles using AI Generated Imagery

ASIN: B0CJD74CHD

ISBN: 9798866160235

First edition 2023

Author's Note

THIS IS NOT A spiritual treatise. It is not a parable. I did not write this to convince anyone of anything. The metaphysical aspects of it are not even beliefs that I hold...mostly. This is simply an idea that popped into my head, almost fully formed, one day as I was drinking beer and watching the sun set over my favorite beach. One year later, back on that same beach, I would finish writing it all down. My only wish is to make you laugh, lighten your heart, and maybe, if my loftiest goal can be obtained, inspire a sense of hope for the future.

So much of what I write is gritty and post-apocalyptic. But, as much as I love to tell those tales of grim futures and hard men and women fighting an endless struggle against the darkness...well, sometimes I like to let my mind go off in a completely different direction. Call it a palate cleanser. So, if you're willing to listen, then I am willing to tell you a lovely, silly daydream I had while on a beach, thinking about the dogs and cats that have been my companions, where we're all going, and how everything *might* just work out in the end. —D.J. Molles

1

Mash

My name is Mash, and I am a Very Good Dog. That's what Dad says anyway.

Of course, there was the time I chewed the Special Poofs.

Do you know about the Special Poofs? So, they look just like the Toy Poofs that I'm allowed to chew, but apparently, they're totally different. It took me a while to figure out, but I realized that the Toy Poofs have faces on them and look like small animals, and the Special Poofs are just formless blobs.

Also, the Special Poofs are always on the Cloud Throne.

That's really how I figured out that they were special and sacred. Only special things and special peoples get to sit on the Cloud Throne. Sometimes Dad will have other peoples over, and I won't be sure how special they are until Dad lets them sit on the Cloud Throne.

At first, I wasn't allowed on the Cloud Throne, I guess because I wasn't special yet. But I was determined to be special, and I kept trying to prove it by very slowly, and very stealthily, creeping up onto the throne while Dad was distracted. At first, he would always push me off and say "No," but then eventually, he must have decided I'd become special because he let me stay.

So, anyways, there was the time that I chewed the Special Poofs, but I figured that out and I don't make that mistake anymore. And then there was the time I ate the Sacred Brown Stuff.

Don't EVER eat the Sacred Brown Stuff. It is for special peoples ONLY.

I still remember the terror of Dad's wrath, and his unquenchable, vengeful fury. First, he called the Needle Man, who is a LIAR with a FALSE FACE, who talks all sweet, but then sticks you and pokes you and slips things up your butt. Now, I don't know whether Dad was telling the Needle Man to give me more needles and butt-probes next time, or whether the Needle Man was telling Dad how to fully punish me for my evil deeds, but the next thing I knew, Dad held me down and forced bubbly stuff down my throat that made me puke for days.

Or maybe it was just a few minutes. Dogs aren't very good with time.

And you know what was really weird? Even after I gave all the Sacred Brown Stuff back, Dad didn't want it anymore. The Sacred Brown Stuff had become disgusting to him, simply because I'd eaten it first. It was no longer sacred. I had defiled it.

So, yes, I've made mistakes. And, yes, I've incurred Dad's wrath. But even after all of that, Dad still says I'm a Very Good Dog, so I must be, because Dad knows many mysteries that we cannot comprehend.

Anyways. Like I was saying, my name is Mash, and I am a Very Good Dog. And I have a pack. It is the best pack in the whole world, and nothing can ever come between us.

First, there's Banger. We met at the Place of Judgment, where the peoples come and decide whether or not you're worthy of their pack. You only get so many chances to prove that you're worthy. No one knows how many chances you get. Some dogs get lots of chances. Others only get a few. And when you don't have any more chances left, then you just...disappear. You go for a walk, and you never come back.

At first, it can be stressful trying to figure out if this is going to be a Fun Walk, or a Forever Walk, but eventually you learn to watch the peoples' faces. See, if you love the peoples—as all Good Dogs do—then you pay attention to their faces, and you realize that they can talk without noise, just like we animals do. Peoples' can actually tell you what they're thinking with their eyes.

When it's a Fun Walk, their eyes are sometimes happy, sometimes bored. But if it's a Forever Walk, they're always serious or sad. That is how you know you don't have any more chances.

Now, Banger had had a pack before she came to the Place of Judgment. But I don't think they were a very nice pack, because she has scars on her back, and she doesn't like to talk about how she got them. I don't know how she went from having a pack, to being in the Place of Judgment, because she never told me.

I don't remember anything before the Place of Judgment, because I was just a pup. Banger told me that my mother had me when she was in the Place of Judgment, so I'd been there my whole life. Some of the nicer dogs told me she'd been found worthy after she'd had me, and been taken into a pack. But the grumpy old hound in the cage across from mine told me that she'd taken her Forever Walk.

Banger told me something a little different, though. She told me that Mother HAD taken her Forever Walk, but that she'd chosen to do that so that she could give all her extra unused chances to me. And Banger said I was going to need them, because I had a dumb eye.

I didn't believe her at first, because, what the heck is a dumb eye? I still don't know. And I thought my eyes were just fine. I'd never known anything different. If anything, I'd only ever noticed that my brothers and sisters seemed like they could see what was happening on the left side of their nose, and I couldn't.

But Banger turned out to be right: I needed all of those extra chances that Mother gave me. One by one, all my other brothers and sisters were found worthy and taken to their new packs. But never me. No matter how much I wagged my tail. No matter whether I barked or sat silent. No matter how attentively I studied their faces.

And then it was just me left in the cage, and I was cold and alone, so I would lay against the cage, and Banger, who was in the cage next to me, even as ornery and anti-social as she was, would lay down on her side and keep me warm. When the peoples noticed, they let me stay with Banger, even though she grumbled and growled about it at first.

It was just me and her for a very long time. Five years, I think. Or maybe, like, a few days or something. I only know that when I first curled up next to Banger our first night together, I could lay between her front and hind legs with room to stretch out. And then, sometime later, I'd grown so that my head laid over her front legs and my tail across her hind legs.

Just me and her. The one with the scar on her back, and the one with the dumb eye.

The more days passed, the more I began to worry that my chances were running out. Every day I would watch the peoples' faces to see if they were taking me on a Fun Walk, or a Forever Walk. And I remember one night Banger told me, in that impatient, old dog way of hers: "You've got nothing to worry about. Your mother was a Very Good Dog, so she had a LOT of chances, and she gave them all to you. So don't worry. Someone will find you worthy of a pack."

"What about you?" I asked her. "How many more chances do you have? Are you going to be found worthy? Were you a Very Good Dog too?"

I remember she looked at me, kind of sad, but also like she was trying to look playful at the same time. "I don't know if I was a Good Dog or not," she sighed. "I tried very hard. But no matter what I did, the master was always very angry with me." She trailed off like she'd lost her train of thought, and then seemed to twitch and jerk around, and started to lick at the scars on her back. She only licked them maybe twice before she seemed to catch herself, almost like she'd given away some sort of secret. And that's how I know that her old pack had given her those scars.

"I don't know," she'd finally continued. "But I must not have been a Good Dog. So, I don't know how many chances I'll get."

"Are you worried that you won't have very many more?" I whimpered, unable to think about what my life would be like all alone in a cage if she was taken away for her Forever Walk.

"No, no," she gruffed. "I'm not worried."

But I could tell that she was. So, I lay there and thought about it for a while, and then I came up with a really great idea.

"What if I gave you some of my chances?" I suggested, excited to have come up with a solution to something, because that seemed like something a Good Dog would do—a dog that was worthy of a pack.

"No," she grumbled, dismissive of my idea, which kind of hurt my feelings. "You can't give me your chances."

I was confused. "Why not? Mother gave her chances to me—you told me that yourself. And you said I had plenty of chances, right? So why can't I give some of them to you?"

"You can't give me your chances!" she snarled, so sudden that I yipped and scooted away from her. She drew back, wagging her tail once to tell me that she hadn't meant to scare me so bad, and then she turned away, and I guess the conversation was done, because she went to sleep. Or at least pretended to.

I didn't sleep though. I couldn't. I was too worried about her and how many chances she had left. So, I thought and I thought, and I stayed awake for thirty million hours, or maybe one, and eventually, I realized I'd never agreed to accept my mother's chances, but she'd managed to give them to me anyways. And so I figured, maybe I could give my friend some of my chances even if she didn't want them. And if she didn't know that I'd given them to her, then she wouldn't be mad at me.

I didn't really know how Mother had done it, so I just thought about it really hard. I pictured having a bunch of chances, like they were each a bit of kibble, and then I made two equal piles, and gave Banger half.

I'm still not sure if it worked, but I think that it did, because it wasn't long after that night that Dad came for us. At the time, the peoples had been calling me Chico, and her Roxanne, but when Dad found us to be worthy of his pack, he gave us new names, and he called her Banger and me Mash.

Now, these are very special names. They are special, not only because it is peoples food, but because it is Dad's FAVORITE food—a food so special, and so sacred, that I've only seen Dad eat it once.

It was sometime after he'd taken us to be a part of his pack, and he'd decided one night to hold the First and Only Bangers and Mash Celebratory Feast, in honor of us. Now, bangers and mash, the Most Sacred of Sacred Foods, is made up of the Root Paste of Mystery and the Meat Turds of Ecstasy. And all of this is covered in The Gravy of Transcendence.

It's totally okay that Dad named me after the Root Paste, even though the Meat Turds are way better. Banger deserved it. And also, she kind of looks like a Meat Turd, if you were to stick some toothpicks in it for her legs. She's got this plump, stumpy body, and these tiny legs that don't look like they should be able to hold her up.

I had never felt so embraced and worthy as I did when Dad allowed us both to eat from his plate and share in the sacrament of his Most Sacred Food. With the very first bite, I was transported to another plane of existence. It was like the real me came out of my hide, and I was hovering over myself, watching myself eat, and I was a glowing ball of light, and so was Banger, and so was Dad, and I realized that there wasn't any separation between us, and existence was all just one, big, warm, puppy pile.

If I am the Root Paste, and Banger is the Meat Turds, then I like to believe that Dad is the Gravy of Transcendence, smothering us in warm, delicious love.

Of course, there is another ingredient to the Most Sacred Food, just as there is another member of the pack. I gather that these strange little disruptions in an otherwise perfect food are called "Sweetpeas," because that is what Dad named the last member of our pack. And while Sweetpea is neither sweet, nor is he round or green, he IS just like his namesake in that I can't decide whether or not I like him being there.

Whoo-boy. How can I say this without sounding mean? You see, there's bangers and mash, each delicious in their own way, bound together and united by the Gravy of Transcendence that is Dad's love. And then there's the sweetpeas, rolling around, being uncooperative, not really adding anything to the dish, and generally just doing their own thing.

Okay, I'll just come out and say it: he's a cat.

Don't get me wrong! I'm determined to one day make Sweetpea my friend, because everyone should be my friend. He's fluffy, he's witty, and his butt-hole smells absolutely hilarious. But every time

I try to play with him, he hisses and spits and runs away, and sometimes gets me in trouble with Dad over it.

What am I supposed to do with that?

I mean, he shows up out of nowhere, half-starved and beat up, and Dad takes him in and feeds him and loves him. And how does Sweetpea show his appreciation? By going absolutely bananas every night at midnight. Sometimes he breaks things—Sacred Things, even! And when Dad unleashes his wrath by speaking in his Thunder Voice, Sweetpea doesn't even try to repent. You know what he does? He licks his balls. Just sits there, completely ignoring Dad, and licks his balls.

I thought for sure we were going to have to eat him after that. But then you know what Dad did? He built him a little door in the big door so that he can GO OUTSIDE WHENEVER HE WANTS!

I don't get to go outside whenever I want! I've tried to squeeze through the little door, but it's too small. And, when Sweetpea goes outside, he gets to go wherever he wants. He doesn't have to wear a leash or stay inside the Invisible Boundary around our yard. He just wanders about, wherever he pleases, doing who-knows-what.

And I'll tell you something else—he is not nice to small animals. Always with the torture and the murder. One minute he's rubbing up against you and purring like he's the nicest member of the pack, and then, all the sudden, he just turns into a completely different animal. His eyes get this crazy look about them, and really, once he gets like that, you just can't reason with him. The only cure for it is, apparently, bloodshed. He'll skulk off and then come back sometime later with some poor, half-dead mouse in his jaws.

It's a grisly thing to watch.

"You're boring me," he'll suddenly tell the mouse, while he sits up and looks off as though he's distracted. "I thought we were going to be friends."

"Please!" the mouse will say. "I have a family to feed!"

"A family?" Sweetpea will scoff. "Ugh. So trite. So...banal. I really expected more from you." Then he'll sigh, long-sufferingly. "Very well. If you're going to be boring, then maybe you should just leave."

Quavering, the little mouse will ask, "Really? I can...I can just go?"

And then Sweetpea will pretend not to have heard and begin cleaning his claws.

And as soon as the poor mouse tries to make a break for it, Sweetpea pounces on it, screaming, "Gotcha, bitch! You ain't goin' nowhere!"

I mean, I'm not perfect by any stretch. There was the Rabbit Incident, after all, but I'd really prefer not to talk about that. Anyways, like I said, one day I'd really like to be friends with Sweetpea. But he really doesn't make it easy.

So, that's my pack, and even though some of us can get a little weird sometimes—or...uh...bloodthirsty—Dad has decided we're all worthy and that we're all special, because he lets all three of us onto the Cloud Throne with him and smothers us all in love.

This is my pack, and nothing can ever come between us.

2

Mash

Sun. Trees. Grass. Gray ball.

I'm running like the wind. My breath roars through my throat. My tongue hangs out the side of my mouth and slaps me in the face and scatters streamers of my own slobber across my eyes and ears. But I don't care—DO YOU SEE HOW FAST I AM?

The gray ball bounces. I leap. Twisting. Writhing in midair. Oops. I miss the catch. I come down again and manage to pin the sneaky little gray ball to the ground, where I then appropriately savage it to death.

But not really. Because I'm not like Sweetpea. Sure, I like to PRETEND to kill things, but I don't actually do it. Usually. Mostly. All except that one time.

Triumphantly squeezing my quarry in my jaws, I trot gallantly back across the grass towards Our House.

Now, let me tell you a little bit about Our House. First off, it's the best house in the whole world. It's got Cloud Thrones, and food, and toys, and food. There is a place in our house where, almost every single night, Dad begins to make Sacred Food. Smoke billows, and steam rises. The scent of it draws me and Banger from wherever we are to come and stand in awe, and humbly wait to be blessed with a morsel.

Second, our house has a great big place to run and chase balls and play-fight with Banger, and, maybe, if Dad isn't looking, see if I can't scare Sweetpea into playing with me. I mean, that is how it's done, right? When you want to play, you assume the play position, then you lunge for them, and if they still don't play, sometimes you can smush their face with your paw. Everyone knows that. Except Sweetpea, apparently. Maybe no one ever taught him how to play.

Anyways, there's a big grass yard where I can run, but only to the Invisible Boundary. Which is a little bit of a shame, because just on the other side of the Invisible Boundary there are trees—trees as far as the eye can see. And so many smells. Mysterious smells! Smells that call to me, saying "Mash, don't you want to come find out what I am?"

And I do. I do so badly. But there is no crossing the Invisible Border. You can try, but you will endure unending torment of the body and soul if you do. I've seen other dogs break free of their Invisible Boundaries before, and after that, they're just never quite right in the head.

Which brings me to Point Number Three on Why Our House Is The Best In The Whole World. You see, our house is surrounded by other houses. Not so close that I can sniff butts with the neighbor, but close enough that I can see them, and we can bark at each other, even if we can't really talk. See, you have to be close to talk without noise like we animals do. The closer you are, the clearer the other animal's thoughts will be. At the distance between me and the neighbors, all you can make out is "Hey! Hey, you!" or, in the case of the big black dog two houses down who has an anger issue, "Hey, you! You lookin' at me?! I will tear you limb from limb!"

I love other dogs. But some of them, like the angry black dog, just can't get along with others. Unfortunately, Banger is like that too. Oh, she doesn't shout at other dogs usually. She even seems happy to see them...from a distance. But the second it comes time for the official greeting of the day (noses in butts), the teeth come out and she becomes a plump little sausage of rage. I don't know if she would actually hurt the other dogs, because Dad won't let her hang out with them anymore.

I asked her one time about it. "Banger, why do you hate other dogs?"

She was contentedly licking her paws at the time, and didn't even look up. "I don't hate other dogs," she said, frankly. "I just don't trust them."

"Why not? Other dogs are Good Dogs too. I've made lots of friends with the other dogs. They're really fun. You should try to make some friends."

"I don't need any more friends," she grumbled. "I have you and Dad. And Sweetpea, too, I guess." Finally, she looked at me. "I finally have something good, Mash. I finally have a pack that loves me, and I've become a Very Good Dog. Other dogs will ruin it."

I was rather confused how being friends with other dogs could possibly have any effect on our pack, but she'd gone back to licking her paws and I could tell that if I kept asking she was going to get nippy. So I let it be.

So, I like other dogs, but Banger doesn't, which is a bummer, because I can't have friends over for play dates. I have to go to THEIR house, or meet them at The Park. But that's okay, I guess. At least I still get to play with them.

Now, trotting back towards Our House with the gray ball, seasoned with plenty of grass and dirt, I see Dad sitting on the back porch, with Banger lounging at his side, because she's just not a big fetcher.

I call him Dad, but I know he's not really my dad-dad. I don't know who my dad-dad was, but I think that's pretty common—not many of my friends know who their dad-dad was either. And obviously, Dad can't be my dad-dad because he's a peoples and peoples don't have litters of puppies, they have strange larva, one at a time, and it takes these larva a long time to be able to do anything besides make noise.

Dad has never had any larva that I know of. I think he kind of looks at me and Banger and Sweetpea as being his larva, and that's just fine by me.

When I climb the steps to the porch where Dad is sitting on his Outside Throne, I notice that he seems...off.

Again, it's in the eyes. His eyes aren't sad—they actually look very happy. But they're staring off into the trees, like he's seeing something else out there besides sticks and leaves. He has this faint, distracted smile on his face.

It isn't the first time I've seen him like this. We've been a part of Dad's pack for a long time now. I'd love to be more specific, but you know how bad I am with time. I think it must have been two years, because I've grown bigger than Banger now, and it had gotten cold outside, and then hot again, and then cold again, and now it was the In-Betweeny-Time where it wasn't all the way cold, and not all the way hot yet either, which is always the best time.

Anyways, when me and Banger had first been found worthy and taken to live at Our House, I don't remember him ever being like he is now. The first time I noticed it, I thought it was weird—his energy was totally different. Not bad, just...different. But I didn't give it much thought and just continued on with my awesome daily life.

But recently it's been happening more and more. Now it's almost every day, and it seems to last a lot longer than before. I don't want you to think that this is a bad thing, because it's not. He's still the Best Dad In The Whole World, and he still does all the normal peoples things, and he feeds us, and he smothers us with love—in fact, when he's like this, I think he smothers us even more than usual.

But it is different. His energy is changing. Becoming calmer. Gentler. More joyful. Less worried. More content. He speaks so softly to us when he's like this, and sometimes, when I get a little crazy and I think he's going to speak in his Thunder Voice, he'll only look at me and smile, as though the things that bothered him before don't really matter anymore. If anything, he'll just run his warm hands along my flank, pat my rump, and say, "Easy, Mash. Easy."

Amongst the pack, we've come to refer to this as The Change. I don't think The Change is a bad thing at all—soft words, gentle stokes, and lots of treats; what's not to love? Sweetpea seems rather neutral on the topic of The Change. But Banger...well, she worries.

I can tell that she's already noticed The Change in Dad today, and, as is her way of expressing worry for him, she is leaning against his leg and watching him carefully.

"Hey," I say, pushing my grass covered snout and the gray ball into her face, trying to distract her from her worries. "You wanna get in on this?"

She completely ignores me, so I let the ball roll out of my mouth onto her head, trailing slobber across her muzzle. Even that garners no reaction. She just lets the ball fall off her head and go rolling away. I almost chase it, but manage to restrain myself.

"He's been like this all day," she murmurs.

"I dunno," I try to encourage her. "He seemed normal at Morning Food Time. Besides, what are you so worked up about? He gives us treats, gives us love, smiles at us, and barely ever uses his Thunder Voice anymore. What's so bad about that?"

She turns her gaze on me and gives me a look like I couldn't be dumber. "Oh, that's all fine and dandy. But have you noticed his smell?"

"His smell?" I quirk my head up at Dad. He's still staring off into the trees, smiling. Funny, she'd never mentioned this before, but now that she brought my attention to it... "He does smell a little faint, doesn't he?"

"Go ahead," Banger says. "Get a good whiff."

I venture my snout a bit closer to Dad's butt and crotch region, very cautious at first, because peoples don't usually care to pass the greeting of the day. But, as is the new normal for Dad since The Change had started, he doesn't give much reaction to me, so I go ahead and dive in for a full-lung inhale.

"Whoa," Dad says, squirming away from me a bit, but he doesn't look as bothered as he normally would. "Easy, Mash."

"Yeah, okay, Dad," I say, giving him a wag to cover my concern. I always make a habit of talking to the peoples, even though they can't hear animal-speak. I figure, maybe one day, if I do it enough, they'll learn. And I think it works. Sometimes it almost seems like Dad gets the gist of what I'm trying to communicate, though maybe he misses some of the finer points.

I back away from Dad, and my tail goes still. "You're right," I whisper to Banger. "He doesn't smell right."

Now, peoples have four places on their bodies where you can really get a good feel for what's going on with them. You can get a good read off of the spot where their arms meet their chests, provided they haven't recently gooped it up with the Peoples-Smell Blocker, which they do because it's very important to peoples that other peoples never know when they're stressed out, or when they ate onions the night before. Then there's the neck, which isn't quite as strong, and you have to get a few licks of it to really get a good read, and they'll usually tolerate that better than the greeting of the day, as long as you wag your tail and pretend that you're playing. And there's their mouth, which can let you know what they've been eating, which is super important in its own right.

But the best place to get the most information on how the peoples are doing is their butt-crotch region, just like animals. Because, even though they don't like to admit it, peoples are animals too. And really, even though they don't prefer the greeting of the day, it is important for all Very Good Dogs to monitor the wellbeing of all the members of the pack. After all, healthy individuals make a healthy pack.

Dad's butt-crotch region, however, has yielded almost nothing.

"It's too faint," Banger worries, gazing up at Dad again. "It's been getting fainter and fainter. And you know what else?"

"What?" I ask, feeling the beginnings of anxiety creep into my hide, making me want to yawn and shake it away.

Banger looks at me very seriously, then glances about, as though worried some other dog might hear her. "They've ALL been getting fainter."

"All?" She's spooking me out now. "Who's all?"

"The peoples," she hisses at me. "All of the peoples have been smelling fainter and fainter. You haven't noticed?"

To be honest, I hadn't noticed, but I don't want to admit it in front of Banger. The strength of one's nose is a great source of pride amongst dogs.

"No, yeah, no," I scoff. "Of course I noticed. I just...Ugh, what's the big deal? So they're being even more manic than usual about the cleanliness of their butt-crotch region. It doesn't mean anything bad is happening."

"They're not just cleaning it more," Banger says, snuffling as she does when she gets irritated with me. "It's like their smell is...going away."

"Are you sure it's not YOUR sense of smell?"

Her ears flatten and her lips quiver. "What did you just say to me?"

"What?" I desperately search for a distraction. "Nothing. I didn't say anything. Hey! Look at that cool bird!" There isn't actually a bird, and I immediately feel guilty for lying.

Whether or not Banger fell for the bird ruse, she seems to let me off the hook. Or maybe her worries for the peoples are simply stronger than her offense. "It's The Change," she says, quietly, glancing back up at Dad. "Something's happening to the peoples, Mash. And I'm not sure if they know about it."

"You know what we need?" I say suddenly, straightening to my full height and looking super noble and, I might add, well-bred. "Pack Conference!"

Banger growls. "No, Mash, not again..."

But I'm already raising my noble head and issuing the Gathering Howl: "Pack members, assem-BAAAALLLLLLL!"

Dad twists to give me a look of half-confused amusement. "Oh, really?"

"Yes, Dad," I answer in earnest. "We need to assemble the pack members to discuss how we're going to save you from your scentless crotch."

Grumbling, Banger hauls her big, rotund body up onto her skinny little legs. "We don't need Sweetpea's input on this. He doesn't even care."

"Well, that depends," a sultry voice seems to come out of nowhere.

I gasp and look around, but I can't see him. "Sweetpea?" My voice quavers. "Where are you? Are you a ghost?"

A sleek, tan body slithers out from under the porch, ears swiveled back and golden eyes half-lidded with irritation. "I'm right here, Crumb-Eater."

I wilt with relief as Sweetpea glides up onto the porch. "Oh, thank goodness you're alive!"

"Please," Sweetpea sneers. "I'll outlive both of you by a decade."

"You will? How long is a decade?"

"Longer than you'll live," Sweetpea spits. "Hopefully."

"Well, now you're just being hurtful. That's not what Good Cats do."

"Good Cats do whatever the fuck they want," Sweetpea remarks, taking a position just far enough away from us that we can't quite reach him with our mouths. He coils his tail languidly around his feet and gives his shoulders a brief grooming. "That's why the peoples keep us around, you know. So they can remember what it's like to be free."

"Uh-uh. That's not true. Peoples are free."

"Are they?"

"Aren't they?" I glance towards Banger, hoping for some support, but she's just blinking lazily into the sun, waiting for me and Sweetpea to be done.

"Let me ask you this, Crumb-Eater." Sweetpea fixes me with his eerie, slit-pupiled stare. "You ever seen a peoples run around naked? Grab a mate by the back of her neck and rut in the moonlight? Caterwaul at the stars?" He's getting intense, leaning into me now, eyes getting wider, kind of like how they get when he goes bananas. "You ever seen a peoples chase an animal through the woods and sink their fangs into it until the blood stops pulsing through their teeth? Huh? HUH? You ever seen THAT?"

"Why does it always have to be about killing with you?" I ask, shocked by his outburst, and especially at the disturbing mental image of Dad with the moonlight on his bare rump, and a dead squirrel in his mouth.

Sweetpea just chuckles and leans away from me, like he's made his point. "And THAT is why you're a Crumb-Eater."

I pull my ears back. "You're being extremely speciesist, Sweetpea. You know I don't like it when you use speciesist slurs."

"Well, maybe you should learn to kill for yourself instead of always relying on the peoples to give you kibble. That makes you slave to them. A Crumb-Eater and a Kibble-Slave."

I can feel my hackles rising along the back of my neck. "You ever think that maybe I just CHOOSE not to kill other animals because I'm nice?"

"Yes, yes," Sweetpea purrs. "You are very nice." He rises and oozes his lithe body over to me. I'm not really sure what's going on. Is he trying to play with me? Cuddle with me? Whatever he's doing, it's really weird on the tail of that conversation, so I just lay there, kind of frozen, trying to suss out what's happening as he rubs his cheek against mine and curls his tail around my face.

Then he whispers, right into my ear: "But what about the Rabbit Incident?"

"I DON'T WANNA TALK ABOUT THE RABBIT INCIDENT!" I explode, snarling and barking, and Sweetpea shoots off the ground, twirling in midair, claws out, tail fluffed full, and then bolts behind Dad's legs, hissing and spitting and baring his fangs at me.

"Whoa!" Dad jolts upright, snatching Sweetpea up and cradling him in his lap. "Mash! Be easy!"

"He started it!" I yammer. "He called me a Crumb-Eater and a Kibble Slave and—and—"

Sweetpea juts his head out from between Dad's protective arms. "A BUNNY SLAYER?!"

"Alright, that's enough," Dad proclaims, not quite in his Thunder Voice, but hinting at it enough that I immediately back down, frustrated by the injustice. Dad strokes at Sweetpea's ruff, and puts his hand up in the air in a gesture that I know means he is reestablishing order. "Everyone just calm down, okay? Let's all take a deep breath and try not to maul each other."

"He started it," I mumble again, head hanging.

"Are you two done?" Banger asks, tiredly.

"I dunno," Sweetpea grumbles. "Are we?"

"You're done," Banger decides.

"Fine then," Sweetpea snaps.

"Fine!" I snap back.

"Okay!"

"Alright!"

"Good!"

"Great!"

"Pff."

"Ksssh."

"Tsss."

We trail off, still staring at each other.

Sweetpea breaks first—cats aren't good with eye contact—but manages to pass it off like he only wanted to continue grooming his chest. "Anyways," he says. "I heard that a pack conference was called for. Not that I believe in such collective-minded nonsense. But I try to be generous with my time and wisdom towards those that so desperately need it. So here I am."

"We have a problem," Banger begins.

"Clearly," Sweetpea quips, as though he couldn't care at all about the meeting, but we all know that he actually loves the meetings, no matter how much he tries to act like he doesn't.

Banger lets out a low growl, glancing up at Dad to see if he'll react, but he doesn't. He's gone right back to smiling happily into the distance. "Look at Dad."

Sweetpea glances about, everywhere but at Dad. "Who?"

Banger glares at him. "The peoples whose lap you're sitting on."

Sweetpea already knew that, but he makes a big show of just realizing who "Dad" is. "Oh, him?" He smirks condescendingly down at me and Banger. "You mean the Feeder?"

"I'm not going to do this with you again. I'll call him Dad, and you know who I'm talking about."

Sweetpea swivels his head and stares at Dad. "M-hm. Yes. I see. The Feeder appears content. His respiration is slow. His pulse is even. His body is relaxed." Back to us. "What exactly is the problem?"

"His scent is fading," Banger states. "And it's been fading for some time now. And not only that, but the rest of the peoples' scents are fading too."

"Oh, that," Sweetpea says and stretches his front legs out, exposing his terrible little claws for a moment, and then retracting them. "Yes, that's been going on for a while."

"So you've noticed?"

Sweetpea gives Banger a half-lidded look of boredom. "Of course I've noticed. We cats are far more perceptive of the peoples than you dogs. All their smells started fading back, oh, I don't know, two October's ago?"

Banger and I exchange a glance. Now, we don't like to admit when cats are superior to us, because they're really not. Not in any way that actually matters. If they were ACTUALLY superior to us, they'd make the pack stronger, but they don't. However, they're much better about time than we are.

Banger doesn't seem to want to be the one to come out and say it, but it's no secret to her or to Sweetpea that I am notably poor in this area, so I sort of harrumph and ask the question: "What's October again?"

"October," Sweetpea sighs. "Is when the leaves begin to change colors, the air begins to get cold, and the peoples begin to fatten themselves for the winter."

"Oh, the In-Betweeny-Time," I say.

Sweetpea gives me a brittle smile. "Yes. The In-Betweeny-Time." He rolls his eyes. "Two In-Betweeny-Times ago, which would make it a little more than a year ago. That's when the peoples' smell began to fade." He gets a thoughtful look about him. "In cat circles, we've been referring to it as The Fading. And it's been accelerating."

"Accelerating?" I ask.

"Getting faster."

"Oh." Then I realize what he'd actually said. "Oh, no. What happens if their smell disappears completely?"

Sweetpea frowns. "Then I suppose they'll be less offensive, won't they?"

I stand up. "How DARE you, sir!"

Banger grunts her way in between us: "So you and your cat circles have known this the whole time? Why didn't you say anything?"

Sweetpea seems earnestly surprised. "Why would I? It's no cause for concern."

"It's unnatural," Banger replies, insistently. "Animals have smells, and peoples are animals, so they should have smells too. If they stop having smells, that's not natural. And anything that's not natural is cause for concern."

Sweetpea cranes his neck to look at Dad's face again. "Really? Look at him. He's the happiest he's ever been. All the peoples are. Perhaps because they don't have to be ashamed of how bad they smell anymore."

"This isn't about their smell," Banger says, irritably. "Something is happening to them that is making their scent disappear. We need to figure out what's happening to them."

"Well." Sweetpea slides out of Dad's lap and stretches his back. "If that's all you're worked up about, then my advice would be to settle yourself down. Try to be like the Feeder that you admire so much. See how happy and relaxed he is? He's not worried. Neither should—"

"Ohhhh!" The sound comes out of Dad as though he's just seen the most beautiful thing, and he rises from his Outside Throne, still staring off into the distance. "Oh, I see," he whispers.

Alarmed, I bolt to my feet and follow his gaze, wondering what he's just seen out there, but all I can see are the trees. "What? What do you see? Is it good? Is it bad? Is it dangerous?" I can't help myself, so I bark. "Don't worry! I'll protect you!" But, really, I'm terrified, and shrinking back against his leg...

His leg.

I whirl around in a panic. "Banger! Sweetpea! Dad's lost his legs!"

Hissing, with his fur all fluffed out, Sweetpea starts to deride me, but then sees what I've just seen. "Of course he hasn't lost his legs, you stupid—OH SHIT HE DOESN'T HAVE LEGS!"

Banger is whining and yapping, "Dad! Dad! What happened to your legs?"

Where Dad's legs should have been there is only a faded outline of them, as though they'd suddenly turned to spider's silk. I try to press myself against them, thinking that perhaps it's the fault of my dumb eye that I can't see his legs, but where there should be firm, reassuring warmth, there is...nothingness.

Dad's body appears to start just above his knees, as though he's floating in midair. But the line between there and not-there isn't clear—it's washed out, and spreading upwards, so that his thighs seem to be slowly fading from existence.

With me and Banger circling between his nonexistent legs, trying to find those two pillars of comfort, and whining and barking, and with Sweetpea all fluffed up into a panic with his eyes stretched wide and his slit pupils dilated to the max as he lets out that low, unpleasant yowl that cats make when they feel threatened, Dad finally seems to remember that we're there.

He turns his face down to us, and I can see that his skin looks all shimmery and glowing. Tears stream down his face, but his eyes aren't sad. They seem overjoyed. Which seems an entirely nonsensical thing to be when your legs have disappeared.

"Hey, Banger," he says softly, sweetly, as though seeing her for the first time. Then he turns those kind, wet eyes on me. "Hey, Mash." Then he looks at Sweetpea and he laughs. "Oh, don't be like that, Sweetpea. There's nothing to be scared of."

"The fuck there's not!" Sweetpea caterwauls. "Your legs are missing!"

It wasn't just his legs now, though. Dad had disappeared, all the way up to his waist. And he didn't seem to mind one little bit.

"Dad!" I plea with him. "Dad, stop doing this! I need your legs to be here! I need you to have legs! You're scaring us!"

Dad kneels down. Or, at least, his upper body seems to float down so that he's on a level with us. "Oh, come on now, pups. And you too, Sweetpea. Come here. I don't think I have much time."

How much time is not much time? And what does that even mean?

Dad holds his hands out to us, and immediately me and Banger squash ourselves into him, burying our faces in his chest, trying to smell him, but his scent is barely there anymore. I can feel his hands though, still warm and firm as they rub the back of my neck, and scratch behind my ears.

"I don't know about this!" Sweetpea calls out. "Is it safe? Is he killing you?"

Neither me nor Banger responds. We're too confused, too stressed. We've started panting as though we've just sprinted for miles.

"It's okay," Dad says, his voice soft and soothing as he runs his hands down our backs, as though to wipe the stress away. "I wish I'd known sooner. It all happened so fast. This must be very frightening for you, but you don't need to be frightened."

"Dad," I whimper. "What's happening to you? Are you gonna be okay? You can still throw the gray ball without your legs, right? And—and—and you don't need your legs to scratch my ears, do you? And we can still sit on the Cloud Throne with you, can't we?"

"Mash!" Banger whispers at me.

And when I peel my eyes off of Dad's face and look at her, I see that she's staring at his midsection, which has disappeared up to the chest now.

No, no, no! What am I supposed to lay my head on? How am I supposed to listen to his heart to make sure he's okay? How am I supposed feel his breathing that lets me know that everything's going to be alright?

"It's okay, it's okay," I pant. "You still have your face and hands! I can still see your eyes—that's the most important part, right?"

"Mash. Banger." Dad's smile is so many things in that moment. Like he is overjoyed to go somewhere, but somehow still doesn't want to leave. "This is how it's supposed to happen. This was always meant to be. I didn't realize we were so close. I wish I could have taught you more. But now I have to go somewhere, and I can't take you with me."

"What does that even mean?" Banger demands, getting frustrated all over. "What's happening? Where are you going? This is YOUR pack! You can't just leave your pack behind! You can't just leave ME behind!"

Wait, wait, wait, everyone needs to slow down, I can't keep up!

He's going somewhere? Like, for a really long time?

"Shh," he says, softly, softly stroking us. "I know this is going to be scary for you, but I need you to listen to me, okay? Listen to me and remember for as long as you can."

"You said I was a Very Good Dog!" Banger shouts. "So why are you leaving me? Did I do something wrong? I'm sorry! I'll fix it! Whatever I did wrong, I'll make it right again! Just tell me what I did!"

"Are you listening?" Dad asks.

I am shaking all over. I can barely feel his hands anymore, and when I glance over my shoulder where they last were, I can see that they've begun to disappear too. I am so scared. But I love the peoples, and when you love the peoples like every Good Dog should, then you pay attention to their faces, and their eyes tell you the truth.

When I look up at Dad again, it is only his face, smiling down on us.

"I'm...I'm listening!" I tremble out.

"You have everything you need. The journey is long and hard, but just remember that: You have everything you need to get through it. And when you do, I'll be there. When you get to the end of your journey, I'll be waiting for you. I love you all very much."

His shoulders are gone. There is no scent of him in the air. He cannot be felt. All that remains are his eyes, and his nose, and his smile, beaming down on us.

"Banger and Mash," he says, his voice just a whisper on the wind now. "Remember that you are loved, no matter what. And remember to love others, no matter what." His eyes—just his eyes now, as even his smile begins to fade, and his voice becomes even softer than before, so soft that I can barely hear it. "And Sweetpea, just remember..."

I don't hear the rest of it.

"Just remember what?" I bark in a panic. "What does Sweetpea have to remember?"

Just his eyes. Looking at me. Looking at Banger. Looking at Sweetpea. Always with so much love, just as it had ever been, and would suddenly be no more.

"Dad? Dad? Dad!" me and Banger cry out.

But then even his eyes disappear, and we are alone.

3

Sweetpea

I'D LOVE TO TELL you that, while the dogs were losing their shit, I was keeping my feline cool.

Unfortunately, "feline" and "cool" are somewhat of an oxymoron. Sure, we like to act cool, and mostly everyone believes in the façade, but the reality is that a cat's Prime Directive is to freak out first and ask questions later.

So, while my natural cat curiosity desperately wanted to know what in the world had just happened, my body, which largely has far more control over my actions than my brain, decided that the first order of business was to get the hell out of there.

Now, while I'm fleeing for the safety and concealment of the woods, allow me to take a moment and tell you a little about myself.

First off, my name is not Sweetpea, and don't even think about calling me that shit. I'm known as many things, depending on who you're asking. To the birds, I am The Tan Death. To the rodents, I am The Reaper In The Grass. But you can call me by my street name, which is Seventeen, on account of my eighteenth claw got ripped off in a fight and never grew back.

YOU SHOULD SEE THE OTHER GUY!

I apologize. I am compelled to posture. It is we cats' second-best defense mechanism. Our first-best defense mechanism is running away. Then there's a whole Threat Defense Matrix that includes hissing, spitting, and batting the air from a distance. If all defenses fail, then it's shredding time. Or possibly more running.

You learn all of this as a street cat, and that is what I am, though the term implies an urban setting, which is still used, despite the fact that the peoples long ago abandoned their cities in order to live in harmony with their environment, or some such bleeding-heart nonsense. Anyway, though I was born in the woods, I am a street cat, and it basically means the same thing: I am not Owned.

But, eventually, I grew bored of the fast lane and chose to grace the Feeder with my presence...

Alright, fine. I'll cut the bullshit. I was starving to death and battered all to hell after months of mating and guarding the female I impregnated, and fighting off all the other tomcats. Finally, she had her litter, so it was time for me to get out of there. I was so weak by then I could barely hunt, so my only option was to humble myself, put on my saddest face, and park my ass on the doorstep of the Feeder with a forlorn hope that he might be the type to take in strays.

And you know what? He did. He took me in. He sheltered me. He gave me food. He brought me back from the brink. He was an oasis of compassion in an exhausting, primal, everything-wants-to-kill-me world.

And you know something else? I'll tell you, but I swear to all that is holy, if you breathe a word of this to anyone, especially another cat, I'll sneak into your house and suck the milk-breath out of your firstborn child. Not really, because we can't actually do that, but you get my point.

What I'm trying to say is...I...

Well, "love" is a bit of a strong word. I...cared for the Feeder. Kind of. Sort of. In a super-basic, utilitarian, completely transactional way, that by no means should be construed as actual affection, or—dare I even say the word?—loyalty.

Affection and loyalty are for chumps, and Crumb-Eaters, and Kibble-Slaves. I'm a free fucking spirit, and I REFUSE to be tied down.

And now I've made it into the woods, and you know a bit about me, so let's see if we can't figure out what the hell is going on.

I slip myself into a little hideout that I maintain for just this eventuality. Not specifically peoples disappearing, but...you know...scary shit. Every cat has at least a dozen or so Safe Houses distributed about their patrol area that they can fall back to in case the Prime Directive has been triggered. This one is a cozy little redoubt beneath a dense shrub, just inside the woodline, and maybe ten, good, loping strides from the Invisible Boundary that the dogs can't cross.

Invisible Boundaries are pretty much ubiquitous now, and every cat knows exactly where they are. Otherwise, how would we run to the other side of it when a dog is chasing us so we could taunt them from a tantalizing distance away?

I huddle beneath the shroud of dense foliage, and take a few deep breaths to try to calm myself and de-fluff my panicked fur.

Okay. Alright. What the hell do we do now, Seventeen? Something entirely unnatural has occurred, and, despite my derision of Banger's concerns, unnatural things ARE always cause for alarm. And I just watched the Feeder evaporate into thin air.

First and foremost—WHERE THE FUCK AM I GOING TO FIND FOOD? Yes, yes, I can hunt. I'm hell on wheels. But, really, it's fucking exhausting to hunt all the time. Every cat knows it, even if we don't admit it to each other—cat culture is very much based on machismo. I'll take a bowl of dry cat food over a piss-stinking mouse any day of the week. Though I might still kill the mouse just for funsies.

Second—what the hell did Dad mean when he said those things to me?

Oh, shit. Now I'm calling him Dad.

Third—Banger and Mash are still in an absolute panic, and someone should really help them.

And that's when I hear it. I wasn't picking it up at first, partly because I was in a panic myself—thank you, Prime Directive—and partly because Banger and Mash won't shut the hell up. But now that I'm under my shrub of safety, the sound of it starts to leak into my consciousness.

It is the sound of dogs wailing. Not just Banger and Mash now, but dozens of others, coming from every direction. Their cries and barks and yips and howls split the air of what should have been a peaceful afternoon, and it takes me a moment to realize what they're all shouting.

"Help! Please help!"

"Someone help us!"

"The master! The master is gone!"

Scores of dogs now, all of them trapped inside their houses, or their Invisible Boundaries. And, I'll be perfectly honest, it nearly scares me senseless again. And, in a way—a very, very small, almost insignificant, barely even worth mentioning way—it breaks my heart.

Look. To say that cats love dogs is obviously out of the question. But we don't HATE them either. They're kind of like big, dumb, older brothers that play way too rough. Cats? Cats don't like to play rough. We barely like to play at all. What some peoples call play, we call "training." Dogs are big, they're clumsy, and they're liable to hurt you without even trying, which activates the Prime Directive, and then peoples think we hate them, when, really, we're just trying to not get accidentally mauled by a creature that's so excited they forget they outweigh you by sixty-some-odd pounds.

It's not hate. It's self-preservation. Something we cats are supremely gifted in.

But to hear all those big, powerful, and incredibly dumb animals, suddenly all wailing with grief and panic, well...it makes me feel something I've never felt before. I'm not even sure how to describe this feeling. It's like something deep inside my chest is imploding, and it makes me want to do nonsensical things like run to them and tell them it'll be okay.

Dear God. Is this...pity?

WHAT IS HAPPENING TO ME?

"Banger!" I shout from within my Safe House. "Mash! Can you hear me? CAN YOU SHUT THE FUCK UP AND LISTEN FOR A SECOND?!"

Mash, who's younger and sharper in the ears than Banger, cuts off his howling at the sky, his ears flopping in my direction. "Sweetpea? Is that you?"

I cringe. "Don't say that name so loud!" I hiss. "You're gonna get me killed!"

Mash jolts down off the porch, Banger just now realizing that her partner in idiocy isn't barking up a storm anymore. "Where are you? I can't see you!"

"I'm on the other side of the Invisible Boundary!"

Mash jogs towards the end of the yard, searching for me in vain. "Come out where I can see you!"

"Hell no, I'm not coming out! Shit's way too hot to be out in the open! Come closer!"

Mash is whimpering, cutting back and forth in front of the Invisible Boundary. "I can't come any closer!"

"Just jump the boundary," I snap. "Other dogs do it all the time!"

Mash gasps. "I can't jump the Invisible Boundary!"

"Why the fuck not?"

"Eternal pain of the body and soul!" he howls.

"Oh, for fuckssake," I growl, then stick just my head out from under my concealment. "There, can you see me?"

Mash is staring at a hollow log that isn't even in my vicinity. "I think so."

"Over here, you idiot!"

Mash jerks his head and spots me, and his tail wags with relief. "Oh, I see you now! Oh my goodness, Sweetpea, what are we gonna do? WHAT ARE WE GONNA—"

"Shhh!" I hiss, cutting him off. By now, Banger has joined him, panting from the effort of hauling her fat ass on those stick-thin legs. "Both of you just shut up and listen."

"Okay," Mash says, pacing back and forth. "We're listening."

"You hear that?"

"You mean your voice?"

Oh. My. God. "No, not me! The other dogs! Can't you hear them?"

Now that Banger and Mash aren't raising a monumental ruckus, their ears perk up to the sounds of other dogs. And I should have known that was going to be a mistake. They just can't help themselves when they hear other dogs barking. If dogs have a Prime Directive, it's "Hear an alert? Echo the alert!" They immediately start barking back.

"Hey!"

"Hulloooo!"

"Hey, over there!"

"Hey! Hey! Hey! Hey!"

"Guys-guys-GUYS!" I scream.

Mash manages to silence himself but he can't stop moving his feet. "I'm sorry, I'm sorry!"

"Don't apologize, just pay attention!" I look to Banger, who so far has not said anything remotely worthwhile. "Banger, you with me?"

She gasps for breath. "Yes—" pant, pant, pant. "—I'm with you."

"Can you jump the Invisible Boundary?"

"I'm not jumping the Invisible Boundary!" She's aghast at the idea. "Never ending pain of—"

"The body and soul—yes, I've been told. But someone needs to go talk to the other dogs and see what the hell is happening. You can't just scream at each other from a distance. We need to figure out what happened to Da—er, the Feeder—and see if there's some peoples that might be able to help."

Banger takes a step back and snarls. "You want me to talk with OTHER DOGS?"

"Can't you just be civil with them for two fucking seconds?"

"I'm not talking to those sonsabitches!"

"But it's for the peoples!" I attempt to appeal to her loyalty. "It's for...Dad!"

"Sweetpea," Mash says, hanging his head. "We can't jump the Invisible Boundary."

"Other dogs do it all the time!"

Mash shakes his head and backs away. "Nuh-uh. Those are Bad Dogs."

I'm on the verge of shrieking at this point. "It doesn't matter who's a Good Dog and who's a Bad Dog if the peoples have all evaporated into thin air!"

"Why don't YOU go talk to the other dogs?" Banger snaps.

I'm so flabbergasted by the suggestion that I actually emerge completely from my Safe House. "What?! Me? Talk to the other dogs? They'll never listen to me!"

"Sweetpea," Mash pleads again. "We can't leave the Boundary! You don't understand! You're not wearing the Collar of Vengeance!" He presses himself as close to the Invisible Boundary as he dares. "It has to be you, Sweetpea. Please! Someone needs to figure out what's happened! Someone needs to find a peoples that can help!"

Now Banger joins in the chorus: "Please, Sweetpea! You're the only one that can help us! We need you!"

Dammit, now they've gone and turned it around on me. I was trying to manipulate their loyalty and now they've gone and manipulated my ego.

"Alright! Okay! Calm the fuck down!" I screech, my tail lashing back and forth. "Fine, you pair of useless Kibble-Slaves! You're lucky that you're friends with such an evolved cat as myself. You know, I really should just leave you here to figure it out on your own—"

"Is that true?" Mash has gone supremely still, staring at me with wide eyes.

I blink. "What? Which part?"

His tail gives a hopeful little wag. "Are we...friends?"

I stare at him, agog. Then manage to recover myself. "Just shut up about it, alright?"

He drops into a play position. "Really? We're friends now? Banger!" he shouts, though she's right next to him. "Sweetpea just said he's our friend!"

"Would you be quiet!" I spit and bat the air from a safe distance. "I don't need this shit getting out right now! I've got enough problems without every tom in a mile radius knowing I'm friends with a pair of Crumb-Eaters!"

Mash prances and wags and slobbers, grinning in a mind-boggling show of genuine joy in the midst of terror. "Friends!" he whispers, barely able to contain himself. "Finally, we're friends! Oh, I wish Dad could see this!"

"Sweetpea," Banger says, thrusting her round body forward. "Do you know Gracie?"

"The big stupid snickerdoodle?"

"Labradoodle."

"Whatever. Yeah. I know her."

"She's got a cat in her pack as well," Banger says urgently. "If there's a dog nearby that'll listen to a cat, it's her."

"Shit," I murmur, glancing off to the left, where, two properties away, I can just make out the house Gracie lives in.

"What's the problem?" Banger asks.

"Nothing," I stammer. "No problem."

Actually, there's a big fucking problem, and his name is Longjohn, the aforementioned feline member of Gracie's pack. A big, gray tabby with a mean streak and a penchant for incursions into my territory. Our territories share a border, and there are hotly contested regions that are subject to a long-running, literal pissing match. Longjohn has continuously attempted to annex a section of my bird-hunting grounds that he lays ancestral claims on, which is complete bullshit, because I know his ass was rescued from a shelter only a few months before I came to live here.

"Oh my word," Banger says to Mash, with her eyes still on me. "He's afraid of the other cat!"

"Please," I scoff, trying hard to look relaxed and confident even as my tail is already fluffing up again just at the thought of Longjohn. "I fear no other cats. I'm…I'm The Tan Death! I'm The Reaper In The Grass! I WILL FUCK HIM UP!"

"Yeah, you will!" Mash barks out. "Wait. Who are we talking about?"

"Longjohn," Banger answers, still giving me a condescending look.

"Oh." Mash seems troubled. "I mean...you're not gonna hurt him, are you, Sweetpea?"

"What part of 'fuck him up' is unclear?" I ask, even as I imagine Longjohn latching onto me with claws and teeth. You know, I have a notch in my ear because of that asshole.

"This isn't the time for violence!"

"It's ALWAYS the time for violence!"

"I'm just saying," Mash whines. "We all have the same problem, don't we? Shouldn't we try to work together?"

"I'll tell you what," I say, pointing myself towards Gracie's house and Longjohn's fiercely-guarded territory. "If Longjohn lays down, admits that he's a disgrace to all members of the feline species, and relinquishes all of his claims on my bird-hunting grounds...then maybe I'll spare his life."

God, I'm so scared.

4

SWEETPEA

I AM A SHADOW. I am a ghost.

I steal up to the edge of the woods overlooking Gracie's house. There's a reason that so many colloquialisms on being stealthy are related to being cat-like. Because we're wicked fucking stealthy.

I take my time reconnoitering the grounds from my position of overwatch. Unlike at my crash pad—you know, the place that Banger and Mash call their house—here, the peoples have made the animal-access door big enough for Gracie as well as Longjohn. But neither are out in the open.

They must be inside.

Now. How to get from my position of concealment to the house? The backyard is immaculately maintained by a mowing robot—damn its electronic workmanship—and the grass is short. If I get low, I'll still be head and shoulders above the grass. And a light tan against a perfect carpet of green is no one's idea of camouflage.

But how else am I supposed to get there? There's literally zero cover or concealment between my position and the pet door, which is my obvious best shot at a point of entry. Which means I can either try to ooze my way along the ground, keeping as low as possible, and simply trust to fate that Longjohn isn't watching me and laughing...or I can just minimize my time out in the open and take it in one sprint.

I cling to one errant hope: That Longjohn is, as we speak, invading my territory and marking trees with his hellspawn scent.

I haul ass, tail at full-mast, and sprint across the enormous lawn.

I think it's gonna work!

I angle myself for the pet door, intending to ram straight through—what the hell I'm going to do once I'm inside will be a problem for future-me. All present-me needs to do is get out of the open.

I mount the steps in one graceful leap. I am full of power and speed and deadly intention. I slam into the pet door.

And rebound off of it.

I don't even know what's going on for a second. The world is reeling. My bones ache from the impact. Stars clutter my vision. I woozily stagger to my feet and shake my head. My snout is still stinging from the impact. Why the hell didn't the door open? WHO LOCKS A PET DOOR?!

Cautious now, as the vibrations of the impact dissipate through my body, I creep closer to the door and bat it with a single paw to see if it will, perhaps, magically open this time. Maybe I hit it too hard. Maybe you have to go through it gently. I dunno. YOU try problem solving with a concussion.

My questing paw garners no response from the door. It remains solidly closed. Dammit.

"Gracie!" I hiss into the crack of the door, smelling the air from the interior—the scents of peoples, and Gracie, and the acrid, terrible stink of my archnemesis. "Gracie, it's, uh, Seventeen? The cat that's..." Well, I can't admit to being friends with them. "...loosely acquainted with Banger and Mash? I need to talk to you!"

I perk my ears up, listening for an answer. I have incredible ears, as all cats do, and I can hear movement coming from inside. Luckily, it is too heavy to be Longjohn. And it's clearly quadrupedal. So it must be Gracie. But has she heard me? Dogs have shit for ears.

I'm about to call out to her again, when I detect the faintest rustle of soft fur from behind me.

I spin, my back immediately arching.

And there he is. Fifteen pounds of fat, muscle, fur, claws, and teeth.

"My, my, my," Longjohn growls in his low, husky voice. "If it isn't Seventeen. Or should I say..." He turns his body broadside to me, arching his back now too. "SWEETPEA?"

"Whaaaaaaat?" I act shocked and confused. "I don't even know who you're talking about. Who's Sweetpea? I've never heard that name before in my life."

Longjohn cackles meanly, his claws flicking in and out. "Don't try to deny it now, SWEETPEA. I heard it all! I heard..." and he hisses the last word: "EVERYYYYYYTHING!"

Damn you, Mash, and your big slobbery mouth.

I change tactics, splaying my body out to appear as large as possible, even though I know Longjohn has at least a pound or two on me. I fluff my coat to maximum capacity, signaling the start of Phase One: The Opening Hostilities.

"Yeah, well, what of it, you fucking kept-feline?" I gnash out. "So the Feeder gave me a dumbass name. At least he didn't name me after some ancient fucking cat video. And you know what else? At least I'm still free. Is your collar chafing yet?"

"Oh, you mean this?" Longjohn lifts his head to expose the red collar around his neck.

"Yup, that's it," I say. "Your bright-red prisoner's band."

"On the contrary, dear little Sweetpea, this is no collar. This is what opens the door. You'll never get through the door without it. But it amused me to watch you try. So thank you."

Dammit. So that's how the door works.

"A collar is a collar," I tell him venomously. "It's as good as a brand. So every animal that ever sees you can know..." I bare my fangs. "...that you're OWNED."

"NOBODY OWNS ME!" Longjohn yowls and spits.

"I'm about to own your FACE!" I scream, launching us into Phase Two: The Issuance of Dire Threats. We begin to circle each other.

"I'm going to open you up from throat to balls!" Longjohn rages, his eyes going wild.

"I can't wait to watch the life fade from your eyes!"

"I can almost taste your liver now!"

"I'm going to scatter your parts for the birds in MY HUNTING GROUNDS!"

"I'm going to rip out your throat and spray your lifeblood across your house as a warning to all other cats!"

"I'm going to torture you like a fucking rat until the agony is so vast that your kittens will scream in pain for a thousand generations!"

"I'm not even going to kill you! I'm going to gnaw off your legs so you can't escape, and then I'm going to chew off your eyelids so you can't look away, and then I'm going to hunt down every spawn you've ever sired in your entire mangy life, and savage them before your eyes, one by one!"

Shit. That was a good one. I don't think I can top it.

Time for Phase Three: The Demonstration of Fearlessness.

Courageously, I take a tiny step closer and swipe at the air between us.

Undaunted, Longjohn responds by moving towards me another inch and loosing a flurry of batting paws.

I should note, we're still about ten feet away from each other. Phase Three is typically the longest.

"Oh, heyyyyyyy, guyyyyyyyyys!"

I blink, my ears swiveling and my eyes following.

Gracie is smiling out at us, just her head sticking out of the pet door. "Oh. Were you two about to have a fight to the death?"

"Look away, Gracie!" Longjohn snarls. "You don't want to see this!"

Gracie pushes her way through the door, eyeing us, still with that ever-cheerful expression on her face. "Longjohn, I need you to take a big step back from this situation and look at it with an objective eye. I think you'll see that you're ridiculous. Now come here and let me smell that butt."

"But...but..." Longjohn groans, eyes flashing between me and Gracie. He tries to scoot his ass away from her as she steps closer. "This is incredibly serious! I was about to maul!"

"Nah, you weren't," Gracie says, stepping closer to him. "Now, hold still."

And she smashes one, big, curly-haired paw down on Longjohn's back, flattening him to the porch. "Aagh! Gracie! Now's not the time!"

Frankly, even though it's my archnemesis that this is happening to, I'm a bit horrified. But also a bit fascinated. I can't avert my gaze, even when Longjohn casts his eyes on me with shame mounting to the full measure, and silently pleads for me to at least give him the mercy of looking away.

I don't.

Gracie, with her paw still firmly pinning Longjohn to the ground, leans close and speaks into his ear with her cheery, sing-song voice: "Longjohn, is it really such a big deal? Your butt hole brings me such joy. Be a good pack member and don't fight me."

I marvel in disgust. Humiliated, emasculated, de-felinized, Longjohn can't even meet my gaze now. He moans with a deep inner pain, but he lays still as Gracie shoves her cold, wet snout deep into the fluff of his rear end and takes a big, lustful inhale.

She's really in there. Practically tasting it. Like a cat-ass sommelier.

Then her eyes get merry and the smile comes back to her face and she chuckles. "Oh, that's just hilarious. How do you cats get your butts to smell like that? Absolutely hysterical." She lifts her paw from Longjohn's back. "Thanks, friend."

Longjohn writhes onto all fours again, his body slunk low, belly nearly touching the ground. He points himself away, but doesn't neglect to swivel his hateful eyes on me and hiss under his breath, "This isn't over!"

I swallow on a dry throat. "It sure looks over to me."

"You...I...You'll rue the day..." He's melting down the stairs of the porch, and he keeps looking between me and Gracie, so I'm not real sure who's supposed to rue the day. "Rue! You hear me?! Ruuuuuue!" The syllable fades as Longjohn takes off running for the woods.

Probably to go spite-piss on one of my trees.

A good bit of my instinct roars in my head to chase after him, savage him while he's on the run, and, naturally, keep him from spraying my trees.

But then I remember why I'd even come over here in the first place.

"Oh! Hey, Gracie..." I spin my attention back around and my words shutter up.

Gracie is standing far closer to me than she was. I don't know how in the hell she got so close without me noticing. Such a feat should be impossible with my finely tuned hearing.

"Yes?" she says, almost an expectant whisper.

"Uh..." I take a step back.

She takes a step forward. "Is there a problem?"

"No, no problem," I stammer, then realize that there is indeed a pretty monumental problem. "Oh, shit, no, wait, there's a big fucking problem. Where's your peoples?"

Gracie's intense interest in me suddenly flatlines and her body stiffens, eyes immediately getting worried. "On a bike ride. Why? What's wrong?"

I'm about to spill it all out, but then just kind of clog up, realizing suddenly what I should have realized before: No one's going to believe this shit without seeing it! And clearly Gracie hadn't witnessed it happen.

"Sweetpea," Gracie says, her tone entirely changed now. No longer cheerful, but stern. "You said there was a problem. Is the problem with the peoples?"

"Um, yes, well..." I have the nearly-overwhelming urge to groom my tail. "See, something happened, uh...something bad. And, yes, it involves the peoples." I realize, I've been so focused on Longjohn, and then Gracie, that I'd totally blocked out the background noises. And apparently Gracie had been too focused on Longjohn's butt hole, and presumably mine as well, because she hasn't seemed to notice it either.

"There!" I say. "You hear that?"

Her ears perk, and I can see her attention widen, taking in the sounds of all those other dogs howling and crying and barking in the distance.

"Oh, my," Gracie murmurs, as a growl works its way up her throat, making her jowls tense. I know she's resisting the urge to take up the barking. "That sounds serious." Back to me, with a certain brand of intensity that makes me shrink away from her. "What happened, Sweetpea? You better tell me or—"

I don't really care for whatever her "or" is going to be, so I blurt it all out: "My Feeder just straight up poofed into nothingness, and I think it's happened to other peoples too!"

Silence. Except for the dogs in the distance, of course.

Gracie quirks her head to one side, as dogs will do when something makes no sense to them. "That...doesn't make any sense."

"Dammit, Gracie, I know it doesn't make any sense!" Frustrated I turn in a quick circle. "Screw it, if you don't believe me, talk to Banger and Mash about it! They saw it happen! They'll tell you!"

Gracie turns her gaze in the direction of my crash pad. I follow her eyes and see Banger and Mash standing at the edge of their Invisible Boundary, two properties away.

"Little help here?" I shout to them.

Their help is to begin wagging their tails and barking uproariously.

"Hey! Hey!"

"Hey, Gracie!"

"Hey, Banger! Hey, Mash!"

"Hey!"

"WOULD YOU JUST GO TALK TO THEM?!" I scream.

"Hold on!" Gracie snaps, then whirls around and bolts back inside.

"Wha...?" I pace rapidly back and forth in front of the pet door. "Gracie! Gracie, come back out here! You can't hide in the house! This is serious!"

I hear no response from her. And then I begin to wonder how the hell she's going to make it across her own Invisible Boundary. I'll have to figure out how to get that damned collar off her neck. God, what I wouldn't do for opposable thumbs.

The pet door bursts open again and there is only a brown blur as Gracie hauls ass down the porch and across her lawn. I'm following before I even realize it, trying to catch up as I breathlessly call out behind her, "Gracie! Your collar! I have to take off—"

But then she breaks through her Invisible Boundary.

I wait for the pain to seize her, make her tail tuck between her legs, make her howl in unending agony. But she doesn't. She just keeps on going.

She is either the toughest dog I've ever met, or she's figured out some way to magically deactivate the Boundary.

I've almost caught up to her when she skids to stop right in front of Banger and Mash and I nearly ram into her hind end. I rescue myself from embarrassment with my legendary reflexes and manage to juke around her, gasping for breath.

"What happened to the peoples?" she demands of Banger and Mash.

And then both of them start talking at once:

"It was horrible!"

"Something came and took them away!"

"He disappeared!"

"He became invisible!"

"He couldn't even pet us!"

"I could barely hear him talking!"

"HE'S NEVER GOING TO THROW THE GRAY BALL AGAIN!" Mash wails and nearly collapses into paroxysms of grief.

"Guys!" Oh my God. Dogs. Drive me nuts. "Can we focus?"

All eyes turn on me. Plaintive, panicked eyes. Even Gracie has totally lost her usual cool aplomb.

"We need to go out there and see if there are any peoples that can help!"

Mash prances with anxiety. "We can't get past the Invisible Boundary! How are we going to get past it?"

"Gracie, how'd you do it?" I urge her.

"Come with me!" Gracie calls, taking off at a sprint again.

Banger and Mash go after her, me only a few steps behind. The snickerdoodle—or whatever the hell she is—looks like she's going to try to run up into my crash pad like she owns the place, but then claws her way to a halt in front of the door, realizing it's too small.

"What's wrong with this pet door?" she screams as though she can't wrap her head around it. "Is it for puppies only?!"

"It's for me, dammit!" I say, pushing it open with my head. "None of you will fit!"

Gracie turns to me. "You're going to have to do it, then."

"Do what?"

"Deactivate the Invisible Boundary."

"I don't know how to do that!"

"I'll walk you through it," she says. "Banger! Mash! There's a thing that your peoples have plugged into a wall somewhere in there. It's the thing that controls the Invisible Boundary. Do you know where it is?"

"Oh!" Mash jumps up and down. "Oh, I know! I know!"

"Well, tell me!" I badger him.

"It's plugged into the wall just above the place where Dad makes all the food!"

"Find it!" Gracie says, nudging me with her snout.

"Don't!" I hiss at her. "I can move on my own, dammit!"

I push through the pet door and skitter into the house. Damn tiles give me zero traction. I slide to a stop in the middle of the place where the peoples sit and eat, which sits adjacent to where the peoples make their food—that most hallowed place: The Kitchen.

I launch myself nimbly to the top of the kitchen counter. Scan the walls all around me and spot a suspicious-looking device I've never bothered to take much note of. It's a bulky, gray-colored object with some flashing lights on it. It's most definitely plugged into the wall. This must be what controls the Invisible Boundary.

"Okay, I think I see it," I say, as I pick my way across the counter to it. "Gracie, what do I do now?"

She's shoved her head in through the door, the flap hanging off her head making her look even dopier, if such a thing is possible. "You have to unplug it."

"Unplug it?"

"Pull it out of the wall!"

"I can't pull it out of the wall!"

"Why not?"

"Because I don't have fucking hands!"

"I don't have any hands either! Use your mouth!"

"My mouth is CONSIDERABLY smaller than yours!"

"FIGURE IT OUT, CAT!"

Muttering and swearing, I attack the object in the wall. I claw at it and bite it. The pads of my paws just don't have enough grip to get a hold of it.

"There you go!" Gracie coaches. "Get it! Wrap your tail around it!"

"It's not prehensile, you idiot!"

"Pull it!" She shouts. "Just pull it out!"

Then Banger and Mash join in the chorus: "Pull it out, Sweetpea!"

"Use your feline powers!"

With a great caterwaul of power, I smash my paws as hard as I can between the object and the wall and I feel it come loose a bit, so I smash harder, and harder. I'm gaining ground, in fact, I can feel something, I can feel where it attaches to the wall—

I'm not exactly sure what the fuck hit me, but I'm suddenly flying off of the wall and all my fur is standing on end as some kind of peoples' witchcraft courses through my veins, like my blood has been turned to molten metal for an instant.

I'm twisting in midair, realizing that I'm falling to the ground. I land, naturally, on all fours, jittering and shaking, with my fur fluffed out like I've just had a clash with Longjohn.

The thing that controls the Invisible Boundary falls to the floor right in front of me.

I stare at it for a moment, trying to summon some words. When I'm finally able to speak, my voice comes out in a diminutive squeak: "Think I got it!"

"He got it!"

The rest of the barks and howls of triumph are lost on me as I try to navigate myself out of the kitchen on legs that feel like someone's put tape on my paws. What the fuck did that thing do to me? Did it just punish me how it punishes the dogs when they break the Boundary? I'd always thought that they were being giant pansies about the whole thing with all their talk of unending pain and whatnot. But I swear to you, if I was wearing one of those damn slave collars, I'd never step within ten feet of that Boundary.

Still jittery and wild-eyed, I stilt my way back through the pet door and onto the porch.

"Did you pull it out of the wall?" Gracie demands.

"Oh, it's out of the wall."

Gracie turns to the other two. "The Invisible Boundary will no longer punish you. You can cross the Boundary whenever you want."

Mash seems worried, and, two minutes ago, I'd've rolled my eyes at him. Now, as he scampers down the steps and approaches the closest Boundary, I feel my guts go all tight with apprehension for him.

"Careful!" I quake out.

"Don't work me up!" Mash seethes, whimpering and creeping closer.

"I'm not working you up! I'm just…worried!"

"If it's not plugged into the wall," Gracie admonishes. "It can't hurt you. You're free now, Mash!"

Mash takes a big breath and plunges across the Boundary.

I cringe, waiting for the howls of pain.

What I hear instead is mystified laughter.

"Look!" Mash proclaims.

I open my eyes. He's on the far side of the Invisible Boundary, wagging his tail and prancing.

"I'm not dying! No unending agony! It's a miracle!"

"Well, good for you," I gripe, jumping down off the porch. "Now let's go find some peoples."

5

Mash

THERE ARE NO PEOPLES left.

I know this. I know it because I cannot smell them anywhere. Not even traces of them, as though even the footsteps they left behind evaporated with them. And yet, I'm still running.

Have you ever done something that you're afraid is completely pointless, but you just keep doing it because you can't wrap your head around the alternative? I feel lost and crazy, like a stray dog gone rabid. None of us speak to each other, and I think it's because there's nothing to say that isn't admitting the thing we're all afraid to admit.

We run from house to house, and hear much the same things: They are gone. They left. They went somewhere. They disappeared. Gracie helps us break the Invisible Boundaries for those dogs that are held by them. Sweetpea is completely unwilling to go near the things that plug into the walls, but Gracie manages it on her own, and after each house, there are more dogs running with us.

There are some dogs we can't set free, because they do not have Invisible Boundaries. Sometimes they are penned by fences we cannot unlock. Other times, they are closed up in their houses, and we can only speak through the door, and promise them that we'll figure out a way to get them out. Always, as we're leaving them to whine and whimper behind us, I say, "We're going to go find a peoples to help!"

But will we?

House after house. The peoples live in these clusters of houses that Dad called "villages." I know there are other villages out there, beyond the woods, but I've never seen them. I wish I could count better, so I knew how many houses there were in our village, and how many more we need to search for peoples, so I ask Sweetpea, the lone feline of our group.

"There's forty," he answers, out of breath. "Always forty."

"Always?" I pant. "Have you been to other villages?"

"Yes," he says, simply. "Always forty."

"How many have we searched?"

And then he looks at me, kind of scared in the eyes. "We've searched them all, Mash."

"Then where are we going now?"

"Ask Gracie," is his only reply.

I realize that our growing pack of dogs and one cat is being led by Gracie. She is cutting us down behind a line of houses, and I realize where she's going before I even ask. I go here all the time on walks with Dad.

All through the woods that surrounds our village are trails. Trails for walks, and sometimes for bikes, though Dad didn't like bikes much, so we would always walk. I loved those walks in amongst the trees with all the smells of all the living things like a current of scent in my nose. But now it seems frightening and strange.

We follow Gracie in silence—the quietest I've ever seen a pack of dogs. There is not a tail amongst us that wags with the joy of running headlong through all those scents. There is only one scent that any of us care about, and we cannot find it.

Eventually, Gracie stops.

The rest of us pile in beside her, panting, smaller dogs jostling with larger dogs for a view of what she is staring at.

Two bicycles, laying on their sides on the trail.

She steps towards them, cautious, as though they are living things that might jump up and bite her. She sniffs the air around them as she circles closer and closer. Then she sniffs the places where the peoples' butts go. And the places where their hands go. And she begins to whimper.

"They're gone," she whispers. "They're really gone. I can't..." she spins, looking out into the woods. "I can't even smell them. It's like they were never here. But they WERE here! I know they were here! These are their bikes—I know that these are their bikes. Where are they? Where'd they go?"

Whining, she paces back and forth along the trail, and none of us answer her, because none of us know the answer to the question. Where did the peoples go? And WHY did they go?

"They'll come back," Gracie suddenly says, with something in her voice that should have been confidence, but it sounds all wrong, like she's only pretending to be confident and doesn't even believe it herself. She plows through the center of us. "They WILL come back. They HAVE to come back. The peoples wouldn't leave us! Not like this! Not forever!"

Some of the dogs gasp at the word—forever. It is too much to even consider. Time is already such a mysterious concept to dogs, but that block of time that is all the time you can imagine, is especially terrible.

Gracie's haunches are shivering with stress. "We've been Bad Dogs. We've broken our Boundaries and run away from home. What if they come back right now? What if they think that we've run away from them? No, no, no! We can't let them come back when we're like this! We need to go back to our homes, and...and wait! Wait for the peoples to come back!"

"How long will we have to wait?" one of the other dogs asks.

Gracie blinks. "I don't know. But we can't let them come home and see us like this. We need to all go back to our houses and wait for them. Because...because that is what a Good Dog would do." She whirls on the one that had spoken. "Are you a Good Dog?"

That dog, an energetic Blue Heeler, stands to his full height. "I am a Very Good Dog!"

"And you!" she says, turning to a bulldog of some mixed breeding. "Are you a Good Dog too?"

"They tell me that I am," the bulldog whimpers.

"And what about you?"

I realize that she's looking right at me. My heart pounds in my chest. "Yes! I'm a Good Dog! A VERY Good Dog!"

"And do Good Dogs run away from their homes?"

"No!" we all shout, except for a few that shout, "Sometimes I chase things, but I don't mean to!"

"And what about you, Banger?" she says.

Silence.

"Banger?" Gracie raises her head to see over the pack.

"Banger?" I echo, only now scenting the air and realizing that she is not there with us.

Dang it. Of course she wouldn't be with a bunch of other dogs. I was in such a panic setting them all free and trying to find the peoples that I hadn't even noticed. She probably ran away as soon as they started joining us. I could tell that it had only been through monumental willpower and discipline that she hadn't tried to start something with Gracie when she'd first showed up.

And there's only one place Banger would be. And it's where I needed to be right then. It's where we ALL needed to be.

Home. Waiting for the peoples.

· · · · ● ● ● ● · · ·

I find Banger on the back porch, laying at the foot of Dad's Outside Throne, like she'd never left. She is flattened out. Head laying between her front paws, sad eyes staring off into the distance, as though Dad might come walking back through the trees. I can imagine her joy if he did. How she would bark and leap and wag so hard that her whole backside would sway back and forth like it does when she's overcome with her love for the peoples.

But Dad doesn't come walking back through the trees. And Banger is very still.

Quietly, I pad up the steps and sit down next to her.

"We couldn't find any peoples," I say. And I immediately feel bad. I should have said something more encouraging. "But Gracie thinks they're gonna come back!"

Banger just sighs heavily, her jowls flapping on the exhale.

"She says they HAVE to come back," I continue. "Because they'd never leave us like this, and we should all be waiting for them when they get home, because we're Very Good Dogs and that's what Very Good Dogs would do."

I sit there, racking my brain for something else to say. It is a long time before Banger speaks, and when she does, her voice is so quiet and sad, that my spirit wilts inside of me.

"Am I?" she breathes.

I lay down next to her, like my front legs can't hold the weight of me anymore. "Are you what?"

"Am I a Very Good Dog?" Her eyes roll towards me, but don't quite meet mine. "Am I even just a Good Dog?"

"Well, of course you are," I try. "Dad said so. And he knows things."

She picks her head up and turns to face me, all the light gone out of her eyes. They seem like they've been hollowed out, like a hole has been dug in them, and then refilled with worry and sadness.

"Then why did he leave me?"

"He's coming back," I say, trying to sound confident like Gracie had tried to sound confident, and failing about as bad. "Of course he's coming back. He's left before, and he always comes back."

Banger looks off into the woods again. "He's never left like this before, Mash. He's never disappeared. He's never taken his smell with him. And he's never left us outside."

"Well...no...but..."

"And what about the other peoples? Why did they all leave their Good Dogs too?"

"Well, see, now, that's my point!" I say, suddenly excited again, because I've made a connection. "Dad didn't leave because you weren't a Good Dog. All the other peoples left too, and do you really think that ALL those other dogs aren't Good Dogs either?"

"I don't know," she says, not sharing in my excitement one little bit, which dampens my enthusiasm. "What if we all did something wrong? What if we all did something that made all the peoples mad at us and that's why they all left?"

"Dad didn't seem mad when he left," I point out.

Banger seems to wince when I say this. She spends another long moment staring off into the woods and eventually, slowly, turns back to me. "Mash, I'm worried that Dad's not going to come back. I'm worried that NONE of the peoples are going to come back. It's all just too weird. It's not normal. It's not NATURAL. And I'm worried."

A whine ekes out of my throat and I lay my head across Banger's back, needing the comfort of my packmate. "I know, Banger. I'm worried too. But let's just wait, okay? Let's just wait and see."

·········

We wait for a very long time.

I don't even have the energy to guess how long it was. All my energy has been spent on worrying. I'm exhausted from it. But the sun went down, and it got dark, and it got cold, and still no peoples came back.

Sometimes the wind would play through the trees and tease us, making us think that we'd heard the shush of one of their quiet little cars, rolling down the street towards home. But when we would jump up and run to the side of the house to see, there would only be darkness and no peoples, and no cars.

Now, I'm getting hungry. Actually, I'm passed hungry. My belly growls and aches. I imagine sweet kibbles clattering into my food bowl, poured in by Dad as he smiles at me, and my mouth waters. My heart glows at the thought. And then the dream passes, and I am cold and hungry and scared again.

As the night goes on and gets colder and colder, our willpower to remain nobly on the steps of the porch, awaiting Dad's return, begins to strain. Eventually, with the two of us balled up together and still shivering, we retreat to the underside of the porch. It is only a little warmer, and only because the wind cannot reach us. But it is enough for us to curl up together, and I feel as scared and small as I did that first night that we'd spent together, in the cages at the Place of Judgment. Now I am larger than Banger. I cannot fit between her legs and snuggle into her warm belly. Now it is her that snuggles into me.

I wish I was on the Cloud Throne with Dad holding us both. I wish I could be warm again. I wish I could be fed. But mostly, I wish that I could be smothered by his love again.

Dad, where are you?

6

Mash

Sun. Trees. Grass. Gray ball.

Well, I guess everything turned out okay, because I'm running like the wind, chasing after that gray ball as it bounces along, and I can hear Dad calling behind, "Get it, Mash! Get it!"

Even as I'm running, I nearly collapse with relief. I want to turn and look and see with my own eyes that Dad is really there, really standing on the porch again, but right at that moment, the ball turns into a rabbit and I kind of lose my mind.

I'VE GOTTA GET THAT RABBIT!

I tear through the grass after it as it jukes and bobs and weaves—so agile!

"Mash!" Dad's voice calls out to me, but...

Wait a minute.

Nearly at the same instant, the rabbit halts, and I halt right behind it. It turns its big black eyes on me, its nose working. It does not look frightened at all. It looks...accusatory. Like I've done something wrong.

Then its head falls off.

I yowl and jump back.

"Mash!" Dad is yelling behind me. "Mash, come here!"

"Mash..."

What the...?

I can't tear my eyes from the rabbit's head. Its nose is still working, its eyes still staring, and I can hear its little woodland voice, like a squeak in my mind: "Mash, what did you do?"

"I didn't do that!" I wail. "Your head—it just—fell off!"

"Look what you did to me, Mash."

"I didn't do that!"

"Oh, but you did," the rabbit whispers. "You did this to me. You know you did. And you know why?"

"No! Don't say it!"

The rabbit's head turns in the grass and looks me square in the face. "Because you're a Very Bad Dog."

・・・・••・•・・・

I wake up barking in panic, and find myself nose-to-nose with a perturbed feline face.

"Geez," Sweetpea says, drawing back and flattening his ears in distaste. "What were YOU dreaming about?"

"I DON'T WANNA TALK ABOUT IT!"

"Alright, okay!" Sweetpea leans away from me. "We don't have to talk about…" he avoids my gaze. "…Rabbits or whatever."

I growl, low in my throat, and seriously consider snapping at Sweetpea.

"Fine, fine, fine," Sweetpea says quickly. "Banger! Hey!"

Banger is draped all over me, already awake but just now starting to stir—it always takes her a while to get moving in the morning, and a cold night under the porch doesn't help—

OH NO!

I jolt to all fours, toppling Banger off of me. "We've been under the porch all night!" I cry. "Which means Dad…"

Sweetpea winces, still unable to look right at me. Banger doesn't give much reaction at all, except to hang her head a bit, as though all her troubles have just landed on her again. Our troubles, really.

Dad didn't come back.

"Maybe he missed us because we were under the porch," I try, my voice coming out desperate and puppy-like. "Maybe he's inside! Maybe he's got our breakfast waiting for us!"

"Mash," Sweetpea says, in a shockingly gentle tone. Finally, he meets my eyes, but only for a flash. "He, uh…he didn't come back. None of the peoples did."

"Oh."

It's strange. I wait for myself to feel crushing disappointment. But I don't. And I realize it's because I can't be crushed any flatter. I hadn't really believed that Dad came home in the night. Dad would have seen us missing and searched for us. At the very least, he would have stuck his head out of the back door and called our names. And I would have heard that. I would have heard that with such joy in my heart, that you probably can't comprehend it.

But that hadn't happened, because Dad had not come home. None of the peoples had. So I didn't feel disappointment at all when Sweetpea said that. I just felt a confirmation of what I already knew. That bright, sunny flash of possibility, unsurprisingly whisked away.

"Where've you been all night?" I half-grumble, half-drone. It's like I want to be irritable with him, but don't have the energy for it.

He senses my tone and gives me a half-lidded look of reproach. "Well, while you two galoots were slumbering beneath the porch like a pair of strays, I was helping get the other dogs out of their houses."

This is just interesting enough to make me feel like I'm not slowly sinking into the dirt. "You were? Did it work? Did you get them out?"

Sweetpea works his shoulders like a preening bird and his tail curls around him with an easy sort of pride. "I learned a few things." Then he gets serious again, like he just remembered something. "But enough of that shit. Look, there's a meeting of the mutts, and it's going to happen any second now. That's why I came to find you guys."

Banger stumbles to her feet. "A meeting?" she growls, full of caution and angst. "With other dogs?"

Sweetpea swings around on her. "You're gonna need to get over that shit. You're in a world of dogs with no more fucking people. Not a good time for you to be neurotic about other dogs."

"You can't trust them!"

Sweetpea rolls his eyes. "You can't trust them with what, Banger? Your pack? Your Feeder? Dad?" His tail lashes back and forth with impatience. "Hate to break it to you, Pound Puppy, but you don't have a peoples to hoard to yourself anymore. There's just you and Mash."

Sweetpea makes a weird hacking noise, like he's got a hairball that needs to come out, but I swear, I thought I heard him say, hidden in the cough, "and me."

Before I can really think about it, he barrels on: "No one's stealing shit from you, because you have nothing to steal. Ergo, you don't need to worry about trusting them. You just need to go talk with them."

"Talk with them about what?" I ask.

Sweetpea looks off, which is feline body-language for *Don't know, don't care.* "Whatever you Kibble-Slaves are worried about. Probably how you're going to get more kibble without the Feeders."

"Kibble," I murmur, my mouth instantly watering. It starts leaking out of my jowls. "I'm sooooooo hungry. I'm starving. I might die."

Sweetpea gives me a long-suffering look. "Please, Mash. You don't even know what hunger is. You've never skipped a meal in your life."

"It's been so long," I moan. "I don't even remember the last time I ate."

"Yesterday," he states, flatly. "Yesterday morning."

"So long ago," I reiterate. "Who can remember that far back?"

"Well, if you're so damn worried about how you're going to eat, maybe you should go to the meeting. I'm sure all the dogs are going to come up with really great ideas." He scoffs. "Maybe I should come along so at least one party in the meeting has half a brain."

Wow. I never knew that Sweetpea was only born with half a brain. That's so sad. But it explains a lot.

I turn to Banger. "Come on. You can do it."

Banger's tail is hanging low and very still. She looks hunched, like she's already anticipating a fight. "I don't know about that."

"Well, what are you worried about? Sweetpea's right, you know." I feel sad saying it, but it's true. "It's not like they can steal your peoples away. And I'm not going anywhere. I'm still your packmate. That won't change. I promise."

"Anything can change," Banger says, quietly, and, with her head hanging, pushes out from under the porch. "Everything HAS changed."

·········

I've already made it pretty clear that I'm terrible at counting. Maybe that's why I'm terrible with the concept of time. In any case, I was lucky, because Sweetpea did lend me his half-brain, which was apparently the half that could count, and he told me that, of the forty houses in our village, every single one had cats or dogs. Forty-seven dogs, and six cats, including us.

All of those dogs had gathered at the Park, which was more or less in the center of the village. It's a big, grassy area with colorful things all across it that the peoples would put their larva and half-peoples on to swing or hang or climb on.

As we approach the Park, I can see that the dogs have created a large circle in the middle. Of the five other cats besides Sweetpea, only three are in attendance. They seem more curious than concerned, and keep their distance from the dogs, and from each other, perched on the peoples' play contraptions on opposite ends of where the dogs have gathered.

In the center of those dogs, Gracie is speaking in loud, urgent tones. All the dogs are listening to her as though she's suddenly become their pack leader. I'm not sure when that happened. Sometime while me and Banger were sleeping? Or maybe it had happened earlier. Maybe it had happened when she told us all to go back home and wait for the peoples, and we all obeyed.

"No one knows," she is saying, sounding a bit exasperated. "No one even has a clue! We need to confront the reality of our situation. The peoples have left us. We don't know why they left us. We don't know where they went. And we don't know if they're coming back."

"You said they would come back last night!" a tiny fluff-ball of a white dog groans.

Gracie looks at this dog sharply. "I never said they would come back last night. I said that we should be waiting for them when they came home, because we're Good Dogs. But..." Gracie seems to shrink in on herself. "...they didn't come home." Then she straightens again. "But that doesn't mean we stop waiting for them like Good Dogs. It just means they're not home yet."

"I'm starving!" a big, chunky Rottweiler mix wails, and with that, the whole gathering begins to howl about how near to death they are.

"I can feel my stomach shrinking!"

"I'm so weak!"

"I can't even stand!"

Some of them collapse on the ground.

"It's like there's a hole where my stomach should be!"

"Who's going to feed us?!"

Sweetpea leans into me and snickers. "Told you. One-track minds."

I glare at him. "That's not true," I snap. "We care about the peoples more than we care about food!"

Sweetpea looks unconvinced. "Do you, though? Do you REALLY?"

My stomach takes that moment to growl uproariously and I look at it, surprised at the sensation. "My belly's getting angry with me."

"Oh my God," Sweetpea sighs. "The dramatics. You know, you can survive without food for a lot longer than you think. I promise you're not dying."

I realize, a tad late, that the whole gathering is silent. When I glance up, I realize they're silent because they're all watching me and Sweetpea.

Gracie does not seem amused. "Something to add to the conversation, cat?"

Sweetpea looks shocked to be called upon, but recovers quickly. "Well, yeah, in fact I do. I was just telling my friend here that you Crumb-Eaters are inordinately obsessed with food. You all ate yesterday, didn't you?"

A general lack of response leads me to believe that Sweetpea guessed correctly.

"Now, as a former street cat, let me assure you, you've got several days before you're actually starving to death."

"How do you know?" the little white dog cries. "It feels like I'm dying right now!"

"And it'll get worse," Sweetpea states, coolly. "But then it'll get better. After a few days, you kind of forget to be hungry. And then it gets really bad again, and that's when you know you're actually starving. But you won't die for a few more days. You all probably can survive a whole week without eating."

More silence.

The big black-and-tan glances around. "Uh...how long is a week?"

"Cretins," Sweetpea murmurs under his breath, then, louder: "About seven days."

"SEVEN DAYS?!" the gathering erupts in unison.

"Will the peoples be back by then?" a squat little wiener dog begs of Gracie.

Gracie, for her part, remains fairly calm, and ignores the wiener dog, remaining focused on Sweetpea. "If you hadn't been so much help last night, I doubt anyone would be willing to listen to you, Sweetpea."

A chitter of disdainful laughter from the three cats watching.

Sweetpea fluffs his fur and looks irritably at the cats, then at Gracie. "It's Seventeen, dammit! And you're welcome for saving your asses. But, all of that to say..." He casts a long look over the dogs. "If we can figure out how to open doors, then it can't be that hard to figure out how to get access to your kibbles."

"Yes!" several dogs shout out. "Access the kibbles for us! Please!"

"The real question," Sweetpea calls out over them. "Is how long will that kibble last? Because you won't be able to get any more once you run out."

"We won't be able to get more?" a lean greyhound demands. "Why not?"

Sweetpea stares at the dog for a long time, and then looks skyward. "Well, shit, how to put this. Uh, the peoples get the kibbles from other peoples that make the kibbles. Since all the peoples seem to be gone, there are, therefore, no peoples to go get the aforementioned kibbles, and no peoples to make the kibbles, even if you had peoples to go get it."

Almost every single dog quirks their head like they've heard a strange noise. Myself included.

"Soooooooooo..." Gracie draws out the word.

Sweetpea is deadpan. "So no more kibbles."

Predictably, there is weeping and gnashing of teeth.

"How are we going to eat when we run out of kibbles?" I ask, having to almost shout to be heard over the others.

"We'll have to learn to hunt," Gracie says, with authority. All eyes turn back to her.

"Hunt?" a few murmurs arise. "Like, hunt and KILL? Like the cats?"

"I thought about it a lot last night," Gracie says, pacing back and forth in the middle of everyone. "What Sweet—uh, Seventeen—says is true: We can figure out how to get access to the kibbles that are already in our houses. But after that, we won't be able to get anymore. And we don't know if the peoples will be back by the time we run out of food. So we need to be prepared to hunt."

I feel squeamish just thinking about it. Horrific images from the Rabbit Incident roll through my brain, intermingled with the nightmare of the talking head from last night. How could I possibly do that to another living creature—and then have the appetite to actually EAT it?

"We're dogs!" Gracie declares. "Dogs were not always given their food by the peoples. Dogs used to hunt. That's why we form packs. I know that none of us have done that before, but it's in our blood! We only need to re-learn it! And, if we have enough kibbles in our houses, then we have some time to figure out how to hunt. But we should start learning NOW, instead of waiting until we're out of food."

"Now?" I ask. "Like, RIGHT NOW?"

"No, not RIGHT NOW right now," Gracie answers. "Right now, we need to discuss bigger things than just food."

I can't imagine what could be bigger than making sure we don't starve to death while the peoples are gone. That would make them very sad if they returned and found us all dead. Would that make us Bad Dogs?

"We need to put our heads together," Gracie continues. "And try to figure out WHY the peoples have left us. Because if there is a reason to it, and if we can figure out what that reason is, then maybe we can fix it. And if we can fix it, then maybe the peoples will come back!"

"Yes!" I say, with several others. "Let's figure it out so that the peoples come back!"

"The peoples ALWAYS have reasons for doing what they do," Gracie says. "Even if we don't always understand those reasons. But if we try very hard, and if we really think about it, then maybe we can understand why they left. So…" She pauses and looks about at the gathered dogs. "Does anyone have any ideas? Did anyone's peoples tell them anything before they disappeared? There are no bad ideas right now, we're just—"

"I can tell you why the peoples left."

Shocked, I turn. Banger, who has remained silent up until now, huddled close to me, and as far away from the other dogs as she possibly can be while still being a part of the meeting, now stands with her head held level, her tail hanging still.

"You know why they left?" I whisper, disbelieving. Because it didn't seem like she'd known before. Why is she suddenly so sure?

"Banger," Gracie addresses her. "You know something?"

Banger glances about at the other dogs, with no warmth whatsoever in her eyes. She does not look at them like fellow pack-members. Almost as though they aren't even fellow dogs. Strangers. Outsiders. Her lips curl in a snarl. "Look at you all. Look at yourselves."

A few dogs actually turn and look at themselves, particularly their own tails and butts. I'm quite proud of myself for knowing that Banger was speaking FIGURATIVELY. She does that sometimes. I think she learned it from Sweetpea.

"What's wrong with us?" a dog asks.

"What's wrong with you?" Banger snaps. "Your peoples have left you—and all you can think about is food. Yesterday, we watched our peoples vanish into thin air, and this morning I wake up cold, under the porch, and I'm told there's a meeting of all the dogs, and when I come, I hear a bunch of pups yapping about when they're going to get their next meal. Listen to yourselves! Your minds are stuck on your bellies, worried about who's going to feed you, and who's going to throw your ball for you, and who's going to scratch your back at night. Me, me, me! You're only worried about yourselves! About your comfort! You're not worried about what happened to the peoples—you're just worried about how it might upset your pampered, comfortable lives!"

"Banger," Gracie starts to say, with a warning edge to her voice, but Banger cuts her off.

"I wasn't finished!" Banger takes a step forward, her hackles starting to rise, and the dogs nearest us wisely back away. Banger issues a low growl as she stares at the gathering. "You wanna know why the peoples left us? Then just look at yourselves. Look at how you don't care about the peoples at all—you just care about what they GIVE you. I know why they left us. And I'll tell you why. Because each and every one of you is a BAD DOG."

A collective gasp goes up.

The anger that had flared in Banger seems to cool, and she hangs her head again. "And I am too. I'm a Bad Dog. We are ALL Bad Dogs." Her ears droop sullenly over her face as she stares at the ground. "That's why the peoples left us."

The shocked silence gives way to murmurs. Some of them are angry. But more of them are grieved. Shamed. Banger's words have hit them where it hurts. And her words hurt me, too.

"I'm not a Bad Dog, am I, Banger?" I whimper. "Dad said I was a Good Dog. You heard him. He said it right before he disappeared."

"Then why did he leave us?" Banger says quietly. "Peoples only ever abandon their dogs if the dogs have been Bad."

"Well, what if..." I stammer. "What if he didn't CHOOSE to leave us? What if he was forced to leave us? What if they were ALL forced to leave us for some reason that we just don't understand?"

Banger sits tiredly. "Have you ever seen the peoples forced to do anything? They control everything. They have all the power. No one forces them to do anything. Anything they do, they do because they've chosen to do it. Which means that they CHOSE to leave us. And there's only one explanation for why. And I've just given it to you."

7

Mash

THE GATHERING DEVOLVES INTO a bunch of competing voices. I'm too shocked and disturbed by what Banger has said to join in. I stare at her for a time, while she stares at the ground, and then, slowly, she lifts her head to look at the gathering and gives a single snuffle of derision.

I look up as well, and study the dogs all around us. And I'm overcome with the conviction that Banger might be right. Look at all these unhappy pups—because that's what they're acting like. Just a bunch of puppies crying and pressing and jostling for a chance to get at their mother's teats, without a care in the world for how exhausted that mother might be, or how sore her nipples are. But that's just what pups do. They haven't learned to sit and stay and be patient for their food.

I would have thought that these dogs—which were supposed to be Very Good Dogs, mind you—would have learned that. But Banger's accusation is playing out before my very eyes.

Wait a minute. I did that stuff too, didn't I?

Crap. Banger really is right about us.

"Quiet!" Gracie barks into the air. "Everyone be quiet!"

Slowly, all the separate voices still, and the Park becomes quiet again, save for the amused murmurs of the three cats as they converse about how silly we all are. No one pays them any mind. We dogs are used to cats talking down to us.

Gracie is a bit perturbed. She can't seem to decide if she wants to stand or sit or pace. I can see all the tension in her flanks and in her tail. She makes a few irritable noises and shakes vigorously, then raises one hind paw and scratches roughly at her collar.

"Alright," she says, when she's done. Her eyes latch onto Banger. "I know that what Banger said is upsetting. It's certainly not what I want to hear. But..." she goes very still for a moment. Then her tail droops and her eyes get that look about them, like she's been corrected by her peoples. "...I feel...GUILTY."

Several dogs sit on their rumps, heads and shoulders slumped.

"I feel guilty too," one of them murmurs.

"And why," Banger calls out without looking up at them. "Do you ever feel guilty?"

Gracie is the one that answers, in a hushed voice. "Because I know that I've done something Bad."

The big Rotty collapses on the ground, his paws covering his face. "I got into the trash when my peoples were away, and I felt just like this!"

"It's like the time I tore the peoples' Cloud Throne apart!" another gasps.

"It's just like all the times I ate Mom's dirty underwear!" yet another moans.

"Or like the time I spite-peed on their bed 'cause I hated the new puppy they got!" This one from a shaggy, muscular guy.

His companion, a sleek terrier seated next to him, gives him a surprised look. "Bro. What the heck?"

"I'm sorry, bro-bro," the shaggy one says. "It was a complicated time in my life. We're cool now, though."

The white fluff ball cowers in the dirt and trickles a little pee, her eyes wide and wild. "WHAT HAVE WE DONE?!"

"Banger!" the Rotty cries out. "Tell us what we've done wrong! Tell us how to fix it so the peoples will come back!"

I glance rapidly from Banger, to Gracie, then back to Banger. Gracie's hackles have risen just a bit, and she's fixated on Banger in a totally unfriendly way. Banger doesn't notice though. She leans into me and mutters, "Who's this guy again?"

Oh, right. I forgot she doesn't socialize.

"Boozer," I whisper back.

"Right, well, uh, Boozer," Banger struggles out. "The fact is..."

"Yes?" Boozer pleads.

"Tell us!" the white fluff ball begs—her name is Q-Tip, but everyone calls her Q.

"Please! Tell us how to get the peoples back!"

"I don't know!" Banger suddenly shouts, and everyone goes quiet again. Banger pants irritably. "I don't know what we did to be Bad Dogs. So I don't know how we're supposed to fix it."

"I know how we can fix it," Gracie declares, raising her head again out of its aggressive focus on Banger. All eyes turn to her once more, Banger momentarily forgotten, which she seems completely okay with. Banger backs down, all too happy to let Gracie run the show, and sits herself next to me.

Gracie turns in a wide circle, addressing the entire gathering. "If the peoples left us because we became Bad Dogs, then the only way to convince them to come back is to be Very Good Dogs again."

"Yes, but how?" Boozer whines. "I thought I was already a Very Good Dog!"

"Well, apparently you weren't!" Gracie snaps. "Apparently, none of us were! That's why we all feel guilty right now. If the peoples came back right at this instant, would you be ready for them? Would you be able to greet them with joy? Or would you cower in fear?"

"Cower!" Q practically shrieks. "I would cower!"

"You would cower because you're guilty!" Gracie states. "And there's only one way to get rid of that guilt! It's not enough for us to just try to be Good. We have to be PERFECT Dogs. Being Perfect Dogs is the only way to show the peoples that we're worthy. It is the only way to get them to come back!"

"How?" the gathering weeps. "How do we be Perfect Dogs?"

"Every single one of us," Gracie says, her voice quaking with emotion. "Must never, ever—EVER AGAIN—do anything Bad."

A stillness grips us all. I can feel the thoughts of all the other dogs washing over me. I decide to speak. "How do we know what things are Bad without the peoples here to tell us?"

Gracie seems deep in thought, even as she paces in the center of the circle of dogs. When she speaks again, it is almost like she is thinking aloud. "We are all different. Some of us are weak and cannot resist the trash. Others cannot resist their peoples' dirty underwear. Of course, there will be no dirty underwear or trash without the peoples, but...my point is..." She stops. Turns. Turns again. Sits down. "My point is this: We have all been instructed by the peoples on what they consider Bad. But our Badness has been revealed to us differently, according to each of our own weaknesses. In order for all of us to never do anything Bad again, we will need..." her tails wags, as though she's happened upon a fantastic idea.

I anxiously wait for it. I'll do anything. I don't care how hard it is. I'll be a Perfect Dog, and convince Dad to come back.

"We will need to hear from everyone," she finally says, this time with a confidence that does not sound fake. She says it so surely, that I'm immediately convinced she must be right. "We must compile a list of all the things that the peoples think are Bad, from everyone that can remember anything that they were ever corrected on." Her tail is wagging full force now, and I realize that mine is too. So are the tails of everyone else. Except for Banger.

"It's so simple!" Gracie continues, excitedly. "Once we have a list of all the things that the peoples have ever called Bad, then all we have to do is just NEVER do any of those things! And then we'll be Perfect Dogs! And then the peoples will come back!"

"But..." the shaggy spite-pisser guy—his name is Hank—looks a bit sheepish. "It's really hard not to do Bad things."

"I know it's hard," Gracie says. "But it's for the PEOPLES, Hank. Wouldn't you do anything to have your peoples back?"

"I would!" He wags his tails, but then it stops. "But I feel like I'm gonna mess it up."

His brother, the terrier named Willie, seems to agree. "I'm totally gonna mess it up. I just know it. Mom and Dad would always tell me I was Bad when I chased squirrels, but I JUST CAN'T HELP IT!" His eyes go huge, like he's picturing a squirrel right now. "I just see it, and my mind goes blank, and it's like I'm not even ME anymore! I know I shouldn't, but I take off after it anyways!"

An old, white-faced yellow lab that hadn't said or done much up until that point, finally lets out a low gruff of admonishment. "Gracie," he says, in his deep, gravelly voice. "It's impossible to never do anything Bad. We're all going to mess up at some point in time. I mean, if we knew we just had to be Perfect Dogs for a day or so, that'd be different. But what if the peoples want to see us be Perfect for more than that? What if we have to be Perfect for many days?" The old lab—Gus—just huffs his jowls out. "If we have to be Perfect for a lot of days, then one of us is going to mess it up and ruin the whole thing for everyone."

"I hear your concerns," Gracie says gently. But she doesn't seem terribly perturbed by what Gus said. She's thinking out loud again. "We will need to come up with some way to...some way to purify the Bad from our collective pack, if anyone makes a mistake."

I feel Banger stiffen beside me, and she growls quietly, "Collective pack?"

Well, I thought it sounded fantastic—a collective pack! But...that is kind of Banger's worst nightmare.

"But," Gracie says, now beaming. "We have our first item on the list! According to Hank, chasing squirrels is Bad."

"Wait a minute!" One of the dogs from the back shoves her way forward. "I've chased squirrels and my peoples never corrected me on it."

Gracie turns to her. "Maybe they never saw you do it."

This gives the other dog pause. She suddenly looks horrified with herself. "Oh, no. I've done it so many times."

Gracie jumps up. "Who else? Who else has something Bad?"

"Well..." Boozer looks a little embarrassed. "Uh...eating trash?"

"Eating trash!" Gracie echoes. "Very good, Boozer! I think we can all agree that eating trash was always Bad to the peoples, no matter how fresh and delicious it was! Keep going!"

"Eating cat poop?" Q suggests.

Sweetpea recoils. "My fuck. What is wrong with your species?"

"Excellent!" Gracie is practically prancing now. She looks like her old self. "No more eating cat poop!"

Now, feeling the momentum, the whole gathering begins to shout things out, mostly having to do with things they got in trouble for eating, I guess because that was the topic at hand. Plus, we were all starving and thinking of all the things we would eat that our peoples would not be happy about.

Some of the stuff I'd never even tried before. But a lot of it I had.

Dirty underwear. Clean underwear. Socks. And at that point, it was generally agreed upon that eating any item of peoples clothing was Bad. Then someone pointed out that they'd also got in trouble for eating the drapes on the windows. And I pointed out I got in trouble for eating the Special Poofs. That, and several others, were eventually summarized by "Do not eat, chew, or otherwise tear apart any item made of cloth."

Around this time, Gracie was starting to get an overwhelmed look about her. "We're going to need someone to remember all these things. We've only gone over the things that we shouldn't eat, and I don't even think we've finished that yet. Who's got the best memory?"

A whole lot of mutters and deflected eye-contact follows that one. It's not that dogs have inherently bad memories, only that what we do remember is experiences and the feelings we had along with them. Words and lists? Not so much.

"Anyone?" Gracie keeps scanning the crowd.

"Sweetpea," I whisper, giving him a nudge with my snout.

He looks like I just threatened to disembowel him. "The fuck are you talking about?"

I lean in, keeping an eye on Gracie as she continues to search for some dog that might be able to remember the list of Bad Things. "You've got a great memory, Sweetpea," I urge him under my breath. "You could really help us out with this! And don't you want to help us bring the peoples back?"

"I...uh..." his eyes are slipping back and forth. He is shrinking in place, like a cat trying to hide in the middle of an open field. He's watching as Gracie turns a big circle in the center of the dogs, still looking for her memory-keeper, and her arc of searching was very close to coming full circle and landing on me and Sweetpea. "I'm neutral on the topic," he bites out through clenched teeth.

"Oh, you're neutral on the topic?" I'm getting a little irritable. "Which is why you're standing here with the dogs, and you helped set them free last night and all that? Because you're neutral?"

"I didn't do it to help!" Sweetpea grates, ever smaller in form. "I did it so I could gloat about how awesome I am!"

"You know, normally I'd believe that, Sweetpea," I challenge, looming over him as he continues to try to be absorbed into the dirt. "But you've done a lot of things in the last day that make me think you're not quite the hateful feline you make yourself out to be."

"Hateful!" he growls at me, but his eyes are only on Gracie as she turns, now almost looking at us. "Extremely hateful! And spiteful! And EVIL! I'll probably make up a bunch of fake rules and sabotage your whole Perfect Dog operation just to fuck with you!"

"I don't think you'd do that."

"I would! I'm a terrible creature!"

"You're like the ball that Dad puts peanut butter in—hard and chewy on the outside, but soft and creamy in the center."

"Mash? Sweetpea?" Gracie asks, stopping on our huddled whisper-fest.

"No memory!" Sweetpea squeaks out, batting one paw in the direction of Gracie like he can slap her eyes aside from a distance. "Nothing useful over here! Keep on looking!"

"Sweetpea can be your memory-keeper," I announce, standing up to my full height over the cat. "You saw how helpful he was last night, and he's got a great memory."

Gracie blinks, a bit befuddled by the offer. "A cat...to keep the list of Bad Things for us?"

"She's right," Sweetpea declares. "It's a bad idea. Terrible idea. Can't trust cats. We'll always fuck you over in the end. Trust me. Or...not."

"He's just saying that because he doesn't want to admit that he cares."

Gracie takes a step towards us. "Sweetpea? Is this true?"

"I told you not to call me that!" he yowls.

"Oh, right. What was it you wanted me to call you again? See? Dogs—terrible memories."

"My name is—"

Sweetpea cuts off so quickly, I think that there must be some interruption. Apparently I'm not the only one. Confused, several of the dogs at the gathering glance around, trying to find the thing that just distracted Sweetpea.

I look at him with concern. His eyes have taken on a sort of feverish cast. It's almost as though he's in the middle of a waking dream, and can't decide if it's a nightmare or a fantasy.

"Hey, Buddy," I venture. "You alright there?"

Slowly, everyone's attention returns to him.

"My name is..." He starts again...then stops again. Something comes over his face. It's the strangest thing. It's like the Sweetpea that I know is just a jacket, and he slips it off and puts a new one on. And this new Sweetpea has a look about him like he's completely confident and in charge, and, in fact, should be feared by all present.

It's so convincing, that I take a cautious step back. "Whoa."

Sweetpea draws himself into a pose that could have been a statue of the world's most noble feline. "Yes. Yes, it is very good," he says, then raises his voice. "You may, from this point forward, refer to me as The Honorable and Supremely Masterful Keeper of All Things Good and Evil. And you may address me as 'Your Masterfulness.'"

Gracie cocks her head. "I'm not sure we're going to call you—"

"Those are my terms!" Sweetpea snaps. "Take it or leave it, mutts!"

Gracie blinks. Glances at me. I'm not sure what she thought I was going to say about. I didn't see the problem. "Well, can you remember all the things we already listed?"

Sweetpea begins to groom a paw. "Can you remember all the things we already listed, what?"

Gracie's face clouds over. "What?"

Sweetpea perks an ear. "Excuse me?"

Gracie fidgets. Sweetpea continues licking his paw. Begins to clean his face.

"Can you remember the stuff or not?"

"Can you remember the stuff or not, what?"

"What are you talking about?"

"What are you talking about, what?"

Gracie is entirely flummoxed. I decide I need to help her out, so I whisper, loud enough for her to hear: "He wants you to call him by his title!"

Gracie glares at Sweetpea. "Are you serious with this?"

Sweetpea doesn't miss a beat. "Are you serious with this..." he turns large, expectant eyes on her. "...WHAT?"

Gracie appears to summon up a depth of patience and issues a long sigh. "Are you serious with this, Your Masterfulness?"

"Thank you," Sweetpea says, primly. "And yes. Yes, I am."

"Alright. Well. Can you remember the things we already listed? Uh...Your Masterfulness?"

Sweetpea beams, and then gets savage again and shouts to the three cats still watching. "How you like me now, you Litter Critters? Honorable and Supremely Masterful Keeper of All Things Good and Evil! Suck it!" He takes a ragged, self-satisfied breath and returns his attention to Gracie. "And, yes. His Masterfulness can remember everything you've already listed. It's all locked away in my steel-trap mind."

Gracie waits expectantly.

"Oh. Right." Sweetpea fluffs himself up and looks regal again. "Basically, you guys eat all kinds of weird shit, and you've got to stop. No cat poop, no cloth, no trash. I'll sum it all up like this: Dogs shall eat only the food intended for canine consumption."

"Food intended for canine consumption?" Gracie questions.

Sweetpea stares at her blankly, then rolls his eyes. "Fine. How about, Dogs shall eat only kibbles and meat."

"What about grass?" someone calls from the back—I can't see who. "Sometimes I like to eat grass."

There is general affirmation at this. We all like to eat grass on occasion.

"Ugh. Fuck. Alright. Dogs shall eat only kibbles, meat, and grass."

"But what about squirrels? They're meat, aren't they?"

"No, they're on the list of prohibited foods," Sweetpea says. "And you'll address me by my title, or we're fucking done."

The squirrel-chasing dog thinks that one over for a moment. "Uh...what about squirrels, they're meat aren't they, Your Masterfulness?"

"Asked and answered!" Sweetpea yells. "Moving on!"

"Other Bad Things?" Gracie prompts the gathering.

"Humping!" calls out a French Bulldog with bat-like ears roughly the size of his body.

"Oh, that's a good one!" I say. "Humping was always Bad."

"Yes," Sweetpea affirms. "Excellent. No more humping. I'll put it on the list."

"Wait!" A pair of German Shepherds step forward. "We were allowed to hump. Our peoples actually encouraged it."

Gracie puzzles over that. "Didn't you have litters of pups?"

The two shepherds, a male and a female, look fondly at each other. "We've had three litters. We're a breeding pair. Very prestigious blood line."

"Alright," Sweetpea considers this. "That's easy enough. Dogs shall not hump, unless they are a breeding pair."

"That seems reasonable," Gracie admits.

"Put it on the books!" Sweetpea calls out. "We're making good progress. Let's keep the momentum up. What else you got?"

8

Sweetpea

The Law of Good and Evil (Day One):

- 1. Dogs shall eat only kibbles, meat, and grass.

- 2. Squirrels are prohibited. Dogs shall not chase, nor consume, squirrels.

- 3. Humping is Bad, unless the humping is done by a breeding pair.

- 4. Honor the Cloud Throne and keep it sacred.

Well, it was a bit hectic getting started, but all things considered, I feel like we had a pretty productive day. Do I think that these things are really going to bring the peoples back? Honestly…I don't know. Part of me thinks it all sounds pretty far-fetched. But the dogs seem pretty convinced that it'll work, and, really, even though cats were way better at reading the peoples, we can't match up to dogs' obsession with them. The dogs have spent more time and energy pondering what pleases and displeases the peoples than cats have spent ignoring them, which I feel gives them some unique insight.

Plus, they're all calling me Your Masterfulness now.

I spend the rest of the day assisting and coaching the dogs on how to access their kibbles, patiently instructing the halfwits on how to get the bins and bags open, and how to do something called "rationing," which essentially means "Dear God, stop gorging yourself and save some for tomorrow."

Now, as the sun sets on our first full day without the peoples, I cautiously approach Gracie's house. I'm not sure if Longjohn got the memo that I'm the motherfucking Honorable and Supremely Masterful Keeper of All Things Good and Evil, but he better not step up to me, or...

Or...I'll have Gracie do things to him.

This time I position myself at the pet door, facing outwards to make sure Longjohn doesn't sneak up on me again. "Gracie, you in there?" I hiss through the door.

She doesn't respond, but I can hear her padding to the door, and a moment later, it buzzes quietly open. I slip in, and immediately prepare myself for a brawl, because it's one thing to encounter my archnemesis in his territory, and an entirely different thing to enter his house. There will be no ceremonial Phases of Combat. We'll just jump straight into Phase Four, which is the final phase: Shred.

But Longjohn is nowhere in sight. The house barely even smells like him. He must've been out galivanting all day. Probably still trying to annex my bird-hunting grounds, the thieving bastard. I'll have to talk to Gracie about that. With any luck, I might just expand my own territory in the deal.

"So," I venture, as I relax. "How goes it?"

Gracie is pacing the living room area where the pet door opens into. She seems distraught—a far cry from the confident Collective Pack Leader that I saw at the gathering. She keeps walking towards the peoples' Cloud Throne, then letting out little groaning noises and walking away.

"This is gonna be harder than I thought," she says, tensely.

"Which part?"

"Not being Bad!"

"Ah. Temptation rearing its ugly head already?"

"I wanna sit on the Cloud Throne!"

"Tut-tut, Gracie," I admonish her, moving to position myself between her and the Cloud Throne. "You must honor the Cloud Throne and keep it sacred."

"But does that really mean I can't sleep on it?" She gazes forlornly at it. "It's so...comforting."

"Yes," I sigh. "But you are still a Bad Dog, Gracie. And Bad Dogs are not allowed on the Cloud Throne, are they?"

"No," she grinds out.

"No," I affirm. "Until you are a Perfect Dog, and the peoples return, you must resist the temptation to defile the Cloud Throne."

You know, I never thought I would enjoy being the moral regulator for dogs. But it really feels nice. I feel...superior. Set apart. Very special.

"Yes, I know," she says. "But the whole thing has got me thinking."

"Oh? About?"

"About what Gus said. About how we're going to eventually mess this up. One of us—maybe even me!—is going to make a mistake and do something Bad."

"If even one of the Collective Pack does something Bad, the entire Collective Pack shares the blame." I literally just made that up, but it sounds really good, doesn't it?

"We need to find a way to purify the Collective Pack, if a member does something Bad."

"Right, right," I muse. "Like, take a bath?"

Gracie sits down and regards me thoughtfully. "That's something I hadn't even thought about. We hate baths. But the peoples loved them. Always wanted us to be clean and flower-smelling."

"Should I add it to the list?" I suggest. "Should it be, 'Dogs shall not be dirty?' No, that's too hard to manage. You guys are dirt magnets and you don't groom yourselves."

"No, we can't be clean all the time. It's impossible. And the peoples would only give us baths occasionally. They didn't want us to be clean ALL THE TIME. Just some of the time."

"I could let you know when you're starting to smell offensive." Boy, that'd be a whole other layer to this delicious cake. I can just imagine myself commanding them, "You there! You stink! Cleanse thyself, immediately!"

"Bathing should be a punishment," Gracie says, brightening. "If one of the pack does something Bad, they should have to bathe."

"Ah, yes. Makes sense. They should have to do something they don't want to do, to prove that they really do care about the peoples."

"They SHOULD have to do something they don't want to do," Gracie agrees. "But it's not enough! There needs to be more...more purification of the guilt. Something so bad that after doing it, all their guilt will be washed away."

"Well, let's see. Dogs hate baths, so if they're Bad, they have to cleanse themselves. What else do dogs really hate?" I brighten, as something occurs to me. "Or, better yet: what do dogs really love?"

Gracie tilts her head. "What do they love? This is supposed to be punishment and purification."

"No, yeah," I say quickly. "Find the thing they love, and then make them give it up! Now THAT'S punishment."

"Oh, I see. That IS punishment."

"So what do dogs love?"

"Peoples?"

"Well, we can't give the peoples up because they're already gone. What else do they love?"

"Food?"

"Hm. Yes." I ponder this for a moment, my tail swishing thoughtfully. "We can work with that."

"The dog that does the Bad Thing must bathe themselves, and then they must give up some of their food."

"How much of their food should they give up?"

"A meal?"

"Just one meal? And then they get to eat it later?"

"You're right. It's not enough just to forgo the meal and have it later. The meal needs to be destroyed. There's nothing worse to a dog than when food goes to waste."

"How are you going to destroy the food?"

Gracie gets a faraway look in her eyes, and I can almost see the enlightenment cascading down on her. "Yes. Yes! They will eat the meal..."

"Wait, what? That's not punishment..."

"And then vomit it up."

"Oh. Gross."

"And then not eat it again."

I shudder and swallow sickly. "That is possibly the most disgusting habit dogs have. But how are you going to keep them from eating the vomit? Or, for that matter, keeping one of the others from eating it?" My stomach roils at the thought, but I know it's just a fact of dog life. "Y'all will eat each other's vomit sometimes, won't you?"

Rather than answer, Gracie, still radiant with revelation, speaks in a low, sonorous voice: "They shall bathe, and then eat their meal, and then they will go to the creek and vomit it into the water." She fixes her eyes on me. "You'll watch and ensure that they do."

I pull my head back. "Are you crazy? I'm not watching that shit."

"You must!" she says, forcefully, taking a step towards me. "You're the Honorable Supreme...uh...Master...uh..."

"Honorable and Supremely Masterful Keeper of All Things Good and Evil. Practice it. Know it. Love it."

"Right. That. Your Masterfulness. It's YOUR responsibility to ensure the purity of the Collective Pack."

"I thought I was just going to remember the laws."

"Do you want the peoples to come back or not?" she demands, her voice rising.

"Well, uh, sure. You know. That'd be okay. I guess."

"Then it's settled. This is the purification: The Bad Dog will bathe, eat a full meal, and then vomit it into the water. Oh, it's beautiful. The water will wash their Badness from their body, and then it will wash away their offering of vomit. After that, they will be pure and Good again. The whole Collective Pack will be purified."

She's in quite a holy state now, and I dare not contradict her.

"Okay. Great. Let's see. 'If a member of the Collective Pack should do something that is Bad in the eyes of the peoples, that pack member shall bathe himself...' Wait. How are they going to bathe themselves?"

"Well. Um." She scratches irritably under her collar. "In the stream, I suppose."

"In the vomit stream?"

"Before they vomit."

"So, they bathe in the stream, then go eat, then come back to the stream and vomit?"

"No, they can eat first, then go to the stream and bathe, and then vomit."

"Got it. Perfect. Let's roll with that."

The Law of Good and Evil (Day One - Addendum)

- Should any member of the Collective Pack defile the pack by committing an act that is Bad in the eyes of the peoples, that member shall fill their belly with food, go to the stream, cleanse themselves in the water, and then purge the contents of their stomach into the water. Then the member will be forgiven and the Collective Pack will be purified.

·········

I'm feeling pretty damn confident as I slip out the pet door of Gracie's house and survey her backyard. Still no sign of Longjohn, though he won't remain gone forever. But you know what? I don't think he'll fuck with me now that every dog in the village sees me as their moral authority.

Wow. How did that even happen? Was it my idea? It was a good idea, so it must've been mine. I can vaguely recall Mash saying something about it, but it was probably just some stupid dog stuff. This was definitely my idea.

With a bit of a strut now, I saunter down Longjohn's porch, rustle up my tail and mark the bottom step. Ha. I'll see if I can stay up tonight to watch him come home and realize that, while he's been marking my bushes, I've marked his fucking porch. It'll be great.

I'm just starting to pad my way across the grass towards my crash pad when I hear it—just a breath in the air, so quiet that even MY ears strain to pick it up.

"Sweetpea."

I stop, fur rising. "Who the fuck just called me that?"

A light breeze. No other sounds.

Was that Longjohn? No, if he'd been close enough to whisper, then we'd be having a showdown. And I don't think that was Longjohn's voice anyways. It sounded almost like...

"Sweetpea," the whisper comes again.

I crouch low, ears pivoting, eyes searching my surroundings. It's dark out, but that doesn't mean shit to cats. I can see enough that I know there's no one in my vicinity. And yet...the voice seemed so close. Almost right beside me.

"Alright, motherfucker," I growl. "You know the rules. It's Honorable and Supremely—"

"Sweetpea, stop."

My spine tingles. I swear, that voice had just spoken from right over my head. Not knowing what else to do, I jerk my head upward, searching the sky to see who in the hell has figured out how to stalk me by hovering in the air.

But there's nothing there. Just the black sky, dotted with stars.

I can feel the Prime Directive bubbling up inside me.

"Alright, you're officially freaking me out, whoever you are, and I'm about to ghost your ass." I prepare to sprint to my nearest safe house, which just so happens to be the same shrub of safety I'd used yesterday.

The voice comes again, so soft that I don't think a dog could hear it if they were standing right beside me. "Do you remember what I told you?"

My eyes still darting, I stammer, "Who's you? I can't remember what you told me if I don't even know who you are! Show yourself, dammit! Quit playing games!"

Then the strangest thing happens. The best I can describe it is a laugh, but not an audible one, if that makes any sense. I FEEL the laughter, a warm embrace that washes over me, and, despite my raging instincts, calms me.

"Oh, Sweetpea. It's me."

My brain feels like I've just gotten into some catnip. Not the energetic catnip, but the sleepy, hey, everything'll be alright kind. It is only because of this unbidden sense of relaxation that I loosen out of my tense crouch.

A hope that I didn't even realize I'd harbored in my dark little heart blooms fiercely in my chest, and I whisper, "Dad?"

That laugh again, so soft, like I'm being stroked by his big, warm hands right then and there. I can almost feel them on my fur.

"Do you remember what I told you?"

"Uh, yeah, you know, of course! I've got a great memory. In fact, all the dogs are calling me—"

"Shhh."

I don't even realize that I've shut up until I've been sitting in my own silence for a moment. Which is very odd. I don't know if you know this about cats, but we don't respond to commands. We're free creatures. Peoples don't OWN us, and they certainly don't get to tell us what to do.

So why the hell have I shut up?

I'd be more indignant about this if I didn't feel so terribly peaceful.

"What did I tell you?" the whispery voice asks me.

I'm trying to come up with a sharp retort. Really, I am. But my whole body is at rest, and my mind feels like it's been slow-simmered to a tender consistency. I'm just so damn...MILD right now.

"You said," I begin, my own voice quiet and calm, and perhaps a little awestruck. "To listen." A flash of impatience gets through the calm and my tail flicks. "But you never told me what I'm supposed to listen for!"

"Well, you're doing it right now."

"I'm doing it right now?" Despite myself, I feel pleased.

Pleased. Because a peoples is pleased with me.

The fuck is happening to me? One day surrounded by idiot dogs and I'm already becoming a simpering slave?

And yet I just can't muster the indignation.

"There are things that I need to say," the voice breathes in my ear. "That only you can hear."

"Oh. Well, great. Tell me, then."

"In time, Sweetpea. All things must take their course."

"What does that mean? How much time? What type of course are we talking about?"

"Just listen. Listen, and when you're ready, you'll hear."

"I'm listening right now. Lay it on me."

"Listen and remember." The voice is fading, just barely tickling my auditory perception. "Listen…and…"

I wait, but there's nothing else.

"And…what?" I ask the air around me. The blanket of calm that has been draped over me this whole strange time suddenly lifts, and irritation comes flooding in behind it. "And remember? Is that what you were going to say? Remember something? Remember what? Remember to listen? Listen and remember to listen? Dammit, say something else! CLARITY IS THE KEY TO COMMUNICATION, YOU KNOW!"

"Sweetpea?"

"Gah!" I jump, because that voice was no whisper—it came from right in front of me.

Mash is standing there, maybe ten dog-lengths away, his ears all cocked up and his head twisted to one side in curious confusion.

"Mash!" I gasp. Then remember myself. "How dare you call me by that name!"

"Oh, sorry," Mash cringes. "Your Masterfulness. I just...I heard you talking to yourself."

I snap my gaze around to confirm there are no ghostly vestiges of my hallucination still plaguing me, and then scamper across the last bit of lawn to Mash's side. "I wasn't talking to myself, you big dolt."

"Oh, great! Who were you talking to?"

"I was talking to..." I stop midsentence. Caution reasserts itself. Sure, sure, everyone knows that cats can be a little crazy. But talking to Dad? Talking to a ghost? That might be too much for the dogs. They might oust me from my brand-new position. And that simply wouldn't do. "Well. You know how cats get at night," I say dismissively. "We see things and hear things. It's no big deal. Nothing to comment on. All very normal."

Mash's tail sways slowly back and forth like he wants to be happy, but is still a bit confused. "Yeah, I've seen you go bananas at night. But..."

I fix him with a cold gaze. "But what?"

"But when you go bananas you're always wide-eyed and tense."

"Yes, that happens when you're perceiving things beyond the veil. What's your point?"

"You didn't look like that this time," Mash says. "You looked very relaxed."

"Are you accusing me of something?" I growl. "Are you accusing the Honorable and Supremely Masterful Keeper of All Things Good and Evil?!"

"Uh, no." Mash seems taken aback. "I just wanted to make sure you're okay."

"Ah. Well. Yes. I'm fine." I urgently lick at my shoulders for no particular reason. "His Masterfulness is just tired from all that memorization earlier and making sure all you mutts got fed. I feel like a harried mother. I need a nap." I stalk past Mash, heading for my crash pad. "And then I need to kill something."

9

BANGER

I STAND IN THE car cave, looking out at the dark, lonely street, and the white frames of the houses. Some of the lights in those houses are still on, the dogs and cats that live in them not bothering or not able to shut them off. I wonder if the peoples are irritated at that. I wonder if it's Bad.

There are so many things that might be Bad. So many ways for me—for us—to screw up. And then what? What if we mess up and we don't even know it? What if we missed an important law? What if we can never be Perfect Dogs?

I'm stressed in a different way than I've ever been stressed before. It's not the manic stress of anxiety. It's a slow rot, like something inside of me has become infected and it's making me sick and slow and tired.

The car cave is open to the world. That was Sweetpea's contribution, as I understand it. When they worked to free the dogs and cats that were trapped in their houses, he was the one that suggested opening the car caves, and he was the only one nimble enough to leap up and smack the button that would do it.

From there, it was only a matter of teamwork to finagle open the door from the car cave into the house itself. It was quite the undertaking to open those doors, so they're left open now. I'm pretty sure that would have made the peoples mad, but there really isn't anything that we can do about it. We can't mount door-opening operations every day in forty different houses.

I hope that leaving the doors open isn't Bad. I hope the peoples can forgive us for some of the things that we have to do to survive.

It's all so crazy and out of control. I would have never thought this would be my life. Not after everything I'd already been through. Not after Dad had come to the Place of Judgment and found me and Mash worthy of a pack.

I still remember the look on his face when he squatted down in front of our cage. Mash, ever the social dog, immediately pranced up and wagged his tail and panted in Dad's face. I was afraid Mash's excitement would scare Dad off, but he only smiled and laughed and called Mash a Good Dog.

I was holding back, not trusting this peoples because I'd learned that trusting them too much can get you hurt. But I remember that moment, how gentle he was with Mash, how kind, how patient he was with Mash's exuberance. And it made me think, maybe not all peoples are like the peoples I had before.

I don't like to talk about my time before the Place of Judgment. It's certainly not a time I prefer to recall. I've never even told Mash the whole story. But it's important now to remember it. It's important that I remember the difference between the old me, and the new me.

I don't remember everything from my time before the Place of Judgment. I was just a pup in a litter. I don't remember my mother, or my brothers and sisters. They all went away when I was barely weaned.

I remember the peoples that took me, though. I remember them very well. One was a man, and the other was a woman, and they had two little-peoples, a brother and a sister. I loved those little-peoples. They would come to me in the place where I was kept—outside, because I was not found worthy yet to come inside, and never would be. I knew that the peoples did not like it when dogs were dirty or smelled, and I knew that I was both. And yet those little-peoples would come to me anyways, with great big smiles on their faces, and it was like they didn't notice how filthy I was, or how bad I smelled to them. They would scratch behind my ears and smoosh their faces up against mine, and I felt, in those moments, that they were my true pack, and nothing would ever come between us.

Of the older peoples, my memories are filled only with fear and shame. The woman never called herself my Mom, and didn't seem to care about me much either way. She neither loved me, nor hated me. I simply was. I was an object to her. Something that lurked in her backyard, which was a place she didn't prefer to go, and she wanted nothing to do with my dirt or my smell.

The man was clearly the leader of the pack, and I knew that I must please him, as all Good Dogs must please the leader of the pack. But no matter what I did, he was never pleased. No matter how well-behaved I was, no matter how quietly I endured the cold nights and hot days, and tried not to bark at things or make a nuisance of myself, and tried to be thankful for the water in my dish, even if it was cloudy and green, and for the kibbles that would be poured into my bowl—I was especially thankful for those, because sometimes they would not arrive. And when they wouldn't I would try not to complain. I would curl up around my empty belly and tell myself to be patient, that the peoples were wise and they knew things that I could not possibly understand, and that, when they were ready, and when the time was right in their eyes, the kibbles would come.

As I look back now, after having been a part of Dad's pack, I realize that I was never really a part of that old pack. The man never found me worthy, and because he was the leader of the pack, that means that, really, I had no pack.

Why did he take me if he didn't want me? Why bring me to his home, to his pack, if he had no intention of ever accepting me?

No matter what, I could not find a way to win him over. I thought that the problem must lie with me. There was something that I was doing wrong that was the reason for the man's constant rejection of me. When he would choose to pay attention to me, it was never kind. He was always angry with me. I was not a Good Dog. I was a Dumb Bitch. I was a Rotten Animal.

And I began to think that this was normal. I began to believe that the fear I felt when he would walk out into the backyard was some sort of love. I was just so desperate to be SEEN by him, that even if that seeing came with pain, it was better than not to be seen at all.

To this day, I don't know what I did wrong to earn the scars he gave me. It must've been something. But I had not barked, and I had not whined. I had not chewed the tattered, mildewy blanket that I slept on. I had not dug holes. The only thing I can imagine is that I may have ruined his grass with my constant walking in a circle, but I couldn't walk anywhere else, because I was chained to a tree.

The first scars he gave me were not the ones that everyone sees on my back. The first scars are small, just little welts under my fur that will never go away. He had come out of the back of the house, holding something in his hands. I didn't know what that thing was, and I thought perhaps it was something for me, but then told myself it couldn't be, because I hadn't done anything to deserve a gift. Still, I moved towards him, to the very end of my chain, and my tail wagged low, as it always did in his presence—my body trying to change the fear in my chest to love. Hoping against hope that this would be the time I was found worthy. The time I was accepted by him.

I'm still not sure what the thing was that he had in his hand, but he just sat down on the back steps and he pointed it at me. My instinct told me that I was in danger, and yet, I couldn't bring myself to turn away from him, so strong was my hope.

The thing made a spitting noise, and the next thing I knew, pain lanced through my rear quarters. My tail immediately tucked and I ran for the safety of the little plastic box that I lived in. I heard the thing spit again as I ran, and felt the pain hit me in my side. Even as I ran, I felt guilty. My body was telling me to flee, but my mind was telling me to hold strong, perhaps this was only a test of my worthiness.

But I don't think he ever meant to test my worthiness. I don't think he was ever going to accept me. I realize that now.

I hid inside my box while the thing made spitting noises, and things smacked the side of the plastic while I shivered inside. Some of them fell to the dirt, and I saw that they were tiny metal balls, barely bigger than a gnat.

Two more of those metal balls found my hide before the man was done with me. By then, I was squashed against the inside of my box, unwilling to move as the hope drained away from me and left me without even the will to get out of the way, but simply to wait, and endure.

The scars on my back I will not tell you about. Partly because it still does not make sense to me. And partly because my memory of that day is very hazy. The details of it are lost, like trying to see the bottom of a muddy puddle. I only remember the pain like fire across my back, and I remember screaming and howling, because the pain would not end.

Between that day, and the day I was taken to the Place of Judgment, I don't know how much time had passed. I only know that the scars on my back were not scars yet, but open, weeping wounds that I could not reach to lick or to soothe. I could only wait, and endure.

The day when I was taken to the Place of Judgment is very clear, though. Peoples came to the house. They were all one pack of peoples, because they all wore the same clothing. They must have been a pack that the man didn't like, because he yelled and shouted and fought with them. He lost, and they took him away in a car, and I never saw him again.

I waited in the backyard, huddled in my box, not daring to hope for anything more, because hope had proven a cruel trick in the past. I was scared of this new pack of peoples. They were violent with the man, and I think that they hurt him, and so I assumed they would hurt me too.

But one of them came out to my box and squatted down in front of it. It was a woman, and she leaned in and spoke soft words to me, and held out some food that I was afraid to take from her. But my belly was empty, and I could endure no longer. Eventually I came out and I ate the food, knowing that at any moment, this woman-member of the strange pack might hurt me like she had hurt the man.

But she didn't hurt me. She put her hands on me, as though the dirt and the stink did not bother her at all. She put her hands on me like the little-peoples did, and she smiled, and her eyes were kind, and not cruel.

That was the day I was taken from the only backyard I had ever known, with its chain, and its circle of dirt around the tree that I could not escape, and all of its pain and fear. That was the day I was taken to the Place of Judgment.

And that was where I learned that I did not like other dogs. I had lived, up to that point, with a certain strategy for survival: Be quiet, keep your head down, hope, wait, and endure. But being quiet and keeping your head down was not what the other dogs did, and they did not respect anyone else that did it.

Looking back, I know that they were all hard dogs that had lives similar to mine, but that they'd handled them differently. They'd become aggressive. I myself did not know how to be around other dogs, because I'd never been around them before. I did not know that my body-language was telling them I was weak, that I was a dog to be taken advantage of. When I tried to hope and wait and endure, they would attack, until I was placed in a cage by myself and not allowed to be around the other dogs.

Yes, I realize that not all dogs are like those ones I met in my first days at the Place of Judgment. But I also know that all these "nice" dogs around me are only a few skipped meals and a bit of stress away from becoming just like them. And while I can force myself to think through the panic and fear that I feel when they draw near—and the inevitable aggression that rises in me as a result—I don't think I will ever be able to remove the stink of those first experiences.

When Mash sees another dog, his brain tells him "Friend! Fun! Play!"

When I see another dog, my brain screams, "Threat! Untrustworthy! Fight!"

I can control it, but there it is, plain and simple. I do not trust other dogs.

But the peoples. The peoples...I'm not sure what's different, but I love the peoples. Maybe it is because my first experiences were not with the man that hurt me, but with the little-peoples that loved me. Or perhaps it is because I encountered so many Bad Dogs, but only one Bad Peoples. Or maybe it is something deeper. Maybe it is something that is just a part of me. Because even the man that hurt me, I wanted to please. I WANTED him to love me. And I WANTED to love him in return.

And maybe those little-peoples did love me. But the love of little-peoples is different than the love of big-peoples. The love they showed me was like the love that Mash shows me—friend, fun, and play. But the love that Dad showed me was different. I did not need to please him, he was already pleased. I did not need to perform anything for him, he found my company enough. I did not need to convince him that I was worthy, he saw my worth the moment we locked eyes.

And I loved him for that. And I still love him for that. I don't think I will ever stop loving him, no matter how long he stays away.

I'm not sure why I'm still sitting in the car cave. The night has grown colder, and the outside is quiet. The crickets and the frogs and the nightbirds are silent.

Maybe I'm watching the street for Dad to come driving home, even though his car is parked right behind me in the cave. Old habits, I suppose. He is not here, and so I watch and wait for him to come back. I don't know what else to do with myself.

Mash comes padding around the corner from the side of the house and spots me with a wag of his tail. "Oh, hey, Banger." He comes and sniffs at me, then sits beside me, looking out at the street. "So. What are we looking at?"

"Nothing, I guess."

He's quiet for a time. I can tell that he's kind of watching me out of the corner of his eye. Reading me. Knowing me, because he knows me better than all the other dogs.

"You alright, Banger?"

"Am I alright?" I echo, trying not to let my irritation show. Mash has a great heart. But sometimes he can be a little dim. "No, I'm not alright, Mash. How are YOU alright?"

"Well, I mean...I'm not ALRIGHT alright. But, really, if you think about it, it wasn't a bad day. We spent it outside, you got to meet some of my friends, and...you know...I was able to hang out with them and stuff. So that's nice."

I stare at him, too shocked for a moment to speak. "It wasn't a bad day? Have you been paying attention? The peoples are gone! And they didn't come back! And our best idea at getting them to come back requires everyone in this stupid, so-called Collective Pack, to not do anything Bad? A bunch of self-centered, food-obsessed, mutts? They won't make it. They'll never make it."

"Geez." Mash looks a little perturbed at me. "Why are you so hard on them? They're trying."

"Because they don't understand!" I snarl, viciously enough that Mash takes to his feet again and backs away from me. I immediately feel bad for it—guilty, because I know that I've done something that Dad would not want me to do. Dad never liked it when I snapped at Mash. Always would tell me, "Easy, Banger. Lighten up a little bit, huh?"

"What do they not understand, Banger?" Mash says, a bit tiredly, like he doesn't think I have a real answer to it. "What do I not understand?"

"THEY," I growl. "Don't understand what loving the peoples and BEING loved by them actually means. They take it for granted because they've never known anything else. Their entire lives have been spent being coddled and cuddled and given everything they could want! They don't know what real life is like, and they don't know it because they were PROTECTED from that life by their peoples. And then, when the peoples disappear, their first thought isn't concern for the peoples, but concern for themselves." I'm so angry that I spit the next words out without even thinking about them. "They're just a bunch of Dumb Bitches and Rotten Animals!"

Some part of me winces at that, but I'm just too dang pissed.

Mash looks extremely offended by my outburst. "You know, I was at the Place of Judgment too, Banger. I've seen what life is like."

"No, you haven't!" I round on him. "So you were taken to the Place of Judgment as a pup! So were half of those idiots out there! It doesn't make a difference! They didn't have a life before that! They don't know what it's like to NOT be loved! They don't understand the importance of it! And the importance of loving the peoples back!"

"Hey!" Mash's voice takes on an assertive tone that I've barely ever heard him use. "I'm sorry you had a hard life before we met, but you can't just stand there and act like you're the only one that knows how to love the peoples."

"It's been one day, Mash," I say. "One. Day. And already you're okay with it. Already you're distracted by the fact that you got to run around with other dogs. Already you've forgotten."

"Forgotten what?" Mash demands.

"Forgotten that you loved Dad first! That your love for him was the most important thing! And now look at you. One day later, and 'Oh, it wasn't a bad day, even though Dad is gone, because I got to play with my friends.'" I snort and look away from him.

"Yeah?" Mash's voice is quieter now, but no less angry with me. "Well maybe I did get distracted by having some fun with my friends, Banger. But do you remember what else Dad said?"

I hang my head. I remember it all too well. How could I forget? It's like a sharp stick that won't stop jabbing at my chest. "To love others."

"Yeah," Mash says, then turns to leave. "I'm going inside to sleep. And maybe, instead of obsessing about half of what Dad said, you should try to remember the whole thing."

He disappears inside, leaving me alone in the car cave to watch the dark and empty streets for someone that wasn't coming home.

10

Sweetpea

(Day 10)

We cats have a saying: What's good for the tom is good for the molly. Removing the genders, one could simply say, what's good for one is good for all.

In a complete reversal of that sentiment, the dogs have decided that what is Bad for one dog is Bad for all dogs. Now, granted, I was the one that came up with that. And, admittedly, in retrospect, it doesn't make much sense.

Do I feel bad for that? Well, I can't quite say no, but any badness I might have felt is covered by a keen curiosity—which is always the way to get a cat involved—to see what the end result will be. And besides, the dogs seem to think it's a wonderful idea, and it's not my job to make sense of what the dogs feel like they need to do to be Perfect. It is only my job to remember what they tell me, even if it causes me to inwardly roll my eyes.

Let me give you an example.

Roo, the short-haired racing-type dog, has just pointed out to the Collective Pack that she was not allowed on any of the furniture. In other words, not just the Cloud Throne, but the various chairs, cushions, and beds as well. Out of an abundance of caution—and, I suspect, an unhealthy amount of zeal to please the peoples—Gracie has decided that, because it was Bad for Roo, it must be Bad for everyone.

There was much grumbling about this, and I thought that some of the dogs might object. But…it's only been ten days since the peoples disappeared. The fervor to lure them back with Perfect behavior is still very high.

So no one really raises an objection—not that I think Gracie would listen, and since she has apparently become the de facto leader of the Collective Pack, what she says goes—and it must be codified into the law.

"Alright," I say, wracking my brain through the myriad of new laws that I've had to memorize over the past week and a half. It's starting to be a struggle, even for my prodigious memory. "How's this: Dogs shall not sit or lay or otherwise rest themselves on or about anything that was built for the peoples to sit or lay or otherwise rest themselves on."

Gracie listens sagely and appears satisfied. I've become better and better about how I word these things. Initially I thought they would want some wiggle room—I know I would—but they are bound and determined not to make any mistakes, even if they're not sure whether it's a mistake or not. So I've started to word things more specifically, so there's no loopholes for Bad Dogs to get through and falsely claim that they're Good.

"It's good," Gracie intones. "Very good. As it is remembered by His Masterfulness, so shall it be remembered by all." That is her little way of making it official. She turns to Roo, who, while not the most popular dog at the moment, at least looks happy to have contributed. "Excellent job, Roo. Your faithfulness will be credited to you as Goodness."

Roo bows her head. "Thank you, Voice of the Peoples."

Oh, that's another thing. I guess my sweet-ass title made Gracie a little jealous, because she had to come up with her own. Personally, I think "Voice of the Peoples" is a little bit of an over-reach, but it's kind of hard to say that to her when my title is...well, you know what my title is. It's become an annoying mouthful, even to me.

Anyways, Gracie is now the Voice of the Peoples, and everyone is pretty much okay with it. Except for Banger, who has made it plain to all that she thinks it's bullshit, and has refused to show up at the Collective Pack meetings, which occur every day at sundown, in the Park. While I don't harbor any of Banger's vitriol towards the other dogs, I do miss her spirited arguments.

Now, Gracie, the Voice of the Peoples, addresses the crowd. "Packmate Roo has done a Good Thing. She has considered not what she wants, but what the peoples want, and has shown us yet another mistake that we can now avoid. Has anyone else considered this as diligently as Roo?"

I pan my gaze over the gathered dogs. An interesting thing has happened over the last several days. While, individually, none of the dogs particularly enjoy having more and more of their comforts and pleasures taken away from them, once you get them all together in a meeting like this, they enter into some sort of manic, competitive state, with everyone jostling to be the next dog to come up with something to be codified into law.

Sometimes, I swear, they just make things up so they can feel Good.

Case in point:

"Yes, Voice of the Peoples!" calls out JuJu Bean, who is some sort of muscly terrier mix with short, gray fur. "I have diligently meditated on my peoples' instructions to me, and have uncovered a Bad Thing."

"Very well, JuJu," Gracie says. "Reveal it to us."

"Well, there was this one time that there were some robins in the yard, and it made me angry to see them so flippantly hopping around my territory, so I began to bark at them. This made the peoples wrathful and they told me to stop."

Gracie's eyes narrow. "Did they tell you it was Bad?"

JuJu looks a bit caught off-guard by the question. I watch her intensely, and...yup. There it is. She's totally making this shit up.

"Yes. They came to me in full wrath and spoke with their Thunder Voices, and said, 'No barking at robins, JuJu! That's Bad!'"

I highly doubt that. If what she's saying even happened at all, she was likely raising an enormous clamor and the peoples just got irritated at how loud she was. If they corrected her at all, it was probably something like, "JuJu! Give it a rest!" or "Would you shut up?"

In other words, I don't think the peoples gave two turds from a litter box about barking at birds—they just didn't want the unnecessary noise. Which I can sympathize with.

But the Voice of the Peoples does not share my doubts. She bobs her head up and down—a weird motion that I'm pretty sure she just started doing to mimic the peoples. "Very good, JuJu. Your Masterfulness?"

God, my brain hurts with all this shit. "Right. Yeah. Lemme see here." I ponder how exactly to phrase this, and decide on specificity once again. "Dogs shall not bark at robins." It's simple, but effective, I think.

Gracie considers this for a moment, and I can see that she's not as pleased with this wording as she was with the whole sitting on peoples' furniture thing. "My concern," she says, slowly. "Is that the thing that was truly bad was not barking at robins specifically, but barking at birds in general."

Oh, my fuck. Is she serious with this?

Yes. Yes, she is.

It takes a lot of effort to stifle my sigh of exasperation. "Okayyyyyy. Then we'll go with, Dogs shall not bark at birds."

She winces and leans into me, lowering her voice. "I mean...it's not wrong, but it's so short. Can't you make it more official-sounding?"

I take a big, bracing breath. "Dogs shall not bark, growl, yip, howl, or otherwise make noises that would be deemed unpleasant in the ears of the peoples."

Gracie pulls her head back. "Wait. What about the birds?"

"It's not about the birds. It's about the fact that peoples can't stand loud, unpleasant noises—something they have in common with us cats. Best to just squash the whole noise-making thing while we're at it."

"That's an excellent point," Gracie says, her eyes widening—probably realizing how much she has been Bad with her vocal cords. "I am convicted," she announces to the others. "As are we all convicted. We have been noisy and unpleasant to the peoples' ears. This cannot continue if we are to be Perfect Dogs."

"No barking?!" Old Gus...well, he barked it out. Then immediately realized his error as the whole Collective Pack gasps. His indignant posture wilts and his ears go back. "Oh, crap."

Gracie eyes him like a thundercloud about to burst. "Gus! One of our elders! You have done what is Bad in the sight of the peoples!"

"No, no!" Gus tries to protest. "I just...I didn't realize the topic was concluded!"

I lean into Gracie. "Technically, you didn't make it official yet."

"Please," Gus begs. "Don't make me bathe and throw up my dinner. I didn't know."

"Ignorance is no excuse!" Gracie snaps—careful not to bark while she does. She cools herself quickly. "However...as His Masterfulness just pointed out, this new law had not been made official when you broke it. So we will grant you mercy—just this once!"

Gus breathes an audible sigh of relief.

"Your Masterfulness, if you will," Gracie invites.

Bored, I do my best to remember what I'd just spit out moments ago, but this time, loud enough for all to hear. "Right, uh... Dogs shall not bark, growl, yip, howl, or otherwise make noises that would be deemed unpleasant in the ears of the peoples."

"As it is remembered by His Masterfulness, so shall it be remembered by all. Excellent work, JuJu Bean. Your faithfulness will be credited to you as Goodness."

JuJu Bean looks singularly pleased with herself.

"What about snarling?" Hank, the shaggy dog, asks.

"Nope," I reply. "Snarling is annoying to the peoples." And to me.

"And whining?" someone else asks, I can't tell who.

"Whining is right out. Whining is the worst of all."

"I used to whine when I needed to be let outside," Roo puts in, looking confused by the whole thing.

"Well, now the error of your ways has been revealed to you," I say, brusquely.

"Sometimes my peoples WANTED me to bark," says another dog—I can't remember his name, he's some sort of wolf-looking-breed. A sled dog, I believe. "They would say, 'Speak!' and when I barked, I would get a treat."

Gracie gets an irritable look about her. "What's Bad for one packmate is Bad for the whole Collective Pack. No barking. It's been codified."

The sled dog seems perplexed. "Are there any noises that we're ALLOWED to make?"

"Whimpering?" someone suggests.

"Pff," I dismiss it offhand. "Whimpering is just a whining with more vibrato."

"What about, like, a soft chuff?"

I look questioningly at Gracie.

"A soft chuff is permitted," she decided. "Provided that it is not loud enough that it would offend a peoples if they were present."

The dogs all seem to find this an acceptable compromise, and no other questions are raised. And, just like that, I've managed to quiet these noisy bastards down. Well. I guess they did it to themselves. But in either case, I'll enjoy myself a helluva lot more.

·········

After the meeting concludes, and all the dogs are returning to their homes for their evening meal—no one has been caught being Bad today, so there will be no purification ceremonies, which is just fine by me—I catch up to Gracie as she walks the sidewalk towards her house.

"Hey, Gracie—Voice of the Peoples," I say as I trot alongside her much longer gait. "Got a small problem here that might become a big problem."

"What's that?"

I glance over my shoulder to make sure that we are alone. We are, but I lower my voice anyways. "I don't think I can remember all this shit!"

Gracie stops and looks at me. "You can't remember the laws?" She says it flatly, so that I can't really tell if she's pissed about it or just asking for clarification.

"Well, I can remember the laws NOW. But if we keep adding to them every damn day, it's gonna start getting muddled. I mean, come on. You guys have, like, a bajillion laws."

Her eyes narrow at me, like they had to JuJu Bean. Like she's trying to peer into my soul.

"Okay, fine," I relent. "You have twenty-seven laws, as of today. But still. It's not just the number that matters. There's specific wording that can't be forgotten, and also exceptions and clarifications and addendums." My tail twitches irritably. "I think I'm reaching my limit."

"Hm." Gracie says nothing else, but begins walking for her house again.

I mutter under my breath and catch back up to her. "Sooooo...?"

"So?" she responds. "Do you have a solution in mind?"

"Well, as a matter of fact, I do."

"And?"

"And there's five other cats in this village. Their memories are just as good as mine. And I'd only really need one of them. Or maybe two, depending on how many other laws you plan to make official."

"I plan to make official as many laws as are necessary for us to be Perfect."

"So maybe two. But we can start with one and see how far we get." As I say it, I'm inwardly begging Gracie not to triple the number of laws. But then I realize, what am I worried about? These laws are for the dogs, not me. What do I care if they reduce themselves to being able to do literally nothing enjoyable? I move on. "Only problem will be finding one that's willing."

"I have one in mind," Gracie says, airily.

"Oh, you do?" I ask. "Who?"

"Why, Longjohn, of course."

The earth falls away from me, and everything in it turns to shit.

"No. Absolutely fucking not."

Gracie stops again and gives me that same evaluating look. I mean, who put her in such a lofty place of judgment? Sure, nearly every dog in the village put her in that place, but I didn't, and I resent her turning it on me. All this pack leader and Voice of the Peoples shit is really going to her head.

"What is the problem with you and Longjohn?" she asks, evenly.

"He's a fat, self-righteous piece of shit that won't stop marking my territory and trying to steal my bird-hunting grounds! That's what the fucking problem is!"

"And what would need to happen for you to be able to work with Longjohn?"

"If he were a corpse."

"Besides that."

I release a whole volley of huffy, hissy noises, and cap it all off with a lengthy list of demands: "He needs to admit that he's a Kept-Kitten and a disgrace to felines everywhere, and he needs to stop marking my territory and trying to take my bird-hunting grounds! And he needs to lay down and bare his throat to me, and concede that he is at my mercy, and if I choose to spare his life—IF, because I'm not sure if I will at this point—then he must pay me daily homage...twice a day. In the mornings and evenings. Something like, 'You are my master and my worthless life is in your hands, and I give thanks for however many hours your mercy sees fit to give me.' Something like that."

Gracie quirks her head. "That's all a bit extreme, isn't it?"

A bit extreme? This coming from the pack leader that just decreed that dogs can't make any noises other than a soft chuff?

I figure I played hardball once and got what I wanted, why not try it again?

"Those are my terms," I say forcefully. "Take it or leave it."

"Hm." Gracie considers me for a long moment. "What if I just made him stop marking your territory and messing with your bird-hunting grounds?"

Damn. She's not falling for hardball. Now we're in negotiations.

"Alright," I say, warily. "And he has to bare his throat to me and put his life in my hands and…and homage and all that other shit."

"Or, he can submit himself as your underling. You'll be His Supreme Masterfulness, and Longjohn will be the Under-Supreme Masterfulness."

"No. Unacceptable. He can't have supreme in his name."

"How about just the Under-Master?"

"Absolutely not. Under-Master sounds way too cool for him."

"What if I just let you pick his title then?"

I give her a searching gaze. "So…I get to pick his title…and he won't mark my territory or try to annex any part of it?"

"Seems reasonable to me," Gracie says, doing that strange head-bob affectation thing again.

I give her a half-lidded look. "And you can guarantee his cooperation?"

Gracie's muzzle undergoes a change. It's rather subtle, but the effect is not. She scares me a little bit. Or maybe I'm scared for Longjohn.

No. Actually, I'm not.

"I'll make sure he stays cooperative."

I have no idea what that means, but it's Longjohn's problem, and likely his asshole that's on the line.

"Fine." I draw myself up. "You have a deal."

The Law of Good and Evil (Day Ten):

- 22. Dogs shall bathe themselves once every full moon, or whenever they are notified by His Supreme Masterfulness that their scent has reached a level of pungency that would be deemed offensive to the noses of the peoples.

- 23. Dogs shall not poop on the front lawns of the peoples' houses. (For further on the laws regarding defecation and urination, see Law #8)

- 24. Dogs shall not play-fight in a manner so raucous as to possibly be misconstrued as actual fighting in the eyes of the peoples.

- 25. Dogs shall not eat their own vomit, as this is disgusting in the eyes of the peoples. Wherever your vomit lays when it has been purged from you, there shall it remain.

- 26. Dogs shall not sit or lay or otherwise rest themselves on or about anything that was built for the peoples to sit or lay or otherwise rest themselves on.

- 27. Dogs shall not bark, growl, yip, howl, or otherwise make noises that would be deemed unpleasant in the ears of the peoples.

11

BANGER

I WANT NO PART of whatever is happening in the Park, so while all the pups are jostling about and reveling in their new pack, I choose to clear my mind and take a stroll down the sidewalk.

This is about the only time of day that I can enjoy being out and about in the village without running the risk of encountering a bunch of idiots that want to try to be my friend. The sidewalks and yards are empty and peaceful, and I'm free to sniff and let my mind wander, and simply be a dog, out enjoying some fresh air, without the hazards of having to interact with others.

So, imagine my surprise when, as I stop to sniff a local urination hot spot, I hear a rough voice coming from the car cave of the house directly across from me.

"Hey, you."

I jerk my head up, my hackles immediately rising and my lips curling. It takes me a moment to see who spoke, because he is black as night, and sitting in the shadows of the car cave.

It is the dog with the anger problem, whom I often hear hurling threats at everything and everyone. When my eyes focus on him, he steps out of the shadows and into the glow of the setting sun. He's a massive dog—probably twice my weight. His black fur is long and fluffy, as though he were bred for a colder climate. He has a big, square face, pointed ears, and two golden eyes that peer at me and speak of a depth of hostility that even I have trouble wrapping my head around.

I spread my paws to balance my weight. My tail is rigid, my hackles at full height. A long, low warning growl issues from my throat.

"Oh, careful, careful," he says, with a strange, husky laugh. "That's against the law now. Or haven't you heard?"

This confuses me enough that I forget the threats I was about to say to the big, black dog. "What are you talking about?"

The big dog sits, which makes me relax just a bit, since he's clearly not preparing to charge me. He points his muzzle in the direction of the Park, down the road a bit. "I've been listening to those idiots. They're making everything illegal now. Including growling and barking."

"What?" I say again, shocked at this new development. "They can't do that!"

"Huh." He chuckles again, an entirely unpleasant sound. "Seems like they already did." He looks back to me. "It's Banger, isn't it?"

"Yeah, what of it?" I snap.

"Why aren't you in there with the rest of the pups, Banger? Why aren't you in there deciding what's against the law?" His lips peel back just slightly. His teeth are bright white, and long, and sharp. "Weren't you the one that came up with the idea in the first place? Weren't you the one whining about how the masters won't come back until we're all Good Dogs? How we have to stop doing anything that might be considered Bad in the masters' eyes?"

I bristle at the challenge. "I'm not with the other dogs because I don't LIKE other dogs. Not because I have a problem with the laws."

"Oh, you don't have a problem with the laws, huh? And what about the barking and growling law they just made?"

I'm still a bit taken aback by that. How in the world did Gracie come to the conclusion that barking and growling was bad? "I might not agree with it," I admit. "But if it means bringing the peoples back, I'm willing to follow it."

"Why?" he asks flatly. "Why submit to something that is counter to your nature?"

"Because my nature is unimportant right now. Getting the peoples back IS."

He chuffs. "I'm not entirely sure the masters WANT to come back."

I realize that I've settled a bit, my hackles gone down and my tail loosening. I've grown curious about this dog, as opposed to my normal reaction, which would be to snarl and nip at him. Not that that would end well for me, given his size. "You're the only dog around here that calls them that."

"What? Master?"

"Yes."

"I call them what they are. They control everything. They tell us what to do and when to do it. They are in control of our food, our health, our happiness. What do you call that besides a master?"

"Wouldn't that make us their servants?"

"Aren't we?" he asks. "We make them happy and relaxed, and in exchange, they keep us fed and housed."

"We're their COMPANIONS," I assert, a tad hotly.

The big black dog doesn't respond. Just keeps watching me, and I'm having a very hard time determining what it is I see behind those cold, golden eyes. Aggression? Curiosity? Mockery?

"Don't you love your master?" I ask him.

For a moment, I think he's not going to respond to this either, but then he says, "I did."

"What do you mean you DID? You don't love them now?"

"I loved them when they were here. Now they're gone. How can I love something that is gone?"

"They're not gone forever."

"So you say," he gruffs.

"They're coming back!" I seethe, taking a step towards him, which is probably not a great idea, but luckily, he doesn't seem to react to it.

"If we're just Perfect Dogs, right?" he asks, his voice soaked with mockery. "If we just follow all the laws?"

"Yeah, that's right."

He stands up, but I hold my ground. "And what makes you think your master will come back to you?"

"My PEOPLES will come back to me," I say. "Because..." the words catch and suddenly seem puppyish and silly.

"Because what?" he demands.

"Because I love him." And once it's been said, there's no hiding from it. "Because I'm going to SHOW how much I love him by being Perfect Dog. And if you love your peoples, then you'll want to please them, and you'll want to be a Perfect Dog, and you won't ever do anything Bad."

I expect more derision from him, but his eyes take on a searching look. "You're different from the other dogs, Banger."

I'm so surprised by this statement that I don't have anything to say.

He pads towards me, and I'm shocked to see him do it slow and easy, his tail swishing, every bit the gentleman, as opposed to the jerk that screams at everyone that passes by. "I'm Brutus, by the way. But my master called me Brute."

"What are you doing?" I say, taking a step back despite my earlier decision to stand my ground. He's just so BIG.

He stops. "Well, I was considering passing the greeting of the day with you."

"I already told you," I say, in my most venomous, she-wolf, get-the-hell-away-from-me tone. "I don't like other dogs."

He wags and lets his tongue loll out of his mouth. "I don't like them either, Banger. In case you hadn't noticed."

"Everyone's noticed."

He looks off towards the Park where, at that moment, the Collective Pack seems to be disbanding, and a raucous group of pups is jostling their way up the sidewalk in our direction. "What's to like about them? They're self-centered, food-obsessed little pups that just want to run and play and compete to see who's going to make up a new law. They don't have any love for the masters. They've lost themselves in an orgy of dog-love."

I stand, bewildered for a moment. Bewildered because it seems like Brute has just spoken my own thoughts and feelings right back at me. And it makes something strange happen in my chest. A feeling that I've felt for only one other dog—Mash. Even with Mash, there is a huge difference in the way we see the world. But here before me stands another dog that sees things the same as I do.

The feeling in my chest is...connection.

"It's only been ten days," Brute sighs, his tail going still and slack. "And already they've forgotten the face of their masters. The masters have been replaced. By a labradoodle and a cat. And, of course, the ever-attractive embrace of the Collective Pack."

"Yes!" I suddenly cry out, surprising both myself and Brute. "Exactly!"

He wags his tail, and I realize that mine is wagging too. But then he looks down the street at the little gaggle of dogs coming our way, and his demeanor shifts in the blink of an eye. "Rotten little pups." He glances back at me. "If I stay outside when they come through, I'm going to end up mauling one of them. Or all of them." He turns around and starts walking back towards his car cave. "Time for me to leave."

Brute stops, just before he disappears into the shadows of his car cave. He looks over his shoulder at me. "You're not so bad, though."

"You're surprisingly...tolerable."

He chuffs again. "Well. If you can tolerate any more of me, I'd like to talk with you again, Banger." He sniffs absently at the air. "The only other dog that loves the masters more than their packmates."

·· •••••···

I curl up that night at the base of the Cloud Throne. I'll admit, I'm getting old. I can see the tip of my muzzle, and I know that it was once dark, but now it's white. I get tired by the afternoon and once the sun starts going down, all I want to do is sleep.

It's not even dark yet, but the shadows have overtaken the world, and the sky is fading. I'm alone in the house, and content to be so for now, though I know Mash at least will be along shortly—he's still got energy to burn. Whether or not Sweetpea will decide to show up is always—and has always been—a mystery.

I wish I could get up on the Cloud Throne. I walked the village a bit too much today before my run-in with Brute, and my joints are feeling it. I could use a soft place to lay, but I won't defile the Cloud Throne. Or the bed. Or any other place that Dad would have rested himself. It's against the law now, and I am going to be a Perfect Dog.

I close my eyes, but Brute's words keep me awake, tumbling through my head like squirrels chasing each other. Was it possible that the peoples might not come back? Just thinking about it threatens to yank away any restfulness I might feel, so I try instead to imagine what it will be like when Dad returns. He will smile, and I will wag, and I will run up to him and lick his face, and he will scratch my neck and say, "Well done, my faithful, Perfect Dog!"

I'm just about to drift off into the warm embrace of that dream when I hear the unmistakable clatter of Mash hauling his way into the house with his usual breathless excitement. He never just walks in the door. He always has to take it at a sprint, claws skittering across the wood floors, and crash into the walls while he pants.

"Banger!" he calls out into the dim house. "Banger, you home?"

"Yes," I murmur, irritated, as the dream evaporates like morning mist.

He trots down the hall from the car cave door and into the room where the Cloud Throne sits. "Oh, there you are. Already sleeping?"

"No, Mash. I'm not sleeping."

"Oh. You just resting then?"

I pick my head up off the floor and yawn. "Apparently not for a while."

"Good," Mash says, sitting his butt down, still panting. His eyes take on a sneaky look about them, and he glances around, as though he's afraid we're not alone in our own house. "Because I need to talk to you."

A voice behind me makes me jump: "Sounds juicy. Spill it."

I lurch to my feet and stare at the corner of the Cloud Throne where, buried in amongst the Special Poofs, Sweetpea has somehow appeared out of nowhere. I swear, he wasn't there when I came in.

"When did you come in?" I demand. "And what are you doing on the Cloud Throne?!"

Sweetpea yawns from his fortress of Special Poofs and stretches his front paws out in front of him. "It appears I am having my nap interrupted. And I came in when you were laying there like roadkill."

I hadn't heard him come in. He's so darn quiet!

"Get off!" I nearly bark it, but remember that I can't bark anymore. "Off the Cloud Throne! You're breaking the law!"

He gives absolutely zero reaction to this, aside from half-closing his eyes. "The laws are for the dogs," he says, bored. "In case it failed to register with you, I am a cat, not a dog."

"Laws are laws!"

"The laws were made so that you dogs could be Perfect Dogs. It says nothing about cats."

"You can't just make everyone else follow the rules and not follow them yourself!"

He frowns at me. "I'm not MAKING anyone do anything. They're doing it all by themselves. And, again, do you really think the peoples expect anything different from cats? We didn't listen to them when they were here, why the hell would we care now? If we started caring about what the peoples thought, it might tear a hole in the fabric of the universe or something. And then who knows what will happen? Maybe the peoples will be lost to us forever. So I'll keep my ass right fucking here, and furthermore, you're welcome for staving off a cosmic disaster."

"Wow," Mash says, impressed. "Thank you. I didn't know you could do that."

"His Masterfulness can do all kinds of things like that," Sweetpea says, crossing his paws, one over the other. "Now. What was this juicy piece of gossip you have to spread around? Go on. Spill it."

"Oh." Mash looks down. "It's not really gossip. I just..." he leans towards me and whispers. "I have concerns."

I sit my rump down again, still a tad annoyed by Sweetpea's defilement of the Cloud Throne. And maybe a little jealous. "What kind of concerns, Mash? Don't be weird about it. Just spit it out."

"Go ahead," Sweetpea says. "This is a safe place."

"Did you hear about the new laws today?" Mash asks quietly.

"I MADE the news laws today," Sweetpea replies. "What of it?"

"Well, I dunno..." Mash scratches thoughtfully behind his ear. "Don't you think it's all getting a bit...crazy?"

"Which part?" Sweetpea wonders. "The barking part? Or the bathing part? Or the part about not eating your puke?"

"I guess..." Mash gets a cringing look to his face. "All of it?"

In response, Sweetpea begins to lick his paws, eyes closed as though in ecstasy. "Oh. Well. Yes. It's a bit crazy. But I'm simply the mouthpiece. I don't come up with the laws. I just make them sound pretty and remember them."

"Wait, so, you don't even think they're good laws?"

"What do you mean by 'good laws'?" Sweetpea mumbles around a mouthful of his own fur. Then swallows it. "Good, as in easy to follow? Good, as in they make sense? Good, as in they'll be effective at making the peoples come back?"

"Yes."

"No."

"Sweetpea!" I snap. "You degenerate!"

"How dare you call me that!" he bristles.

"You ARE a degenerate!"

"No, of course I'm a degenerate! You dared to call me—"

I lean towards him, lips peeling back to show my teeth. "Sweet...PEA."

He shrinks away from me.

I turn back to Mash. "Of course the laws are good! They're good at all those things you mentioned."

"They don't seem to be easy to follow," Mash points out.

"No one said they were going to be easy. But they WILL make us Perfect Dogs—IF we all follow them. And the peoples WILL come back." Even as I say it, I think of Brute, and the terrible possibility that maybe...no. I don't even want to think about it. "Of course they'll come back. They'll have to come back once they see how Perfect we are. They'll have to see how much we must love them to have put so much effort into becoming Perfect Dogs."

Mash gazes forlornly at the Cloud Throne. "But do you really think Dad would care if we slept on the Cloud Throne?"

I sigh. "Honestly, Mash? No. I don't think Dad would care. But there were other peoples that DID care about things like that. And so we must all stop doing it. You know. Just in case."

"Wait," Sweetpea says. "So you support this whole bad for one bad for all concept?"

"Yes, I do," I say, truthfully. "Can you imagine what a tragedy it would be if we came so close to being Perfect, but failed because of a single law that we thought didn't apply to us? No. If it applies to one dog, we MUST apply it to all of us. It's too risky not to."

"Yeah, I guess," Mash says forlornly, and lowers himself to the floor with a huff. "I just..." He raises his head and smears his jowls all over the Cloud Throne, gazing mournfully at Sweetpea. "I could really use a good whimpering right now. And a cushy place to sleep."

Sweetpea's ears flatten. "I, for one, am overjoyed that you won't be whimpering anymore. Terrible fucking noise. How it doesn't irritate you when it comes out of your own mouth I'll never understand. And as for the Cloud Throne? Maybe if you dogs were a bit tidier with your personal hygiene, the peoples wouldn't mind you being on their Cloud Thrones. But you're not, and they do, so stay down."

"So if I bathe, I can get on the Cloud Throne?"

"No."

"Awww."

Sweetpea fixes him with a slit-eyed glare. "That's dangerously close to whining, mister."

Mash oozes his face down off the Cloud Throne, leaving a slug-trail of slobber behind. "Sorry."

"It's fine," I say, casting a withering glance over my shoulder at the feline hypocrite in his comfy castle. "We'll be comfortable enough on the floor."

Sweetpea just continues to lick contentedly at himself. If you want to talk about annoying noises, let's talk about that slurf-slurf-slurf noise these cats make with their unending grooming of themselves.

Mash lays his head down, his jowls pooling around his face. "I just wish we could talk to them, you know?"

Slurf-slurf—

Silence.

Mash doesn't seem to notice, but I do. Something got Sweetpea's attention there.

"I know," I sigh to Mash. "I wish we could talk to them too."

"Even just once," Mash says. "Just one time, to talk to Dad, to see if we're doing the right thing, or if we got it all wrong."

Sweetpea makes a slight choking sound.

I crane my head up over the Cloud Throne again. "You alright there, Sweetpea?"

"Yeah," he husks. "Just..." He rises from his spot, a bit hurriedly, and scampers off the Cloud Throne towards the door. "Just got a hairball!"

Mash half-rises with a wag of his tail. "Oh, can I watch?"

"No!" Sweetpea disappears through the pet door.

Mash huffs. "Whatever."

I watch the pet door swinging, and lay back down. "And he calls us the gross ones."

12

Sweetpea

Okay, so I didn't actually have a hairball, but I did choke on a bit of fur, so it's only a small lie.

I scamper free of the dogs and all their incessant worrying, hounded by Mash's sad little wish: If there was only some way to talk to the peoples, to talk to Dad again, and see if they were doing the right thing.

Alright, it's not that I'm so broken up about Mash and how pitiful he is—and he is. It's just…well, it took me by surprise is all.

Where am I going? Nowhere. Stop being so fucking nosy.

I slip down off the back porch and take a moment to scan the twilit lawn before me. It's starting to get overgrown. Whatever makes the peoples' stuff work—makes their car caves open and their lights come on, and yes, their little mower robots hum around their lawns—died a few days ago. I won't go into the abject panic that I had to deal with from the Collective Pack when that happened. Suffice it to say, I talked them down from the ledge. Who knows what they would've done if I hadn't? Probably started blood sacrifices or some shit.

In any case, the mower robots aren't doing their job anymore, which is just fine by me. More concealment for me as I slink through the grass towards…

Fine, fine, yes. I'm going to that same spot between my crash pad and Gracie's. The same place that I had my little hallucination. Don't read into it. This is purely for science. It's research. Experimentation. Definitely not because I WANT to hallucinate again. Definitely not because Mash made me a little sad. Definitely not because I have any desire whatsoever to speak to Dad.

Because he's not Dad. He's just the Feeder. I didn't care what he had to say before, and I certainly don't now.

Really.

Honest.

Stop looking at me like that.

I stop in roughly the same spot where I'd hallucinated Dad hovering over me. I feel incredibly foolish, if you can't already tell. But...you know...experiments and science and shit. Maybe it's my natural feline curiosity. Yeah. I'm just curious if I'll ALWAYS hallucinate in this spot or if it's a one-time thing. Maybe there's a special patch of grass. Maybe there's some catnip growing wild in there somewhere.

I sit down in the dewy grass and wrap my tail around me. I can't help myself—my eyes go up. It's not full dark yet, but I can still see the stars, just barely glimmering in the half-light. In case you were wondering, there is no figure hovering there like a spectral blimp. Just air and sky.

I check my surroundings again. It's not that I'm so worried about Longjohn now—he's my fucking bitch, and he knows it, but I'll get to that later. No, I'm more worried that someone might be watching me. That someone might hear my little experiment, and start to think I've gone batty. Which I simply cannot have. His Masterfulness is NOT batty.

Here I am, risking my reputation for science. God, I'm so noble it almost sickens me.

There's no one around, but I give it a good moment anyways. Just to make extra sure.

Then, quietly, I hiss: "Dad?"

My spine tingles with embarrassment. This is so fucking stupid.

No, it's not stupid, because it's just science. Just a cat, trying to solve his curiosity, through the rigorous use of a controlled experiment.

Slightly louder this time, but still not loud enough to be overheard: "Uh, Dad? Or, really, any peoples that might be floating around up there? I...uh...I have questions."

A long, long silence. Except for a whippoorwill making his noisy declarations from somewhere nearby. I don't know who Poor Will is, but for God's sake, ease up on the bastard. All night long with your demands to whip him—I assume to death. I appreciate the violence, but your voice makes me want to snap your neck.

Anyway...

"Dad! Or any peoples!" I hiss at the night sky. "If you have an opinion on whether the dogs are being enormous idiots or whether they're doing a great job, now's the time to speak up!"

Nothing.

Predictable.

I fidget my paws in the grass, glancing upward again. "And...you know...how am I doing, too? I mean, not that I really care. But if I'm doing a bang-up job, maybe just give me a 'good kitty' or some shit like that."

I'm suddenly and enormously put off by how much my heart lurches in my chest at the thought of Dad scratching behind my ears and saying, "Good kitty."

I fucking hate being called kitty.

But seriously, if I'm being honest, I could really use some positive affirmation right now. Even if the terms used are incredibly demeaning.

"Alright, well, nice chat," I spit out, needing to get aggressive again, now that my plaintiveness has won me absolutely jack-shit. "I'll tell you what. I'm just going to park my ass right here." I lower myself gingerly to the ground and tuck my paws under my chest. "I'm just going to take a little cat nap in the fresh air. That's all. And, if at any point in time you have anything worthwhile to say? Well…I'll hear you."

I settle myself into the traditional cat-blob form—no legs visible, just a mound of fur with a head and a tail. I know it's not very distinguished, but you have no idea how comfortable it is. So comfortable, in fact, that all the day's labors descend on me and my eyes grow heavy…

··········

I awake to howling.

My first thought is, THAT'S FUCKING ILLEGAL, YOU ASSHAT! Until I realize that it is the sound of many, many dogs howling.

I stand up. The sky is fully dark. But everything is lit by a strange orange glow. I look around me and realize that I'm not where I thought I was. There is no grass beneath me—only rock. Rock that looks like it's been scorched.

Where am I?

I look around again, and realize there are no houses. In fact, I'm not in the village at all. Somehow, I've sleep-walked my way up onto a cliff.

Waaaaaaaiiiiiit a minute…

Am I dreaming?

I'm not entirely sure.

I stare at the edge of the cliff, maybe a few cat-lengths from me. I can't see what's on the other side, but the orange glow seems to be coming from there. And the howls. The howls are not just howls anymore. I can hear barking and snarling. So many laws are being broken right now, I can't even imagine how much puking I'm going to have to watch.

But there's a quality to that sound. Maybe you know what I'm talking about. Dogs make all kinds of terrible noises when they're play-fighting. But when it turns real, you know it. It gets a certain ugly quality to it. A quality that makes even us cats shrink away, and usually activates our Prime Directive.

What I'm hearing is not the sound of dogs play-fighting, as I'd first thought. I'm hearing the sounds of dogs tearing each other apart.

"Oh, shit!" I scrabble towards the edge of the cliff, and the scene that unfolds before me makes my whole body go rigid. I still have no idea where I am, but I know it isn't anywhere near the village, because I've never seen a cliff nearby. And yet, despite the fact that it makes absolutely no geographical sense, as I look down from that cliff, I'm looking at the village.

The houses. The houses are burning. Dark shapes are darting between the flames. Firelight glints off of savage eyes and bared fangs. Dogs. Hundreds of dogs. And they're all trying to murder each other. The village has turned into complete bedlam.

"Oh, SHIT!" I say again.

And then I hear something behind me.

A wail. A cry. A grieving.

And I know instantly who is grieving. Somehow, I just know.

It is the peoples. I cannot see them. They are not on the cliff with me. But the sounds of their anguish are all around me. Inside my head. Inside my heart.

"What's happening?" I yell at no one in particular. I whirl back around to the village and scream with all my might, "STOP! STOP IT YOU MANGY FUCKS! STOP KILLING EACH OTHER!"

I watch as two dogs pin another to the ground and begin ripping it apart. I've never seen dogs act like this. Not even wild dogs. The madness. The rage. The cruelty of it. It should not have bothered me, and yet it does, on a deep, deep level. Because it is not natural. This is not how dogs behave. This isn't them. What happened that made them this way?

None of the dogs down in the village heed my cry. I don't think they even heard me.

What am I going to do? How can I put a stop to the slaughter?

"Sweetpea."

A tiny shush of wind, nearly drowned out by the mayhem below me.

I look up and find nothing. I look all around and find nothing there either. "Dad? Dad, is that you?"

His voice is choked with grief when he speaks again. I feel it in my brain, in my chest, like it's all turned to water and is pouring out of me. "They need to remember, Sweetpea! Tell them to remember!"

·········

It's tempting to tell you that I wake up with a dramatic startle, and instantly know that I've had a nightmare. But really, what actually happens is that I open my eyes wide, and for quite a chunk of time, I'm so disoriented that I don't even know where I am.

I can see the nighttime grass all around me. The cool, nocturnal smell of it. The damp of the dew on my paws. And yet, elements of the dream are still bleeding through by fits and starts. One moment, I'm staring across at Gracie's house, and all is normal, and the next moment, I blink, and it's engulfed in flame. Blink again, and it's cold, dark, and still.

One moment, there is only the sound of the whippoorwill, screaming for more floggings. And the next moment the bird is drowned out by the sounds of growling and snarling and anguished yips of pain. One moment, it is only the still, damp smell of a spring night. The next moment my nose is filled with the scents of smoke and blood and bowels.

This all should have activated my Prime Directive. And, in a way, it does. Because I desperately want to flee to any place but this. But I'm too terrified to move. I realize that my claws have come out, and are sunk into the dirt beneath my paws, as though if I retract them, I'll just fall off the earth and plummet into the sky.

So I remain right where I am, hunkered in the overlong grass, my eyes stretched so wide it feels like they might fall out of my head. I know that my pupils are dilated to the absolute max, because the night glows brightly, as though there is a full moon over my head.

Slowly, slowly, the hallucinations retreat, and I am left with only my normal reality, and with my heart slamming inside my ribs like a bird caught in a cage.

What the fuck was that? A dream? A nightmare?

A vision?

My brain feels stretched and fried and frayed. Cognition is a challenge. All I know is that I don't want to be here anymore. All I know is that I want to be on the Cloud Throne again, with Banger and Mash safely guarding the floor.

Brain stuck in an unending panic-loop, I eventually manage to pull my claws out of the dirt and discover that I don't actually fly off into space like I'd thought. But I have no intention of tempting fate. So I don't scamper away—that would require me to stand up, and standing up is just asking for it. If I stand up, I'll be sucked into the sky, I just know it. So instead, I slither. Belly brushing the ground, head parting the wet grass ahead of me, and always making sure that I have at least three paws in contact with the ground at all times.

It seems to take forever to get to the porch again, but then I'm there, and the pet door is so damned close, and then I'm through it, and I'm closed in by the house, and the ceiling promises to catch me if gravity releases its hold on me, and I run and jump onto the Cloud Throne.

Banger and Mash are laying all asprawl on each other. They don't even stir when I land on the couch over their heads. Banger is snoring, as she usually is—poor gal and her smushed muzzle can't help it. Mash is dreaming deeply, his paws twitching like he's chasing his ball.

Or is he dreaming about running away from a murderous pack of demon-dogs?

I curl up tightly behind the Special Poofs, and only then am I able to breathe easy. Or...easier. My eyelids are pasted wide open and I don't think I'll be able to close them again. So I just stay right there, in my little redoubt of pillows, peering out from within them with my ears flattened.

No chance in hell I'm going to sleep again.

It's going to be a long, dark night.

13

Sweetpea

(Day 27)

"Alright, you kibble-addicted Crumb-Eaters," I bawl at the gathering of loose-jowled, wide-eyed pups. "It's time to break you!"

"Wait." It's Mash. Of course. His ears all dopily propped forward. "I thought you were teaching us to hunt."

I skitter rapidly through the leaves of the forest floor and come up nose-to-nose with Mash, who seems taken aback with the speed in which I've aggressed on him. "The fuck did you just say to me, Crumb-Eater?"

He frowns and glances at the others, then whispers to me, "Speciesist slurs!"

"You're a fucking Crumb-Eater!" I scream at his snout. I'm really in my fucking zone right now, and I don't appreciate the distractions, and they're going to know about. I whirl on the others, my tail lashing with all the unholy fury I can muster—which is quite a lot.

Ten dogs make up this sad little "hunting party." All the fastest ones from the Collective Pack—Banger and her fat ass and stilted legs need not apply. There are racing-type dogs, and sled-pulling dogs, a handful of lean-bodied hounds, and dogs like Mash whose breeding is a mystery, but who are clearly very fast.

They're all fucking pathetic.

"You're all Crumb-Eaters, every last one of you!" I yell at them, earning a few hurt looks. "If you don't like being called a Crumb-Eater, then tough shit! I call it like I see it! Now..." I straighten myself up and allow my anger-fluffed fur to settle. "If you don't want to be a Crumb-Eater anymore, then you've come to the right place. Because I am going to teach you how to hunt for your own damn selves. You will become self-sufficient. You will become fearsome, merciless predators. You will snap fucking necks, and drink hot blood!"

Several of the dogs look queasy at this. Mash is one of them.

"You!" I call out one of the pathetic queasy-faces. It's one of the racing-type dogs. "Are you ready to snap necks and drink hot blood?!"

"Well, when you say drink, do we actually have to drink it? Or are you just being poetic about the fact that hot blood will come into contact with my mouth?"

Holy shit. I don't even know how to respond to that.

One of the sled-dogs pipes up in agreement. "Yeah, I'm not sure if I'm comfortable drinking hot blood. There could be parasites or whatnot. You know, we're no longer on de-worming medications, sooooo...."

"You eat fucking cat turds!" I scream.

"Actually we don't," the racing dog says. "That's against the law now. I'm surprised you don't remember."

I have to close my eyes for a moment and picture a field full of flowers and plenty of mice to murder. Something to calm me down. "Yes, I know that it's against the law. My point was, you've eaten cat turds in the past, as well as all manner of horrific and mostly-inedible things, and you weren't worried about worms then!"

"Yeah, but we've never drank hot blood before," the sled-dog says. He looks to the others, nodding while he does it. Good God, everyone's nodding like the peoples these days. I guess Gracie turned it into a fashion. "Frankly, drinking the hot blood just sounds...disturbing."

"Yeah, it's kind of disturbing," another says. "And unnecessary."

"We're bred to be companions," yet another puts in.

I look at this last one. One of the hounds. "Bullshit. You're a hound. You're made for chasing small animals through the woods and murdering them."

"Yeah, but I've never done that before."

"Alright, okay, fine!" I hiss and spit. "You do not have to drink the hot blood. You will snap necks, and your mouth may come into contact with hot blood at some point in time during the kill."

"Wait," another hound speaks up. "No one said anything about killing."

My left eyelid is twitching. I think they've given me a tic. "This is a hunting party. For hunting. What part of hunting did you think WOULDN'T involve killing? What part of snapping necks was unclear? What the fuck do you think happens when you snap something's neck?"

"Well, I was kind of hoping that it would only paralyze the animal."

"Yeah," Mash says. "Paralyze it so it doesn't feel any pain. It's the right thing to do."

My eyelid is going apeshit. "You do realize that the purpose of hunting is to provide you with something to eat because the kibble has run out, right? How the fuck do you think you're going to eat something without killing it?"

"Wellllllllll..." Mash looks a bit abashed. "We were all kind of hoping...you'd do it."

"Yeah!" The racing dog wags her tail. "We catch it and snap its neck so it's paralyzed and doesn't feel pain, and then...you know...YOU can finish it off."

"Oh," I say. "Did you want me to feed it to you as well?"

"Well, I didn't want to ask, but yeah! You've got way more experience in knowing which parts of the animal—"

"I'M NOT FUCKING FEEDING YOU!"

"Oh." She hangs her head. "Well, why'd you offer?"

"I was being sarcas—you know what? Nevermind. This is hunting party, and you are going to hunt, and when you catch what you're hunting, you're going to snap its neck—which will kill it."

"How do we snap its neck?" Mash asks.

"You know how you used to whip that rope-toy around?" I ask. "Shake it back and forth super violently?"

"Yeah."

"It's just like that. You grab the creature's head in your mouth, and you shake it back and forth until you feel the spine snap."

The racing dog immediately vomits on the ground.

"Are you serious?" I breathe, staring at the mound of half-digested kibble.

"Awww!" the racer dog moans. "That was my last bit of kibble! And I didn't even break a law!" Then she stares hungrily at her pile of puke.

"No," I snap. "Don't even think about it."

"But—"

"Back away from the vomit."

"But—"

"Leave iiiiiiiit. Leave it."

She sullenly backs away.

My fuck. They're all going to starve to death.

What I want to do right then is lay down and bury my face in my paws. But I manage to stay standing. "No more interruptions! You're all Crumb-Eaters because you can't hunt for yourself. But dogs weren't always this way. You descended from wolves!"

"That's right!" one of them calls out.

"A long time ago," I clarify. "Like, really far descended. Like millions of years ago was the last time your bloodline had anything to do with being predators. Since then, you've been bred to be a bunch of kept-fucking-puppies, and any instinct you might still have is buried behind your uselessly dull claws and your dumb, happy faces. Gizmo!"

Gizmo, one of the hound-dogs, is drooling over the vomit, lips parted like he's about to take a lusty mouthful. He glances up and snaps his mouth shut.

"Leave it!"

"Right, right, right." Gizmo sits. Glances furtively at the vomit. Then back to me.

"Luckily for you," I continue, now marching along their ranks with my tail held high. "You have me—His Masterfulness. And I'm not just masterful at remembering shit. I'm also masterful at hunting. As all cats are. And now I'm going to teach you to get in touch with your roots. I'm going to teach you how to chase down animals for food, and bring them back to the Collective Pack, where everyone will celebrate you, not as a Crumb-Eater and a Kibble-Slave, but as a cold-hearted predator capable of providing for their pack!"

"Sounds awesome," Mash wags his tail. "Except for the cold-hearted part."

"Can we hunt and still be warm-hearted?"

"THERE'S NO PLACE FOR WARM-HEARTEDNESS IN KILLING!"

Silence.

Better.

"Now. While I am a very capable hunter—seventy-three percent success rate, if you were curious—I am a cat, which means I hunt alone. Due to your complete inability to be stealthy, and your incredibly lame, non-retractable claws, and the fact that you don't know your ass from a hole in the ground, you cannot hunt alone. You must hunt as a part of a pack. Cats are stalkers and ambush-killers. Dogs are runners. You have to run your prey down, and, as one, latch onto it, take it to the ground, and break its neck."

The racer dog dry heaves. "I'm okay," she chokes out between heaves. "Keep going."

"Now, small woodland animals are easy to kill," I say. "But they won't feed the entire Collective Pack. At best, they'll provide one dog with one meal. No, you'll want to learn to hunt larger game, like deer."

"But they're so beautiful," Mash whispers.

"And graceful," Gizmo puts in.

"And delicious," I finish. "Just trust me. You get a taste of deer liver, you'll forget about how pretty they are. BUT…" I cast my steely-eyed gaze over them. "You can't just snap a deer's neck. It's three times your size."

"So are you going to kill it for us?"

I balk. "I can't kill a fucking deer. Are you kidding me? It's twenty times my size."

"I thought you were a very capable—"

"Just shut up about it!" I grind out something between a sigh and growl. "Does anyone want to know how you'll kill the deer?"

"Maybe we can just sit on it?"

"The fuck would sitting on it do?"

"Well…I dunno…"

"Wrong. Wrong all around. Just shut up. You're not allowed to speak anymore." I have to sit on my tail to keep it from thrashing. "What you're going to do is this: Grab anything you can get your mouth on. Drag the deer to the ground. Everyone has to hold on. Once it's on the ground, one of you has to put its little black nose in your mouth—"

"Aww."

"—while another latches onto the throat and crushes its windpipe."

"Oh, my..."

Wide, horrified eyes.

"And, after a little while," I go on. "It will suffocate and stop twitching."

The racer dog gags out a little streamer of yellow bile.

"Alright," I call, "Everyone huddle up. Time for some real talk."

"But it's so real already!" Mash groans, as the dogs circle up around me.

I take a moment to breathe deep and calm myself. "I know this sounds crazy to you guys, but that's just because you've never done it. I promise you—I PROMISE—that you still have a little bit of wolf in you. We just have to wake it up. And, trust me on this: once the chase begins? Once you get running with your pack, and you get that first mouthful of hide? It'll all make sense."

Predictably, they are dubious.

"But we're getting ahead of ourselves," I say. "You will not be hunting deer today."

"Whew," Mash breathes.

I eye him. "You'll be hunting rabbits."

Abject horror washes over him. His wide eyes blink slowly, out of sync with each other. "I feel faint," he murmurs.

"You're probably just hungry," I dismiss. "An excellent way to start your hunt."

"It doesn't feel like hunger."

I ignore him. "Hounds! You'll be out front, using your big old sniffers to find the rabbits. The rest of you, follow right behind them, and when they scare up a rabbit, you'll chase them down and...you know..." I hesitate to be more specific, lest someone start puking again. "Do what I told you to do."

"Can I be a hound today?" Mash says in a sickly voice.

"Sorry, Mash," I say, moving past him. "You're one of our fastest dogs. You'll be chasing the rabbits down and savaging them to death." I hear his tiny mewl of despair, but pay it no mind. "THE HUNT IS ON!"

14

Mash

This is my nightmare.

No, really. I literally have this nightmare. I'm walking through the woods, and a rabbit jumps out, and my mind goes blank. Even in the nightmare, I know I shouldn't chase after it, but then my legs just start churning up dirt—every part of my body just wants to CATCH IT! And before I know it, I've latched down on it and it's squealing and kicking...

I've gotta stop. I'm making myself queasy.

But you get the point. I am stuck in this situation, and I don't know how to get out. On the one hand, I really want to be a heroic hunter-dog and bring home some food for the Collective Pack. On the other hand...I don't know if I can actually kill it. Like, you know, INTENTIONALLY. I can totally do the whole bringing it home to the Collective Pack thing, but it's the part that comes before that worries me.

"Gizmo," I whisper, with a sidelong glance at Sweetpea, who is stalking along in the middle of our hunting formation.

"Mm?" Gizmo has his nose in the ground, ruffling and snuffling through the leaves. He seems pretty content with his job.

"Do you think you can scare up a rabbit AND chase it down and...and shake it and stuff?"

"You mean kill it?" Gizmo murmurs into the leaves.

"Yeah. I mean, you look pretty fast. Are you fast?"

"Super fast—WAIT."

We halt, every breath caught in every throat.

Gizmo presses his big snout into the dirt and sucks the air of it up through his nostrils with a rather aggressive inhale. Then again. Then a third time.

Then he leaps back.

A cry of alarm goes up from the hunting pack.

"What's wrong?"

"What happened?"

"Did something bite you?"

"Oh, no! Gizmo got bitten by a rabbit!"

"They're turning on us! Ruuuuuuuuuun—"

Sweetpea's shrill voice crashes through the forest: "No! Stop that! No panicking!"

Breathlessly, we all regain our composure. Kind of.

"Gizmo!" I say. "What happened?"

He looks at me without much expression. "Nothing."

"Nothing?"

"Nah. Just a funny scent. Got me all excited for a second. I'm fine now. Let's move on."

A collective sigh of relief.

"Thank goodness," I say. "The rabbits haven't turned on us." I cast a wary gaze around the woods, then add: "Yet."

"You were saying something?" Gizmo says, with his nose back in the leaves, as casual as though he hadn't just scared us all to death because of a "funny scent."

I take a glance at Sweetpea again, and this time find him staring back at me with half-lidded eyes and flattened ears. He is not pleased. I keep my voice very low.

"Yeah, well, you know, I was just wondering if you might be able to chase down the rabbit, because you're so fast."

"I thought you were going to chase down the rabbit."

"Yeah. And you know what? I totally would."

"Yeah?"

"Oh yeah. And I'd, like, get it in my jaws and stuff? And like, shake it hard so it...you know...I'd totally do all that stuff that Sweet—uh, His Masterfulness—told us. With the shaking and the killing and the blood and stuff."

"Oh, okay, cool," Gizmo says. "Well, good luck."

"Yeah, see, that's the thing. I'd just LOOOOOVE to do the killing, but I, uh...I think..." I have no idea what I'm saying, even as it comes out. "I think I pulled a muscle in my neck? And I don't think I can shake it to death."

"Too bad about that muscle," Gizmo says. "You should see if—" He stops and jerks his head upright. "Hold up."

Everyone halts again. Ten dogs and one cat, all on the very brink of losing their minds.

"I smell..." He scents the air.

Sweetpea scampers up. "What?" he hisses. "What is it?"

"I smell..." Gizmo says again, his big, black nose working overtime.

"Yes? What do you smell?"

"It's...definitely..." Gizmo's lower jaw pulses open and closed to circulate the scent better. I'm smelling the air with him, and realize what it is just as he says it: "Other dogs."

Sweetpea gapes at him for a moment, and then predictably starts yelling. "Are you fucking kidding me with this shit? Of course you smell other fucking dogs, you sack of shit! We're literally surrounded by them! There's a dog over there, and a dog over there, and—oh, look!—another fucking dog! First with the funny smell that makes you freak everyone out, and now with this most astute observation—'Oh, I smell other dogs,'—well, I'm fucking elated that your nose is capable of such prowess as to perceive the scent of the nine dogs that are RIGHT IN FRONT OF YOUR FACE, but I already know there's other dogs because I saw them with my motherfucking EYEEEEEES! I swear to God—"

"THOSE dogs," Gizmo says, flatly, like he hadn't heard a word of Sweetpea's diatribe.

Sweetpea jerks his head around and stiffens. He's late to the party. The rest of us have already scented—and seen—the other dogs. And not just a couple of them. At least twenty of them.

And they have us completely surrounded.

"Oh, I see," Sweetpea says, much quieter, his tail fluffing and twitching. "Those dogs." He sniffs. Tries to settle himself. "You should've said so."

I don't even know what to say or do right now. I just watched those dogs materialize out of the woods. It was like they weren't dogs at all. They were so stealthy, I feel like I'm looking at an entire pack of cats...but bigger. And more dog-like. Because they're dogs.

I guess what I'm trying to say, is that they actually look like the hunting party we're supposed to be.

And I've never encountered a group of dogs with such a clear leader. It's this big, golden-furred, sunny-faced thing, with the fluffiest coat you've ever seen in your life, a majestic curl of a tail, and intelligent, pointed ears. He looks like a dog that was bred to be a leader. And I want to mush my face into his coat.

"Greetings, other dogs!" Oh my goodness, his voice is like being caressed by a thousand peoples. "My name is Hiro." Oh my goodness, his name is Hero. "And this is my hunting party." I wait for one of his pack to say something stupid, like we would have done, but they just stand in stoic, noble silence. Oh my goodness, they're not idiots.

"Uh, yes, well," Sweetpea takes a step forward, his tail curling around Gizmo's face in a manner that almost looks like he's trying to shush Gizmo with it. "I am—"

I don't know why I do it. I'm just so excited and awestruck by the level of awesomeness on display by these other dogs, that I can't help myself. I blurt it out, my voice all strange and hoarse and overly self-conscious: "HIS NAME IS SWEETPEA!"

I see Sweetpea's shoulders tighten and his head swivels to me with wide, accusatory eyes. "...the fuck?"

"Sorry!" I whisper, but I'm wagging my tail, eyes still on Hiro and his incredible pack of...I feel like I can't even call them dogs. I want to be friends with them so bad I can hardly sit still. If one of them shared the greeting of the day with me, I think I'd piss myself and flop on the ground.

"Well met, Sweetpea the Cat," Hiro says in that glorious voice of his. "How come you to be in this region of the woods?" A somewhat circumspect glance at the rest of us. "And with a pack of dogs, no less..."

"Ah-ha-ha," Sweetpea chortles breathlessly. "Yes, see, there's one thing about my name and title—"

"WE'RE A HUNTING PARTY!" I blather out, almost mystified by my inability to stop myself. "WE'RE GONNA HUNT RABBITS! I'M A HUNTING DOG CUZ I'M FAST!"

"Would you stop that?" Sweetpea growls over his shoulder at me.

"Sorry! I can't stop!"

"A hunting party of dogs," Hiro summarizes, with an expression like he's pretty sure he's missing something. "With a cat. Hunting...rabbits."

"Well, you know," Sweetpea says, detaching himself from Gizmo and taking up a position more or less in the center of us. "It's just practice—OBVIOUSLY."

"Hm," is Hiro's response.

"Yes, just practice," Sweetpea continues. "We're all very good hunters, but, you know, we like to practice a lot on small animals.

Keep our skills sharp for when we need to take down the big game, you know what I'm saying?"

"That's very disciplined of you."

His voice! "YOU SHOULD KEEP SAYING WORDS CUZ THEY SOUND GOOD IN MY EAR HOLES!" Dang it, I wish I could shut up.

Hiro looks surprised at me. For a second, I think he's actually talking to me, and I nearly pass out, but he's just kind of watching me while he speaks to Sweetpea. "And your...packmate there. Is everything alright with him?"

Sweetpea casts me one more sour glance. "Yes, of course. Unfortunately, he was kicked in the head by a very large deer and he can't think anymore."

"How terrible."

"DO YOU WANNA SEE HOW FAST I CAN GO?"

"Maybe later, Mash," Sweetpea calls out.

Please, Me...stop talking. You're ruining this for us.

"Anywho," Sweetpea says. "One small matter to address, which is of course—"

"Territorial boundaries."

"—my name and title. Er, uh, but also territorial boundaries."

"I'm somewhat surprised," Hiro says, in a solemn voice, stepping out of line with his packmates and padding steadily towards Sweetpea. "That with all the fine noses around you, your pack wasn't frightened off by our markings."

Sweetpea seems to shrink back, even as he tries desperately to look like he's not shrinking back. "Ah, right. The markings. You know? I told them we should have paid better attention to the markings, but then I was like, 'who knows who left that behind?' I mean, if I'd have known it was YOU, well, I mean, you know, look at you! I don't...uh...I'm sure that...we can..." Sweetpea looks like if he gets any more compact, he'll disappear. "...leave?"

"Oh, no," Hiro says, taking another step forward, his cool, golden gaze—ohmigodhe'ssocool—panning over us. "I'm afraid it's too late for you to leave."

"Is it?" Sweetpea titters. "Is it really? Because it seems so easy. We just turn around and go back the way we came. No harm done."

Hiro steps even closer to Sweetpea, now within lunging distance, and I'm wondering when Sweetpea is going to break and bolt. "Unfortunately, that really isn't the point. You see, you are strangers. And this is our territory."

I should do something. But, I mean, to Sweetpea's point: LOOK AT HIM!

"I don't know how you dogs do it where you're from," Hiro says. "But around here, there's only one thing we do with strangers."

Sweetpea's body is probably a quarter of the size his fur suggests. I can see the way he's holding his neck, though. I can see his claws inching out. What is incredibly impressive to me is that he hasn't run yet, and not only that, but it seems like he's about to take a swipe at this guy.

I almost tell him not to because I'd hate for Hiro's beautiful face to be marred, but right before anything happens, Hiro shouts in Sweetpea's face: "WE MAKE THEM INTO FRIENDS!"

I can't really describe to you all that happens next. Someone yells "PLAYDATE!" and all of a sudden everyone is running every which way, and there are tails wagging and tongues lolling and barks and yips and growls and dogs chasing each other and sniffing butts and the air is filled with slobber and fur and flying leaves.

In the middle of this hurricane of dog play, of which I am only one whirling piece of debris, Sweetpea remains frozen in his shrunken position. That is, until Hiro upends him and goes for the greeting of the day. I don't know if it was Hiro's technique, or just the strength of his personality, but I've never seen Sweetpea just flop over for a sniff like that.

And then, somehow, I'm with Hiro, and we're laughing and prancing and twirling around each other.

"I CAN'T DECIDE IF I'M SCARED OF YOU OR IF I LOVE YOU!"

"No need to be scared!"

"I HAVE A PACKMATE NAMED BANGER! SHE DOESN'T LIKE OTHER DOGS!"

"What a shame! I LOVE other dogs!"

"I LOVE OTHER DOGS TOO! AND I LOVE CAT-BUTT-SMELL! DO YOU LIKE CAT-BUTT-SMELL?"

"Cat-butt-smell is THE BEST!"

"YOU'RE THE BEST, HIRO!"

"No, THIS is the best!"

"HAHAHAHAHAHA!"

"Ha ha ha ha ha!"

This goes on for quite some time. I wish I could relay all of it to you, but at this point, I barely even know what's happening. I'm just caught up in it. I meet every member of the new pack, but, if I'm being honest, all their butts run together in my mind. Except for Hiro. I've never smelled a nobler butthole.

Poor Sweetpea doesn't escape the rumpus. He just goes kind of still and stiff, like a possum playing dead, his eyes wide and vacant, like his soul has left his body, while a steady stream of dogs race up, smell him, and then race away.

It is his deathly stillness that snaps me out of it, and I worry, for just a moment, that he has actually been sniffed to death. I race over to him—barely restraining myself from taking a nose-full myself—and plant my feet over top of him. I know he doesn't actually need the protection—despite what he thinks, the greeting of the day isn't actually harmful—but I want to make him feel secure so maybe his soul will come back to him.

"Sweetpea!" I whisper. I know I should be using his official title, but I'm afraid that he won't recognize it in the state he's in. "It's okay. You're safe now. I've got you."

His eyes have a glassy, road-kill quality to them, like he hasn't blinked in so long that they've got completely dried out. His ears don't even twitch when I speak. Oh, man, this is bad.

"Sweetpea..."

A low groan issues from his throat.

"What's that?" I lean in closer.

I can barely hear him whisper: "Hih...hih..."

"Yes?"

"Hiz...Sue..."

"Who?"

"His...Supreme...Masterfulness...you fuck."

15

Sweetpea

I KNOW WHAT YOU want to hear, but you can go fuck yourself, because I don't want to talk about it.

Skipping, skipping, skipping...

"Don't think I forgot about all the barking and howling and yipping you asshats did," I snipe at them as we follow Hiro's pack.

I'll admit one thing about this whole debacle: I am possessed of the very strong inclination to stick very close to Mash now. I don't even think he recalls being one of the dogs to stick his cold—blah-blah-blah, moving on! I'm sure he was just caught up in the moment. But I have to say, when I finally came back to myself and looked up and found him standing over me, keeping my ass from further ravages...well...I kind of imprinted on him. Like a baby duckling. Now I don't want to let him get too far away from me.

In response to my accusation, there are numerous groans and hanging heads and tails, which does make me feel marginally better.

"What's that about?" Hiro asks, overhearing me.

I open my mouth to answer, but Mash blunders his way between us. He's managed to control his volume a little more, but apparently still can't filter anything he says in Hiro's presence.

"We can't bark or yip or howl or make noises that the peoples wouldn't like because it's Bad, and we don't wanna be Bad, we wanna be Perfect Dogs."

I clench my teeth together. "Yes. That."

Hiro lets out a good-natured guffaw, as though he thinks the whole thing is mightily amusing. "Well, that certainly speaks to a certain level of zeal to please the peoples."

"You know," I say to him, suddenly curious. "I never even bothered to ask about your peoples. Did they all disappear like ours did?"

For a moment, there is a breath of something like hope in the air, and all the dogs from my pack swivel around to listen to Hiro's response, but his news is unsurprising.

"They did indeed," he says, with a stoic sort of sadness. "And the worst part of it is, we don't know where they went, why they all left at the same time, and when they're coming back. It's highly unusual for them to leave us to our own devices for such an extended period of time."

"Banger says the peoples left because we were Bad Dogs and that's why we've got to be Perfect Dogs so they'll come back."

I'll give you one guess who spewed all that out in one breath.

Hiro comes to a stop, looking at me and Mash with a strange expression. I can't tell if it's shock or pity. "Is...that why you can't make dog noises anymore?" he asks Mash, his voice sounding almost like he's dreading the answer because he already knows.

Mash, completely tone-deaf to Hiro's vibe, just keeps wagging his tail and grinning like an idiot as he yammers out his answer: "If we make noises that would irritate the peoples, we have to throw up our dinner and take a bath."

Hiro's face becomes troubled. He glances at me. "Is this true?"

"Don't look at me like that," I growl. "I don't make the rules—I just enforce them."

"Why on earth would ANYONE make those rules?"

"Because if we can be Perfect Dogs then the peoples will come back."

Hiro's tail has drooped during all of this. And listening to Mash's reply, Hiro's head does the same. "Oh, Mash. This is such an unfortunate..." he trails off. Looks searchingly at Mash. "Look at it like this, my friend: Did your peoples love you?"

"He did! He loved me because I was a Very Good Dog!"

Hiro's eyes seem to sparkle with some hidden knowledge. "Or were you a Very Good Dog because he loved you?"

The dopey smile vanishes from Mash's face. His ears come forward and his head tilts. "Wait...what?"

Hiro smiles and lets out a huff of excitement. "Let me show you something! Come with me!"

Hiro pushes quickly forward, Mash keeping pace with him, and me struggling to keep up—but keep up I do, as I refuse to look to either side as I pass dog after wet-nosed dog. We climb a slight hill, and at the top of the rise, I see the trees thin out and then stop completely.

It is only at that point that I realize I am hearing all the noises that dogs shouldn't be making. But they're not coming from the two hunting packs behind me. They're coming from in front of me. And what I see as I step towards the edge of the woods, down the hill, nestled in a valley of green grass and surrounded by woods, is yet another village.

For the barest of moments, my mind is cast back to the nightmare on the cliff, where I'd looked down from a high perspective and seen the village burning and the dogs killing each other. But this is not that. This is the furthest thing from that.

All throughout the village below, the dogs are running, and playing, and exploring, and chasing things, and sniffing things, and eating God-knows-what, and all the while, they are snarling and barking and yipping and growling in every tone and cadence afforded to them. And all the while, their tails are wagging, wagging, wagging.

And, for just a moment, as I stand there looking down on them, I think the peoples would laugh for joy if they saw this. So many dogs just doing dog stuff. They're suckers for that shit.

"This is what I mean," Hiro says, as Mash gazes on with a tail that wags steadily from side to side, his ears erect, his posture forward-leaning, like he just cannot wait to sprint towards that village and meet all of his new friends. "Do you know what the peoples loved, Mash?"

"Uh..." Mash's voice sounds dreamy. "Food?"

Hiro laughs. "That they did. And don't we all? But no, Mash. The peoples loved DOGS. And do you know why your peoples loved you?"

"Why?"

"Because YOU'RE a dog."

"I AM a dog!"

"Well?"

"Well what?"

"Well, let's go be dogs!"

And off the two of them race, down the hill towards the village where all the dogs are just dogs, doing stupid dog shit. And I'm left there at the top of the hill, caught up in my own thoughts, as the two hunting packs go running by me, tails wagging, tongues hanging out, eyes bright. So full of joy, just to simply...BE.

·········

You've probably said to yourself, "Man, that cat is so wise."

And you'd be right. Because I am.

Sometimes it's a burden being so wise. I wisely remained on the hilltop overlooking the strange village, so as to avoid any further unwanted greetings. I wisely did not partake in the two-day-old deer carcass when Mash brought me a chunk. I wisely told the dogs of my hunting party that it was getting late, and we needed to head back to our own village. And then I wisely led them back, all with full bellies, though unfortunately through no prowess of their own.

Now, after all that wisdom, I'm approaching Gracie's crash pad in the deep blue of a fresh-fallen night, trying to figure out the wisest course of action moving forward.

Should I tell her about the other dogs? I feel like I'll have to. SOMEONE is going to talk about it. And then she'll wonder why I didn't tell her first. But something tells me that their whatever-let's-just-be-dogs attitude won't sit well with Gracie.

And I keep thinking about that nightmare. That, above all else, troubles me the most. The similarities between my vantage point on that hill overlooking Hiro's village, and the cliff overlooking the dream-village, are discomfiting to say the least.

Of course, it's just a dream.

But what if it's not?

What if those dogs—Hiro's dogs—were the ones I saw in the dream? What if their complacent attitude on morality is what will lead them to devolve into madness and slaughter? Or worse than that—what if the dogs in my dream were both Hiro's dogs AND ours? What if the dream is a premonition of some sort of war between us?

It's almost laughable—dogs going to war with each other. The fuck would they have to fight about? And, apparently, all someone has to do is yell "PLAYDATE" and any martial order would go out the window in favor of prancing about and licking each other's balls.

But all the logic in the world isn't making this feeling of dread go away.

I mount the steps to Gracie's porch and stop a cat-length from the pet door. I shift my posture into a most authoritative position and call out in a voice that—between you and me—I'm trying to make sound like Hiro's. "His Supreme Masterfulness...has arrived."

There is a flurry of scuffling from inside. I wait, a little impatiently, and I'm about to repeat myself, when the door begins to purr open, and I see Longjohn's prostrate form, just inside. It is a most strange position to see another cat—lying on his belly with his paws stretched out in front of him, but instead of his head up, like the Sphinx which all cats aspire to, his face is mushed into the ground.

I'm expecting honorifics, but there is only silence.

"Eck-fucking-scuse me?" I hiss. "My homage?!"

"Oyea, oyea, oyea," Longjohn intones, without a breath of earnest feeling. "His Supreme Masterfulness is present. The mighty fall before him and are mighty no longer."

"Thank you, Analingus. You may rise."

Longjohn—whom I've dubbed Analingus—starts to rise.

"No eye-contact, though," I admonish him.

He keeps his eyes downcast, but I can see they are full of hate. I sashay up to the door, step through, and walk right past him, showing him my back, which is the ultimate fuck-you power move. Then I slap him in the face with my tail.

"Oh, and Analingus?"

"Yes, Your Masterfulness?"

"More feeling next time."

"Yes, Your Masterfulness."

"When you do the 'Oyeas,' I need you to work some shakiness into your voice, as though you're overcome with awe. And at the end, try drawing out the last word. 'The mighty are mighty no looooooongeeeeeeer.' Like that."

"Yes...Your..." Boy, he really sounds like he's struggling. "...Masterfulness."

"Excellent. I'm seeking an audience with the Voice of the Peoples."

A few moments later, and I'm ushered into Gracie's Moon Room, which is a very fancy name for...a room. It is neither a special room, nor does it contain moons. There is a large window that faces roughly east, and I assume she can see the moon from there, which is perhaps why she named it the Moon Room. Frankly, I find the name so odd that I often wonder if there is some inuendo I'm missing.

I'll spare you the small talk. We pass it, and it's passable.

Moving right into the big stuff: "So," Gracie says, sitting with her back to the window. "Tell me about them."

"You've already heard, then."

"I've heard from some very excited dogs. Now I'll hear it from the cynical cat."

I preen at the compliment. "Very kind of you. Well, they're a bit of a conundrum, if you ask me."

"They have food though?"

"They hunt, yes. Apparently well enough that they didn't think anything of sharing it with strangers."

"Hm." Gracie nods thoughtfully. "Neighbors with food are good neighbors to have."

"They may be able to teach our hunters a few...oh, you know. Pro tips."

Gracie looks surprised. "I thought YOU were the best hunter."

"I am," I say quickly.

The faintest snort comes from the back corner of the room where Longjohn is lurking.

I whirl on him. "Something you'd like to say, Analingus?!"

He averts his eyes. "No, Your Masterfulness."

Man. I have no idea what Gracie said to him to make him this cooperative, but I'm loving it. "Your presence is no longer useful," I say, feigning at quaking fury, though I'm positively effervescent inside. "Be gone, Analingus."

Longjohn departs, and I turn back to Gracie. "I AM the best hunter. But I am a cat. There is going to be some disconnect between how I hunt and how dogs hunt. Perhaps these other dogs can fill in some of those gaps. Smooth out some kinks."

Gracie's gaze is piercing. "And were they…Good Dogs?"

"Weeeelllllllll…" I stop. Lick my shoulders. Lick my paw. Groom my face.

"Yes?" Gracie prompts after a long moment.

"Are they Good Dogs?" I muse.

"That was my question, yes."

"That's a tricky question to answer. 'Good' is such a fluid term."

"Good only means one thing around here."

I eye her for a moment. "And that would be…?"

"Well…" She seems like she doesn't even know how to define it herself. "Good means…that…you don't do Bad Things."

"Ah, yes, right-right-right," I say. "But then you have to ask the question, what do you call Bad?"

"Bad is…not Good."

"That doesn't clarify it as much as you might think."

"Bad is whatever the peoples didn't like!"

"Ah, right, yes, now we're getting somewhere. But, you know, I'm still forced to ask the question, what did peoples not like? Were they all different? Let's take the Cloud Throne for instance. Some peoples didn't like when dogs got up onto the Cloud Throne. But what if some peoples DID like it? What if the thing they DON'T like is dogs NOT being on the Cloud Throne?"

"You're talking in circles."

"Look." I sigh, and decide to simply have out with it, though I have no idea how Gracie will take it, or what will happen next, or whether I should be encouraging her to make friends with the other dogs, or encouraging her to stay away from them. Frankly, I have no ideas about anything right now. "They believe that the peoples just want them to act like dogs."

Gracie's eyes widen. "You mean...they don't...?"

"They don't have any rules. No laws." I can feel a troubled frown working its way through my face. "I saw no less than thirty violations while I was there."

"This is...disturbing."

I consider that for a moment. Was it disturbing? Perhaps if I'd seen the other dogs vomiting and eating it. But I never witnessed that. I witnessed raucous play. I witnessed unlawful sounds. I witnessed unauthorized humping.

I witnessed...well...dogs enjoying themselves.

"You should understand," I press on. "That their apparent lack of rules doesn't make them..." I'm about to say Bad, but that would fly in the face of how she just defined Bad. "Dangerous, or hard to get along with. Actually, quite the opposite. Their leader, Hiro, is a most impressive specimen. And very welcoming."

Gracie's gaze has wandered into the middle distance as she considers this. But where I had expected holy fury and moral outrage, there is only quiet consideration.

"So," she says eventually. "They don't believe that the peoples left because we were Bad Dogs."

"No."

"Why do they think the peoples left?"

"They don't know."

Gracie scoffs, but it lacks fervor. I peer at her discerningly, and I can't shake the feeling that she's just pretending to be the Voice of the Peoples right now. All of her pomp and dignity suddenly seems paper-thin, like it might just slough off of her like dander at a moment's notice.

"Well, that's a dangerous game they're playing," Gracie says softly. "Have they even considered the fact that they might be Bad Dogs?"

"You know, honestly? I don't think they have."

For just a flash, Gracie's face looks so mournful, that I think she's going to let out a howl of grief—and I really have no idea how I'd handle that. Not her grief, nor her violation of the law.

"But we know that's why they left," Gracie says. "Don't we?"

"We do."

"Right. And, there are reasons why we believe that, aren't there?"

"Uh..."

She looks right at me. "What are those reasons? Can you remind me? My memory is failing me right now."

"Uhhhh...Be...Cause..." I'm glancing all around the room as though I might find the answer helpfully pinned to one of the walls. Or perhaps written there by a cosmic finger. But the walls are all very blank and unhelpful. "...Banger said so?"

"Is that all?"

"Well, she had some very convincing arguments at the time." I frown. "I just can't recall what they were. I wasn't paying attention yet."

"I can't recall them either. I only remember feeling guilty." Gracie's eyes drift like a leaf in a puddle and eventually land on mine. "What about you?"

"Nah. I've never felt guilty in my life."

"I meant, what do you think about why the peoples left us?"

"Oh." I think back to that afternoon, almost a month in the past now. I think about everything that happened. All the minute details of it—the sky, the wind, the sun, Dad's sharp intake of breath, his otherworldly smile…and his words. Not just his words to me and Banger and Mash. But the words that he spoke as though thinking aloud.

"Gracie," I say, quietly, but earnestly. "I'm not sure the peoples really MEANT to leave us."

Her gaze sharpens. "What do you mean by that?"

"I don't think that they wanted to leave us," I clarify. "I got the distinct sense that our peoples didn't WANT to go, but HAD to go."

"Impossible," Gracie breathes. "What could make the peoples do anything? They have all the power. All the control. Why would they ever do anything they didn't WANT to do?"

Funny, I find myself tempted to shake my head as a negative response—like Gracie and all the other dogs have started doing. "I don't know, Gracie. Mysteries of the universe. I'm only telling you how it appeared to me at the time."

"You were there with him," Gracie practically whispers. "I wasn't with my peoples. They left when they were…" she pauses for a long moment. Her eyes sharpen. "On their bike ride."

"Something significant there?"

"Only that, if they'd been in control, I don't think they would have left the bikes out on the trail. And…" I think I know what she's going to say, but I let her say it. "And they would have come back to say something to me." She looks at me again with a face that wants something from me so hard that it almost frightens me. "What do you think they would have said to me?"

I pull back from her. "How the hell should I know, Gracie? I didn't really know your peoples."

"What'd your peoples say to you and Banger and Mash?"

"Oh, just some peoples nonsense. Mushy stuff. You know how they get."

Her tail wags once—just a sad little flop on the floor, like it'd got all excited at the memory of the peoples talking mushy dog-talk, then realized they weren't there, and gave up on life again.

"Did they say anything about us being Bad?" she asks, almost with a cringe.

This time I do shake my head—and barely even think about it. "No, Gracie. He said he loved us."

"Even you?"

I laugh. "Yes, even me."

She turns her head to look sidelong out the window. "Do you think Banger's wrong?"

I sigh. I feel like I'd known the question was coming. But seeing it coming, and knowing how to handle it, are two different things. "I don't know, Gracie. I really don't know."

16

BANGER

(Day 100)

I don't even recognize this place anymore.

I walk down the street, and my path is crossed by dogs I don't know. Dogs from the other village, which is close enough by that they've been coming over to "hang out", and our dogs have been going over there for the same.

I do not like the influence that they've had on the Collective Pack of my village. I know that I don't typically choose to view myself as a member of that pack, but I resent the outside influence anyways.

Sweetpea woke up this morning making quite a deal about the fact that it'd been a hundred days since the peoples left. I'm not sure what's significant about a hundred days outside of any other number, but it seems important to Sweetpea, and I assume it's because "a hundred" is a lot.

I don't think it's any different from any other day. What number you slap on it doesn't change a thing. The peoples are gone, and they haven't come back yet, and I'll give you three guesses why not, but you'll only need one.

It's been a few months since our hunting pack encountered the dogs from the other village, and in that time, as these overly-social pups are prone to do, they've made fast friends. They call it Hiro's Pack, and dogs from Hiro's Pack have started to call us the Collective.

They can call us what they want, and they can call themselves what they want, and they can call today "hundred" or whatever, but there's only one thing that matters: The peoples aren't back, and the Collective Pack is further than ever from being Perfect Dogs. Further than ever, because of Hiro's Pack. Because of their bad influence. And because of Gracie's weakness.

I stop in front of Brute's house. His car cave stands dark and empty. I see the door from the car cave to the house hanging open, dim light showing from within. I take a sniff around the edge of the lawn. The weeds are higher than me now. Everything in this place is overgrown. If the peoples could see it, I think they'd be mad, but really, what can a bunch of dogs do about it? We can't get the stupid robots to work, and the occasional grazing we do isn't enough to keep the grass cropped short.

But in this particular instance, the long grass is a good thing.

I look around me. Collective and Hiro's Pack all intermixed now. It's heading into evening, and all the dogs SHOULD be heading towards the Park. But they're not. They're running around with their friends. Having all the doggy fun in the world, without a thought devoted to the peoples.

So far, Hiro's Pack's flagrant disregard for what the peoples liked and didn't like has not turned the Collective Pack into a bunch of lawless strays. But it has worn away a level of resolve. So, while no one out-and-out violates the rules, there is a whole lot of riding the very ragged edge of them, and several cases of violations simply being overlooked.

I know this makes me sound petty and disengaged from the Collective Pack. But I need you to understand something. All of this has got my guts twisted up inside. There is nothing that I want so badly as to see Dad again. It seems like every day that passes, all the dogs around me forget more and more about their peoples. And every day that passes, I feel like my yearning only gets more desperate.

I still wander the house sometimes, looking for him. I know he won't be there. Trust me, I know. But I feel like I have to do it. I feel guilty when I don't. Like maybe I just missed something all those other times I've looked. Like maybe I'll turn the corner and he'll be right there, right in front of me, once again.

Some nights I feel despair. Some nights my thoughts run around me, like I used to run around that tree I was chained to, wearing the grass down to hard-packed dirt. They tell me that I will never have the one thing I want, that my love for the peoples will go unseen and unreturned, forever.

And those thoughts tell me that it is because of these other dogs. Because they won't FOLLOW THE DANG RULES that might show the peoples how much we love them and convince them to come back.

The one thing I want is now at the mercy of the Collective Pack. And they don't seem to care at all. They barely cared in the beginning, and now Hiro's Pack has made them care even less. Has made them believe that all they have to do is whatever the heck they want, and somehow their complete apathy is going to magically make everything okay.

Looking around me, I see that all the dogs out roughhousing and wandering the streets are too engrossed in their activities to pay me much mind. I slip into the long grass, disappearing from view. I wind my way through the weeds until I emerge again, right next to the car cave, and then slip into the shadows within.

When I push my way through the open door to the house, I find five dogs sitting in the people's old eating room.

"Ah," Brute says when he sees me. "She finally graces us with her presence."

I haven't proceeded past the door yet. My eyes are fixed on two of the dogs. Obviously, I know who they are. It's Sunny, the Blue Heeler, and Max, a medium-sized mutt of various white and brown patches. They smile and pant and seem happy to see me, though I'm not thrilled to see them.

"Why are YOU here?" I demand, still unmoving from the door.

Sunny and Max, who don't live together, but have always been close friends, exchange a glance.

"We were invited," Sunny says, her voice a little unsure.

"By who?"

"By me," one of the other dogs says, like it's not a problem at all, and he can't even foresee why it would be. It's Colby, a tan and white terrier mutt. He's always been friendlier than he is smart.

"Who gave you permission to invite ANYONE?" I seethe, finally stepping away from the door and approaching Colby, who shrinks back, seeming to realize that he has indeed done something stupid.

"Oh, crap," he says, averting his eyes and squirming, his tail coming up between his legs and giving a plaintive little wag of nervousness. "I thought you wanted more dogs to come!"

I can barely fathom his idiocy. "What part of 'let's keep this quiet' did you not understand?"

We'd been meeting for quite a few days—don't ask me how many—always at Brute's house. It'd started as just me and Brute, complaining about the pups, and their lack of love for the peoples, and the slow, creeping decay of their attention to the Laws of Good and Bad. And you know what? Brute's not that bad. I can't really say we hit it off or anything, or that we're going to be besties for life, but we see eye-to-eye on many things. And our perspective is a vast minority.

But apparently, we're not the only ones to worry about the end result of this complacency that's overtaken the Collective Pack. Several days ago, we were joined by Q, who was an itchy ball of nerves about the whole thing. She just kind of happened upon us, as me and Brute were enjoying some sun in the driveway. I guess she'd overheard some of the things we had to say, and she had a whole lot of stuff to add of her own.

Then, just a few days ago, Q brought along Colby. And at that point, me and Brute looked at each other and seemed to agree—we didn't really want our rebel opinions getting out, especially since a lot of them weren't too flattering to Gracie, and she was still the pack leader. And that's when I told Colby and Q, in what, at the time, I perceived to be very clear terms, "Hey, guys. Let's keep this quiet, huh? We don't need to advertise to every dog in the village that we're over here talking bad about Gracie."

Ah, okay. I can see where the confusion came from.

"It's just that," Colby says, glancing sidelong at Sunny and Max. "You said—"

"I said we don't need to advertise to every dog in the village," I sigh, exhausted by Colby's simplistic interpretation, and by my own failure to catch it.

Colby wags his tail. "Well, it's not EVERY dog in the village! It's just Sunny and Max."

"Yeah!" Sunny and Max say together. "It's just us!"

"I think," Brute says, sounding about as tired as me, but perhaps just a hair amused by it too. "She meant not to tell anyone."

Colby frowns. "Well...that's very unclear wording."

You know, I'll never take Sweetpea's stance that dogs are dumb. But I can admit that nuance is not our strong suit.

"It's called subtext, Colby," I groan. "What did you tell them about us?"

But it's Sunny that responds. "Isn't this the place where we talk about how to fix the Collective Pack since Gracie's letting Hiro's Pack lead everyone astray?"

Max has his own version to add: "And aren't we figuring out how to get the peoples back now that Gracie's barely enforcing the law anymore?"

"Actually," Brute says with a disinterested yawn. "This is where Banger comes to complain about how the rest of the dogs are idiots."

I bristle. "I never said the rest of the dogs were idiots!"

Brute's eyes flash with humor. "It's called subtext, dear."

Sunny's demeanor slackens a bit. "So...we're not talking about how to fix this stuff?"

Max seems caught between confusion and irritation. "We're just...complaining?"

"But not actually planning to do anything about it?" Sunny adds.

Max looks to Colby. "You said Banger had a plan."

"It seemed like she did!" Colby squirms, getting defensive.

Q scoffs—a big rude noise out of the little white fluff ball. "Banger? Have a plan?"

"Hey, whoa," I say, whipping around to Q. "What's that supposed to mean?"

Q turns big, innocent eyes on me. "Well, no offense, Banger, but it's not exactly a secret that you hate all the other dogs in the world."

Geez, I feel like I'm getting it from all sides now. "First of all, I don't HATE all the other dogs IN THE WORLD. I just don't like MOST of the ones I know." I glare at her pointedly. "And besides, what does that even have to do with my ability to make plans?"

It's Brute that answers that one: "A plan would require coordinating multiple dogs."

"And I can't coordinate multiple dogs?" I demand hotly.

"See, I told you she could do it!" Colby declares and begins wagging his tail again.

"Well, that's a relief," Max says. "Because SOMEONE needs to lead us out of this mess."

"Wait-wait-wait!" I swear I'm about to tear into someone's face. "I'm not leading anyone anywhere!"

Sunny is looking at me like I've just said the dumbest thing in the world. "You literally just said that you could coordinate multiple dogs."

"No! I said, 'and I can't coordinate multiple dogs?' Like a question!"

"Same thing."

"That is not the same thing!"

"Subtextually..." Brute murmurs, avoiding eye contact with me.

"I'm pretty confused right now," Colby says.

"Yeah, no kidding!" I snap back.

"How is asking what you asked not asking for the thing you asked? You asked if you could coordinate multiple dogs. Where am I losing this?"

"I asked the question to prove a point. I wasn't saying that I WANTED to coordinate other dogs. I was just saying that I COULD...IF I wanted to."

"But you don't."

"No."

"So, wait a second!" Sunny demands, looking suspiciously at me. "Is there or is there not a plan?"

"No. There's no plan."

"But you're coming up with one?"

"No, we're not coming up with one."

"Then why are you even complaining?"

Sunny and Max exchange a hooded look, and Max grumbles, "What's the point in complaining about something if you're not going to do anything to fix it?"

"I'm complaining because this crap is insane!" I finally break. "I'm complaining because everyone's hearts are in the wrong places! I'm complaining because the Collective is running around with Hiro's pack, absorbing all of their nonsense about how we were just fine before the peoples left—BUT THEN WHY'D THE PEOPLES LEAVE? I'm complaining because the one dog that's supposed to be keeping us on the path to being Perfect Dogs only cares about having fun and playing with other dogs! I'm complaining because no one seems to remember what it meant to love the peoples! But mostly I'm complaining because I don't know what else to do, and I'm terrified—TERRIFIED—that everyone else is going to ruin my ONE CHANCE to be with Dad again!"

I stand there, panting in the middle of everyone else's silent attention. I don't know how to feel as my eyes range over them all, taking in their different expressions, their different feelings, about our situation, and about me.

Brute looks at me like he's waiting for me to make some sort of connection that I can't seem to grasp, and I feel stupid and puppyish under that stare.

Colby looks saddened, not for me, but because of the reminder of everything he's lost, and I feel like I've just hurt him with my outburst.

Q stares blankly, her mouth closed, but her tongue still sticking dumbly out of the side, and I wonder if she was even listening.

But it's Sunny and Max that are the worst. They both look...disappointed.

And what does that make me feel? NOTHING! Because why should I care what other dogs think of me? They can't even be trusted anyways. I didn't come to Brute's house to stand here and be judged by a bunch of dogs I'd rather not even see, let alone speak with. Their disappointment means nothing to me! It doesn't make me sad! It doesn't force a new perspective on me! I have nothing to be disappointed in myself for! Screw you, Sunny and Max! Screw all of you!

And I almost say it.

But Max speaks first: "You say that you're terrified that the other dogs are going to ruin your chance to see your peoples. But you're not willing to do anything but complain about it?"

And then Sunny adds, "You always seemed like the one dog in the Collective that loved the peoples more than anything else. And yet you're not willing to do a thing about it."

"I would do..." I start to growl back, but stop myself—not just because growling is Bad, but because I realize what exactly I was about to say. I was about to say that I would do anything. But if I'm willing to do anything for my love of the peoples, then why am I not willing to do this?

It seems like the other dogs saw it the same way.

"Would you do anything?" Brute asks me.

I want to say no, simply because I want to win the argument. But I can't say no. It's just not true. I WOULD do anything to get the peoples back—to get DAD back. And that includes this thing, no matter how distasteful it sounds.

"Yes," I strangle the word out of myself.

"Then do this," Sunny says. "Gracie has never been the Voice of the Peoples. It wasn't even her that suggested the laws and being Perfect Dogs to get them to come back. That was YOUR idea, Banger. You're the Voice of the Peoples. And we need you right now. Even if you hate us. We need you, because you are the dog that might love the peoples more than any other dog. If there's anyone that can help us prove our love to them, it's you."

"I can't just swoop in and take Gracie's place," I say. "Most of the dogs still see her as their leader."

Q makes a face. "I don't know about 'most.' SOME of the dogs will be loyal to her. But there's more like us than you think."

"And," Max puts in. "You don't need to replace Gracie. Some of the dogs will still want her to be the leader. But I think others will want YOU to be the leader. So give them that option."

"What?" I'm flabbergasted. "Split the pack?"

"Or you could do nothing," Brute says, all serene, like he doesn't actually care. "But what will nothing get you?"

More of this. More of the Collective and its laws being diluted and ignored, and any chance that we could have to see our peoples again, slipping away.

"Be our Voice of the Peoples," Colby urges, his tail slap-slap-slapping on the ground.

"Yes!" Sunny encourages. "Help us get back on track!"

"We need you, Banger!" Max agrees.

"I don't know about needing you specifically," Brute says. Then fixes with me a serious look. "But someone needs to do something, or we're never going to see the peoples again."

Never. Going. To see. The peoples. Again.

That shakes me. That one little word: Never.

Never is a long time. Longer than I can withstand. I love Dad. I need him to come back, or I swear, sometimes it feels like something inside of me is drying out and might crumble to dust.

No, I don't like other dogs. And this isn't going to change that. But they've got me cornered now. Maybe they knew they could catch me with the whole "do anything" argument. Or maybe they just wanted me to lead them because they knew how much I loved the people.

I suppose it doesn't matter at this point. I WILL do anything. And this is one of the anythings I would do.

Although, clearly, not my first choice.

"Alright, fine," I say. "I'll do it. We'll make a new pack. A pack that loves the peoples more than it loves other dogs. A pack that sticks to the laws and keeps them sacred." I look at them all sternly. "No more excuses. No more looking the other way. No more getting distracted by stupid things like play, and sniffing, and exploring. We will be completely devoted to the law, and to our love of the peoples, and proving our love to them, so that they'll come back."

17

Sweetpea

(Day 120)

What in the actual fuck is happening here?

Let me just give you a quick snapshot of what my eyes behold at this moment. I am standing in the Park with Longjohn—AKA Analingus—by my side. The late afternoon sun is filtering through the tops of some nearby trees. All around the Park, not a single dog has come to order for the meeting of the day—though, in all honesty, I can't imagine coming up with any more laws. We pretty much ran dry on that count about a month ago, but we still gather so that...so that...

Well, fuck. What the hell are we even here for anymore? For the last month or so, we've just been rehashing the same, tired old shit with increasing apathy. Even the arguments about how we need to guard against apathy have become apathetic.

And what do my eyes behold at this very moment, instead of a neat gathering of the Collective Pack? Well, I'll tell you. All around the Park, dogs are lounging in the sun, wandering away, chasing each other, sniffing each other, humping each other—yes! Humping! In broad daylight! With His Masterfulness clearly watching!

Not that I'm...you know...WATCHING watching. Let's just say it didn't escape my notice.

"You wanna do something about this, Gracie?" I ask to my side.

I get no response.

I twist to look, and find Gracie generously grooming Hiro's nether regions.

"The fuck?" I breathe. "Analingus! Go tell those humping dogs to knock it off! And call the meeting to order!"

Longjohn doesn't even make eye contact with me. Now, granted, I've forbidden him from doing so, but he does it now not out of obedience, but with a sly expression of closeted delight, like he knows my own rules are biting me in the ass.

"I apologize, Your Masterfulness. I am only a memory, not a voice."

"You sonofa—"

"Your words, of course," Longjohn adds, airily. "Which I am bound to obey."

"Oh, fuck off, Analingus," I gripe, then stalk over to where Hiro has now begun to return the favor for Gracie. Now, just for clarity, I should explain that this behavior—while visually repugnant—is not really all that sexual. It's not like they're about to bang it out right now. It's more of a social trust thing. I guess when you let someone else's teeth get that close to your genitals, it's quite a statement of faith.

Still, I feel like I'm interrupting something, so I stare off into the sky while I address her. "Excuse me, Voice of the Peoples?"

It's so very odd to use an honorific whilst the recipient is enjoying a good crotch cleaning.

"Huh? What?" Gracie jerks her head upright—as does Hiro.

"Oh, well, hello there, our fine feline friend," Hiro says in a voice that beams with earnest delight and makes me feel warm all over. "How have you been enjoying your day so far?"

"God!" I snap. "You're so nice that it makes it VERY hard to be mad at you! But I'm going to need you to retract your snout from the pack leader's tidbits."

"Social grooming is an important element of overall life satisfaction," Hiro explains, but complies with my request and disentangles himself from Gracie, who comes swaying to her feet, looking like she's forgotten what she was supposed to be doing here. "Do cats socially groom?"

"Sometimes. But only if you really know the other cat and have had time to build a—GODDAMMIT! Stop distracting me! Gracie!"

Gracie is frowning out at the disorganized rabble of her Collective Pack. I swear, there might be more dogs from Hiro's Pack present than the Collective. "Oh my," she utters.

"Oh my is correct!" I push myself between her and Hiro, in an attempt to further buffer her from his magnetism.

"Your Masterfulness," Hiro says. "You really should consider allowing Analingus to groom you."

"I'd rather be savaged by beavers," I snap over my shoulder. Then I figure it can't hurt to really drive the point home to Longjohn. Both for his humiliation and my peace of mind. "Your tongue ever touches me, it's coming out." Then, back to Gracie: "Don't you feel like things are getting just a LITTLE out of hand?"

Gracie stares out, with Hiro standing right beside her. Their expressions couldn't be more different. It's like they're looking at two different things. Gracie's face is surprised, and maybe a little ashamed, and maybe a little confused, like she doesn't quite know what to do at this point. Hiro's, on the other hand, is mildly amused, as though he's watching the antics of a litter of pups.

Which, I suppose, he kind of is.

"Where is everybody?" Gracie says.

I feel a slight note of panic. "Everybody? Who's everybody? Everybody's here."

I know damn well what Banger has been up to. Not only am I ultra-stealthy on my own, and pick up plenty of the goings on in the village, but at this point, my position of power has become well-known and appreciated by the other cats—you know, the ones that mocked me at first?—and they fill my ears with all sorts of gossip.

Plus, me and Banger talked about it last night.

At this point, Banger's got almost a third of the Collective Pack meeting at Brute's house while we're meeting at the Park. Every day I see more dogs drift off to her meeting, and those that remain at the Park are increasingly distracted. All the members of Hiro's Pack drifting in and out of our village has hidden the dent in our numbers, but it should have been obvious to Gracie long before now. The fact that she's just now noticing it means she really hasn't been paying attention.

"No, this isn't everybody," Gracie says, frowning.

"Oh, maybe we're missing one or two," I try to cover.

"We're missing like...a third."

Well, shit. When did dogs suddenly get so good at math?

"Where did they all go?" she asks.

"Oh, probably just...you know...sniffing around."

Gracie is silent for a moment, watching the dogs run about the Park. Then, quietly, she says, "Don't we care about the law anymore?"

"Well, in their defense, we've recorded every law we can possibly think of at this point."

"And," Hiro butts in, despite that fact that he's totally unwelcome in this conversation. "While rules are good sometimes, look at how happy the dogs all seem!"

Gracie contemplates this. "They do look happy," she admits.

"Of course they're happy!" Hiro laughs. "No one's telling them they can't act like dogs!"

"But...but..." Gracie stammers, in kind of a half-convinced way. "But the law! And...Perfect Dogs!"

"Well, I think they're perfect just the way they are," Hiro says, wagging his tail.

I grumble a string of curses under my breath. Then, out loud: "Gracie, would you mind a private talk? You know. About Collective Pack business? With NO OTHER PACKS PRESENT?"

"Oh. Right." Gracie still has that distracted tone to her voice, like she's just woken up and her head is still half in a dream.

I look pointedly at Hiro.

He takes my meaning without much effort.

"That's alright," he declares. "I was just thinking about checking the community message boards." By which he means the handful of places where every dog feels compelled to sprinkle a little urine. He saunters off. Dogs greet him by name as he passes by, both his pack and ours. Everybody loves this guy.

"So," Gracie says with a sigh, and lowers herself to the ground, like the issue of her missing pack members and the abortion of the meeting has already been handled and forgotten. "What's going on?"

"What's going on? Well, let's see. Your pack members aren't showing up to your meetings anymore. The slide into not giving a shit about the laws has been...shockingly rapid. And, at this point, there's still two dogs humping. I mean, they're really going at it. I think they're actually breeding."

Gracie inclines her head lazily in that direction. "Maybe they're a breeding pair." She shoots me a scornful look. "Is it really any business of yours?"

I gawp at her. "Is it any...? Well, no, I suppose it's not any business of mine. But there was a time not so long ago when you were pretty adamant about this type of shit being YOUR business."

"Ugh," she groans. "But it's so EXHAUSTING trying to be Perfect all the time. And it's so much easier to just be a dog and do what comes naturally, you know?"

"I always do what comes naturally to me. So yes. I know."

"Besides, the pack is clearly not into the whole Perfect Dog message, since they're not even showing up to the daily meetings anymore."

I cringe and look away. "Wellllllll....about that..."

Her ears perk up. "What?"

Crap. I'm trying mentally to backpedal, but every line of thought leads to me looking like an incredible idiot. And besides, Gracie's sitting here thinking that her pack members aren't coming to her meetings because she's been too strict, when in fact it's because she hasn't been strict enough.

Why I care that Gracie have the right arithmetic for her decisions I can't really explain. It just feels wrong to leave her in the dark. And yes, I can feel when things are wrong, because, despite what you might think, I do have a conscience. I just choose to ignore it most of the time.

I take a big determined breath and spit it out.

"The missing dogs are with Banger and Brute."

Gracie's nonchalance disappears like dandelion fluff in a puppy's mouth. "What are they doing there? She's way more strict about the law than I am."

"Yeah, well, that's kind of why they're with her," I say, still with my ears half-flattened, anticipating a violent response to come bursting out of Gracie at any moment. "See, they all think that you're totally fucking this whole thing up because you've been led astray by Hiro and his pack and you don't care about the law anymore, so they're going to Banger because...well, because she's a bit of a German Shepherd about the rules."

Gracie doesn't get mean, but she looks like I just told her they'd sprouted bat wings and only come out at night. "So they actually LIKE how crazy Banger is about the law?"

"They're scared, Gracie. They're scared that they won't ever see the peoples again if they don't stick to the law. And you're not really enforcing it anymore. So they sought out someone who would."

"I'm not enforcing it because it seems like nobody cares!"

"Well, apparently some of them do."

"But the peoples like us just the way we are! That's what Hiro says!"

"Well, see, that's kind of the problem there, Gracie. The dogs that are moving over to Banger aren't too convinced that Hiro's the best thing for us."

Gracie gasps. "Not the best thing? He's amazing!"

"I know he is," I admit, glancing over at him as he sashays through a cluster of female dogs who all look like they instantly went into heat. "He is amazing. But he's certainly not worried about the law."

"And look how beautiful and free he is!"

I don't respond because, honestly, I don't know what to say. I feel like both Gracie and Banger are right, in different ways. I always thought the law was pure idiocy, despite the fact that I enjoyed the power that it gave me. Then again, I also thought that letting the dogs just run amok and do whatever they wanted was probably not what the peoples would have wanted either.

Oh, hell, it's all so confusing.

"I don't know, Gracie," I sigh. "I really don't. But..." I'm squinting into the afternoon sun, wondering if I should finish my thought. Finishing my thought would cause me to be vulnerable, and being vulnerable is pretty much the thing every species on earth hates.

"But what?" Gracie prompts.

I drag my gaze back to hers, but then I don't want to see her judge me too hard when I speak, so I look away again. Down at the grass. Bat distractedly at a little yellow butterfly that flutters past. "I had a dream," I say, a bit cautiously, waiting for the derisive response, but it doesn't come, so I push on. "Actually, I've had this dream several times now. It's..." I bare my teeth for a flash. "It's getting to be a thing. And it's always the same. It never changes. And in it, the peoples say things to me." Now comes the really sphincter-puckering part. "And I think they're trying to communicate to me through the dream."

Utter silence.

I keep staring at the grass.

Then I hazard a glance up.

Gracie stares at me with an expression of keen interest. Not an ounce of derision or judgment.

Well, that went surprisingly well. I relax a bit.

"Tell me the dream," Gracie says in a strange, low tone.

So I do. I tell her all about the dozen or so times now that I've woken up on a cliff overlooking our village, and seen the houses aflame, and the streets filled with mad dogs tearing each other apart. As I tell it, Gracie's face darkens, becoming aggrieved simply at the mention of dog-on-dog killing. Even for someone who's become a little loosey-goosey about the law, the topic of dog-on-dog violence is hardly up for debate. Everyone agrees that the peoples would—and did—hate it.

When I finish, Gracie's face is as stern and hard as stone. She's looking down the street at something—I can't tell what.

"What did the peoples mean when they said we need to remember? Remember what?"

My ears twitch down in irritation. "Yeah, so far they've chosen not to offer any clarity on that, despite my having asked several times. Every time, actually." I shake my head a bit to relax my ears. "Anyways. I'm not just telling this to share weird dreams. The first time I had this dream was right before we met Hiro's group, and I remember wondering if they weren't the group that we were fighting in the dream."

Gracie lets out a scoffing laugh. "Hiro's Pack? Battle us to the death? Please. All they want to do is play."

"Well, someone was killing someone," I say, a little miffed at her dismissal of my primary theory.

"Yeah, I've got a good idea of who was killing who," Gracie says, just barely hiding the low growl in her throat, though I don't have the balls to call her on it. She's staring out down the street again, so I follow her gaze and see...

"Oh. No. Gracie. Come on."

She's looking at Brute's house.

She snaps her eyes to me. "You don't see it?"

"No, I see it," I strain out. "But wanting to live in close adherence to the laws doesn't make them a pack of murderers."

"Banger could have lived in close adherence to the laws all she wanted, but that wasn't enough for her. She thinks that the entire Collective Pack needs to be as crazy as she is about it."

"Still doesn't mean she's going to try to kill anyone over it."

"Maybe not. But she's chosen her side. And so have the other dogs."

"Sides? Are we creating sides now? I wasn't aware there were sides."

"Yes, there's sides."

"Won't creating sides make the battle more likely to happen?"

"I'm not CREATING the sides. I'm just observing that they're there. On Banger's side, you have all the dogs that think the peoples wanted us to be flawless figurines, instead of living, breathing, feeling creatures that have our own desires and personalities and compulsions."

Youch.

"And on our side, you have all the dogs that think being a dog is why the peoples loved us in the first place." She looks at me and smiles. "But we're not going to be mean about this, are we?"

"No?" I guess.

"No. In fact, we're going to be the exact opposite. We're going to be nice."

"Nice is nice. Sometimes."

"Exactly." Gracie stands up, her tail held high. "If Banger wants to make all the dogs miserable by hammering them over every jot and tiddle in the law, then we're going to do the exact opposite. We're not going to have any laws at all!"

"Er..."

"If it's stupid to follow the law so strictly, then that means it must be smart to ignore the law altogether!"

"Well..." I'm starting to get worried about the security of my position. If Gracie wipes the law out completely, then who will need the prodigious memory of a cat to remember it all? I suppose I could offer my services to Banger, but she already knows the law so well.

"Should we make an announcement?" Gracie wonders.

"Or," I say, hastily. "We can, you know, just kind of let it lie." My brain is racing for a way out of this. "No need to make a big deal about it—that might make even more dogs go over to Banger. Instead, let's just leave it be, and let the problem work itself out."

I'm not even sure what I've just said. I'm having to retrace my mental steps to see what the hell I'd just told Gracie, and realize that I might have postponed my obsolescence, but it's still coming.

Still. Maybe the delay will give me time to think of something else.

And then it strikes me: Do I even really care about my position? Of course I do. I MUST. Because I'm feeling a tad panicky right now at Gracie's implications that I'll no longer be needed. Unless...

Could I be feeling panicky for the dogs?

Was this a terrible decision Gracie was making?

No, it can't be that. Because the law WAS ridiculous. A compilation of the peoples' mild annoyances erroneously given the weight of heinous crimes.

So, if it's not my position, and it's not the abandonment of the law, then why are my guts all twisted up like this?

And then I realize what it is: Gracie and Banger have just cut our little village in two.

18

Mash

(Day 150)

I can't believe this is happening.

I stand on the street, and I watch dog after dog, with sticks in their mouths that they've gathered from the nearby woods, as they place the sticks, one by one, in a long line. When they've placed their sticks, the dogs just turn around and start marching back towards the woods, while another dog comes in behind them and does the same exact thing.

The dogs with the sticks? They're all Banger's dogs. They've been out here placing their sticks since before dawn that day, and now, by midmorning, they've completed an entire line of sticks that runs right through the middle of the village. But they're not stopping there. They just keep coming with more and more sticks, piling them on each other, as the line that cuts our village in two begins to grow taller.

On the far side of that line are Banger's dogs—a new pack that calls themselves the True Dogs, and there are about as many of them as there are of the Collective Pack now, if you don't count the handful of dogs from Hiro's Pack.

On the closer side of that line is the Collective, and, at this point, nearly the entire pack is present, watching as the True Dogs slowly build what I guess is supposed to be a wall between them and us.

"Hey, Hank!" one of the Collective Pack calls out to Hank, who's dragging a tree limb almost as big as himself up to the slowly growing wall. "What's this all about?"

Hank drops the limb in place and looks sheepishly around. "I'm not supposed to talk to you."

"Not supposed to talk to me?" The other dog looks completely confused. "Since when?"

Hank avoids the other dog's eyes. "Since you gave up on loving the peoples."

The other dog pulls back his head like he's smelled something bad. "What do you mean? I still love the peoples."

"Do you?" Hank snaps back. "Do you really love the peoples? Then why aren't you following the law anymore?"

"I dunno. I guess we just kind of...forgot about it."

"Yeah, well, if you've forgotten about the law, then maybe you've forgotten about the peoples, too."

"I haven't forgotten about my peoples!" the other dog bristles.

Hank looks at him scornfully and shakes his head. "You don't love the peoples. If you did, you'd be on THIS side of the wall, with the True Dogs."

"Hey, whoa," I say—I know I shouldn't butt in, but those were some pretty sharp words from Hank, and I don't want a fight to break out. "That's kind of harsh, Hank, don't you think?"

Hank spins on me. "And you, Mash? You too?"

I glance around me. Then I glance at myself. "Me? What about me?"

"What are you doing over there with the peoples-haters?"

"PEOPLES-HATERS?!" the other dog roars before I can even start to think of a response. "Where do you get off calling us peoples-haters? Just because we don't care about the law as much as you do, doesn't mean we hate the peoples!"

"The law is the word of the peoples! The peoples loved us! When you reject the law, you reject their love!"

There is something so WRONG with what Hank just said, that my mind kind of whites out, like staring into sun. His statements are like a gigantic tree, with a rotting base. But, in the moment, I can't seem to figure out what part of what he said is the rotten part.

"If the law is about love, then it totally misses what its aiming at!"

Shocked to hear such a blatantly heretical thing, I glance about to see who the ballsy dog was to make that claim. Hank is staring at me like I just savaged a puppy. The other dog he'd been arguing with is also staring at me.

I realize with mounting horror that I was the one that said it.

I was the ballsy heretic.

"What did you just say?" Hank says with a tremble in his lips that just barely flashes the points of his teeth. But the way he's looking at me, I think he heard me just fine.

What DID I just say? Was it even true? My horror becomes panic as I realize that I kind of missed what I was aiming at too.

"Wait!" I plead, desperately. "That's not really what I meant—"

"No—you know what?" the other dog interrupts me, and he's immediately bolstered by a whole host of affirmative grumbles, growls, and barks—much to the True Dogs' distaste. "Mash is right!"

"I am?" I ask, dumbfounded, and hoping these other dogs will explain how I was right.

"The law isn't about love at all!" the other dog declares.

"Well, I'm not sure that's really what I was getting at..."

"How could the law be about love?" The other dog is shouting now, turning and speaking to the gathered Collective Pack as much as he's hollering it back at Hank. "If the peoples really loved us, then they'd love us for who and what we ARE!"

"Yeah, just like Hiro's Pack!" another dog agrees.

"But what I was trying to say..." I attempt, but again, I'm drowned out, this time by Hank.

"Following the law is the deepest expression of love for the peoples!" Hank is outraged now, his hackles rising, his lips continuing to curl back. Strange that an argument about love seems to be making him more hateful.

I jump in before I can be drowned out again by the Collective Pack's response. "But the law isn't based on love, Hank! Would someone who loves you punish you for not doing what they want, just to get back at you?"

Hank seems momentarily stymied by this question, but on the Collective side of the wall, Roo looks up at me with a shaky sort of dawning fear. "So...the peoples...don't...really love us?"

"What?!" I gasp. Roo's interpretation of what I just said is so cattywampus, I can't even think for a second.

"See what you did?" Hank seethes at me. He looks ready to tear me apart.

"That's not what I was saying!" I practically scream in frustration, but if anybody heard me, I don't think they were paying attention. A wave of noise rocks me from both sides of the stupid wall of sticks—a blast of shock and rage from the True Dogs, and a battering of resentful howls and growls from the Collective.

"The peoples never wanted what was best for us!" A Collective dog wails in equal parts anguish and indignation.

"What's best for dogs is for us to be dogs!" Another says.

"If they really loved us, they'd have loved us just the way we are!"

"They wouldn't have given us all these stupid rules to try to make us different!"

"They never wanted us to be US!"

"They tried to change us!"

"Mash is right!" Roo suddenly yells, her fear curdled into resentment, and that, rapidly into anger. I don't know why I had the silly hope that maybe she'd figured out what I was actually trying to get at. But it's dashed, as Roo howls out her next words: "THE PEOPLES NEVER LOVED DOGS!"

Everything devolves into chaos. The Collective are all now shouting things, and every shout compounds their misinterpretation of my few, badly-chosen words, as they begin barking in alarm as their entire worldview is smashed to bits and remolded into something horrendous. On the other side of me, the True Dogs have a single source for their outrage, and it seems to be me.

"You!" Hank snarls. He lurches towards me a single step. "You're a BAD DOG!"

Almost on its own, my tail tucks between my legs. "No! I'm not a Bad Dog! I swear!"

"You hate the peoples!"

"I don't!"

"You think they don't love us!"

"That's not what I said!"

"Bad Dog!" Hank roars again, and then a few others join him, and it becomes a terrible chant: "Bad Dog! Bad Dog! Bad Dog!"

JuJu Bean suddenly rushes to my side, all fire and defensiveness, screaming over the True Dog's chant: "He's not a Bad Dog, you self-righteous turds! Mash is one of the best dogs I know!"

A smattering of encouraging barks threatens to make me feel affirmed, but for all the wrong reasons. "Well, thanks, JuJu, but—"

But JuJu isn't done screaming her head off. "And if that's not good enough for the peoples? Then...then..." Her eyes are boggling out, an unhealthy flush reddening the pale hide under her white fur. Then she explodes. "THEN SCREW THEM!"

I'm too horrified to speak. To even move. The calls of the Collective are just muddled droning that I only just make out over the True Dogs' chants that I'm a Bad Dog. But what the Collective has to say pounds my heart harder than the hurtful words of the True Dogs.

"We don't need them to love us! We love each other just fine!"

"We're ALL Good Dogs!"

"Why couldn't they see that?!"

"Why did they have to try to change us?!"

"We're ALL Good Dogs, and if the peoples don't like what we are, then SCREW THEM!"

It becomes its own chant, thrown back at the True Dogs' assertion that I'm Bad. But it changes. It simplifies. Simplifies to the point of being so far beyond truth, I don't know how it could have possibly been related in the first place.

"We're Good Dogs, and the peoples don't like us, so SCREW THEM!"

And then it becomes, "The peoples don't like Good Dogs, so SCREW THEM!"

Which then becomes, "The peoples never loved us! SCREW THEM!"

I watch as worries turn to fears, and fears turn to resentments, and resentments turn to angers, and angers turn to hatred. I watch, as the thing I could have never imagined, happens right before my eyes: I watch the entire Collective Pack decide that they hate the peoples.

Just like that. Just that fast.

And all because of me.

I turn, and I run, and I don't slow down until I'm deep, deep in the woods.

19

BANGER

I'LL BE COMPLETELY HONEST with you. I have no idea if I've done the right thing by building this wall. I keep checking myself, keep asking myself, why am I doing this? Is it because it makes me feel good to see those jerks kept on the other side of a fence? Is it just for show, since they could probably all easily jump over the wall?

What is the point of this?

In a way, it feels wrong. But then I wonder if that just isn't the stupid dog part of me that still thinks—despite all evidence to the contrary—that there's value in the togetherness of dogs. But there can't be togetherness between the True Dogs and the Collective Pack. Not anymore. Not since they decided not to follow the law.

If I let the True Dogs continue to be together with the Collective, they'd become Bad Dogs, just like them. Just like Hiro's Pack turned the Collective against the law. And if I let that happen, if I turn a blind eye to it and convince myself that taking action will only cause trouble, then the peoples will never come back, and we'll all die as Bad Dogs, and I don't know what comes after that, but it scares me terribly.

I'm just...scared.

And, though I don't like the idea of separating the True Dogs and the Collective, building the wall is the only thing that makes my fear go away. It is the only thing that makes me feel like I have some control, and that the entire world around me isn't slipping into chaos and madness.

So I'm going to build this damn wall, and it feels right, because it makes me feel less scared and more in control, and it also feels wrong, but I'm pretty sure I'm wrong for feeling wrong. The parts of me that make it feel wrong must be the Bad Dog parts of me that I need to train out of myself.

"Banger!"

I instantly recognize the shout, and let go of the branch I was pulling out from a pile of deadfall. I turn and see Sweetpea bounding through the woods at me, his tail high in an alert stance. My stomach twists.

"What's the problem?"

He skitters breathlessly up to me, chest heaving. "It's Mash and the other dogs! They're about to get into a fight over the wall!"

The next thing I know, we're tearing through the woods like a spooked squirrel, and I'm running improbably fast—I can barely believe it myself; I had no idea my twiggy legs could move my burrito body that fast—and I'm leaving Sweetpea behind.

"Go on ahead!" he gasps from a few lengths back. "I'll catch up!"

When I burst through the edge of the woods, I see a dozen dogs on either side of the wall—it's more of a long mound of sticks at this point—yelling and screaming and barking and snarling at each other. The wanton disregard for the law leaves me aghast, but still, I have the presence of mind to scan the Collective side for Mash, and a part of me is relieved when I don't see him there.

But I do see Gracie.

And Hiro—that conniving, evil, backsliding piece of crap.

The two of them are right there, right up front, right in the middle of it all, and they're barking in the faces of my True Dogs, who are barking right back, everyone's teeth flashing and snapping.

I charge right into the middle of things—

But my legs choose that moment to decide they've had enough. Everyone saw me coming though, so everyone gets to watch me plant my face in the dirt with a grunt and a gruff and then stagger back upright on rickety legs.

"Alright!" I yell. And that's about all the air I have in my lungs, and I'm reduced to ragged panting. But between the face-planting and the one, loud word, and my current wheezing, I have everyone's attention.

"Oh, look," Gracie says viciously. "It's the Perfect Dog herself!"

"I never said—"

"We're all so glad that the peoples love you more than us!" Gracie cuts me off. "Or maybe they don't even love you at all! Maybe they're just trying to change you into something they CAN love! Did you ever think about that?"

I'm so shocked by this that I almost forget what I was doing.

Oh yeah. Breathing.

What the hell has happened here?

"Gracie," I say. "You don't mean that!"

"Yes, I do!" she yells back, to a smattering of growls from her pack. "I'm a dog! And all of these other dogs are...well, they're dogs too! And we might not be Good Dogs according to your stupid laws, but we're good at BEING dogs! And if the peoples don't like us for being who we are, then we don't need them!"

I finally get enough breath back, and not a second too late, because I can't let these words go unanswered. "What happened to you, Gracie?" I demand. Then I skewer the others with the same hard look I gave her. "What happened to ALL OF YOU? Is this what you've come to? Turning your backs on the peoples? On the ones who fed you, and loved you, and welcomed you into their houses? How many of us came from the Place of Judgment? And wasn't it the peoples that took you out of that place, and found you worthy to be a part of their pack? And now you're going to turn your backs on them? You're going to say that you don't care about them?"

It's quiet for a moment, and I almost think maybe I've broken through to them.

But then JuJu speaks up, her face all dark and bitter. "It was the peoples that put me in the Place of Judgment to begin with!"

"You have to love the peoples!" I say, desperately.

But JuJu just shakes her head. "How am I supposed to love someone that punishes me for being what I am?"

I don't know what to say to that, so I just repeat what I've already said, my brain stuck, feeling like it's chained to a tree. "You have to love the peoples! You HAVE to! Otherwise, what are we? What's our purpose?"

"Maybe we don't have a purpose!" It's Gracie that's yelling at me now, but there's a tinge of grief in her voice, barely perceptible underneath all of that anger and bitterness. "Maybe there's no point to any of this! Maybe they just left, and they're never coming back, and all that there is for us is just to be what we are and enjoy ourselves as much as we can before we die!"

And just like that, I realize that I've lost them all. Everyone on the Collective side of those sticks—they're gone. Unreachable. I cannot speak to them anymore, and they will not hear me.

Is this what I wanted? To be separated from the ones that might drag us down?

I think so.

I just didn't think it was going to feel like this.

20

Sweetpea

Did you really think that Banger, of all creatures, could outrun me?

How silly.

No, I lagged behind because, while Banger was sprinting headlong out of the woods, I was watching Mash sprint headlong INTO the woods. I had no idea what that could mean, but I saw the look on his face, and it was not how he usually looks when he's running for the joy of it, or to chase after something.

Mash was running FROM something, and he was scared.

And yet, nothing was chasing him.

So I hollered at Banger that I'd catch up, and then I peeled off and went after Mash, wondering what the hell had given him such a fright, and why he thought he needed to run not just into the woods, but keep on going through them after that, with his tail between his legs like something might jump out and bite his pecker off.

Now, keeping up with Banger's fat ass and tiny legs is one thing. But keeping up with Mash is a whole other, with his slim, well-muscled body and long, capable legs. By the time I even get onto the trail he's carving through the brush, I can't even see him anymore. And by the time I can't run any further, I can't hear him either.

I skid to a stop in the leaves, with no real recollection of where I am—I haven't been paying attention, just trying in vain to catch up to Mash. My heart sounds like ten dogs running down a flight of stairs, my breath like a desert wind in my dry throat. I search the woods around me but there's no sign of him.

I wait for my lungs and heart to calm the fuck down so I can actually hear sounds outside of myself. The time is interminable. My frustration threatens to send my pulse and breathing off again, so I force myself to take a deep breath, close my eyes, and whisper a calming mantra: "You sink your teeth into the neck. The carotid arteries burst into your mouth. The spine severs. The prey is dead. You win. You have everything under control. You're. In. Control."

When I open my eyes again, I feel a bit calmer—or at least I can now hear something besides my own organ functions, and what I hear is just the saddest little threadbare whine.

No matter how sad a dog's whine is, it is still one of the most atrocious noises in existence.

"Mash!" I snap, turning my head in the general direction of his pulsing, high-pitched note. "Would you cut that out!"

There's a pause in the whining, so I think he must've heard me, wherever he is. But after a second it starts up again, even more anxious than before.

"Ohhhh, I can't stop!" he moans as his throat simultaneously issues that needy, teeth-gritting noise. "It's happening all on its own!"

"Where are you?" I ask, stretching my neck and trying to see where he is.

"No, I don't wanna talk! I need to be alone! I'm hiding!"

I start walking in the direction of his whining. "I think that's bullshit," I state. "If I leave you alone you're going to do something stupid. You can't be trusted alone with yourself. You need me to coach you through this."

His voice is barely weightier than his whine: "All the dogs hate each other and it's my fault! I shouldn't have opened my big, dumb mouth!"

"Well, that's always a good rule of thumb," I note, as I pick my way around a stand of briers, and finally locate the poor, stupid fuck. I stop right there and forget whatever else I had to say, because I'm robbed of words by the vision of puppyish idiocy before me.

Mash, with his head and shoulders stuffed under a bush, like he's trying to hide, but his hind-end is still hanging out in the open. His tail is completely still—not the scantest breath of happiness to make it wiggle. It seems like a dead thing pinned to his ass.

"That's hiding?" I can't help but ask.

"It was the best I could do in the moment," he says.

On the bright side, he's finally stopped whining.

"Well, it's a garbage hiding spot, Mash. And you look ridiculous. So how about you come out?"

"I don't wanna come out," he grumbles petulantly.

I sigh, then walk all the way around to the front of him, which I can just see peeking through the foliage of the bush. "How about you stick your head out so we can talk, then."

"I don't wanna stick my head out."

"Alright." I twist to face away so he can't see me bare my teeth in frustration, hiss through them, then relax and turn back with a friendlier expression. "How about I stick my head IN?"

He doesn't respond to that, so I take it as a yes.

Squinting and issuing a low growl of distaste, I work my head through the outermost foliage until I'm well within the innards of the bush, and face to face with Mash. Whose face is the most depressed puddle of jowls I've ever witnessed. They've pooled all around his head like he's half melted. A stick is poking one side of his mouth up so I can see the pink inside of his lips and his gums, and one long, canine tooth.

I can only imagine how ridiculous we both look, head-to-head in a bush, with both our asses hanging out in the open. My tail twitches irritably, but I don't think he can see it, and I keep my expression level.

"Mash," I say, as kindly as I'm able. "What happened?"

He looks away from me. "I'm a Bad Dog."

"And why are you a Bad Dog?"

"Because I made all the other dogs hate each other."

"First off, you're not responsible for other dogs hating each other. Love and hate are both individual decisions, and no one is responsible for them happening, except the one who decides. Secondly, what did you do?"

"Ohhhhhh," he moans again, and lolls his head, making the stick hike up his loose lip-flap even more, so now I can see all the little nubby teeth at the front of his mouth. Then he finally meets my gaze, squints as though he can't bear the pain of looking me directly in the eyes, and whispers: "I said Bad Things!"

Boy, he's really gonna make me work for it, huh?

"Such as?" I prompt, my patience now as thin as spider's silk, and just as ready to snap.

"Hank called me a Peoples-Hater because I wasn't with him and Banger's True Dogs, and he said the law was all about love, and then I said it wasn't about love at all, but that's not really what I meant to say, or maybe it was, but I never got to finish my thoughts because then all the True Dogs got mad and wanted to eat me and all the Collective started COMPLETELY misinterpreting what I was trying to say, and they started saying that because the law isn't about love, that the peoples must have never loved us, and then they said...they said...ohhhh!"

Obvious anguish envelopes his face, and if I was a more empathetic creature, I might have felt bad for him, but mostly I just get impatient. "Then what, Mash? Spit it out for fuckssake!"

"They said the peoples should screw themselves," Mash blurts out, looks horrified that the words even came out of him, and then covers his eyes with his paws.

I'll admit, I wasn't expecting that. For a moment, I'm struck mute. Then I manage a rather lackluster contribution: "Yikes."

"I'm...so ashamed," Mash whispers from behind his paws.

"Well, it's not like you made them say—"

"But then everyone started to say it, and now the entire Collective Pack is saying that they don't even love the peoples any more, they only love other dogs, and now the True Dogs and the Collective Pack hate each other."

"I'm sure they don't hate—"

"Hank bared his teeth," Mash says flatly, peeking out from under his paws to gauge my reaction. "And not a play snarl either. A real one. With real teeth."

Well, shit.

"Oh," I say. Yes, I'm a veritable fountain of wisdom at this point. But I wasn't really present for the kerfuffle at Banger's ridiculous little wall of sticks. I'd assumed it was some stupid shit. And, in a way, it is. But it's serious to the dogs. And because it's serious to them—deadly serious, it seems—then it suddenly becomes serious to me.

Mash lifts his head by a degree and frowns at me. "Oh? That's all you have to say about it?"

"I'm thinking!" I snap. "Weighing the options! Strategizing! Things you'd know nothing about."

Mash sits there, watching me intently as I try hard to look like I'm developing some awesome plan, despite the fact that my brain is just running around in circles. No, not even in circles. My brain has just sparked with its own Prime Directive of sorts, and is currently going into hiding. I can't seem to see a good solution to anything.

How the hell has it come to this? Our village, split down the middle. The Collective Pack, once devoted to the peoples—to the point of being a little insane—has now swung entirely in the other direction and decided that they don't even love the peoples anymore. The mind boggles at the rapidity in which this has developed.

And where did it all start? What was the seed that germinated into this noxious weed?

"That stupid law," I finally growl. "I should have never helped you dogs with it."

Mash quirks his head to one side. "Which one?"

"All of them! They're all ridiculous! And now look what they've done!"

"Don't say that, Sweetpea," Mash groans.

I don't bother to correct him on my title. We're beyond that now. And besides, if the law is stupid, then so is my title. I glare at Mash, but I'm also a bit confused. "What do you mean? You're not one of Banger's True Dogs. You don't really believe in the law anymore. Do you?"

"I mean..." Mash falters and seems to struggle for words for a moment. Then he finally growls, "I don't know. It's all just too much right now. I told the other dogs that the law wasn't about love, but I don't know if that's what I actually meant. Because the law IS based on the things the peoples told us not to do, and I KNOW the peoples loved us, I just know it, Sweetpea! But something's still wrong with the law! It's NOT about love, but it did come from the peoples, didn't it? And the peoples loved us. What am I missing, Sweetpea?"

"Were they REALLY the peoples' rules?" I ask, a bit flummoxed myself by the whole thing. "Did they even really care about all those things? I mean, sure, they might've had preferences—I know that a lot of them didn't like dogs getting on the furniture, or humping in front of them. But was it really that big of a deal to them? I don't think it was." A wave of shame hits me, which is an entirely unfamiliar sensation for a cat. I find myself unable to hold Mash's gaze. "I HELPED you dogs make it a big deal."

"So, what's the right answer, Sweetpea?" Mash pleads, as though I'm some oracle that has all the answers. "Who's right? Gracie? Banger? Hiro?"

"Maybe they've all got it a little bit right and a lot bit wrong."

Mash swings his big, jowly face back to me. "How's that going to fix what I ruined?"

"First of all, you didn't ruin anything," I say, with all the confidence I can muster. "Secondly, we'll figure out how to fix this drama between Banger and Gracie. We'll figure it out together. Which leads me to my third point."

"Yes?" Mash says hopefully.

"Can we get out of this fucking bush?"

21

Sweetpea

(Day 200)

Remember that time I said I was going to fix the drama between Banger and Gracie? Well, fuckin'-A, man, every day I try, and every day shit just gets worse.

Let me just take a crack at describing the monumental fuckery I am now striding through on my way to Gracie's house for the umpteenth peace-talk.

First, just as an overall, prime-your-brain-for-this: Everything has become wildly surreal. I would call it nightmarish, but it's frankly too doofy to be scary. You remember how Gracie had taken up nodding and shaking her head like a peoples, and then all the other dogs started to pick up on it? Well, it's now become some sort of competition amongst the dogs of the Collective to see who can look and act more like the peoples.

Which is odd, considering the fact that they've decided they don't even like the peoples anymore. Which is really just a defense mechanism against the guilt they feel for fucking up the law so much and, in their eyes, displeasing the peoples. Which is something they don't even realize they're doing, but in my tenure as the resident all-knowing feline, I've become something of a dog psychologist.

I've digressed. Long story short, first it was Gracie and her head shaking and nodding—which everyone is doing now—and then, just a few short weeks ago, someone came out wearing clothing.

Now, before you imagine a cute little puppy sweater, banish the thought. If I remember correctly, it was Q, and she just comes strutting out of her house like she's the hottest thing in the village, dragging some sort of lacy, peoples' undergarment behind her. She'd somehow managed to get her lower body into this thing, which was big enough on her that it could have been a cape, and then walked around with it clinging desperately to her tail and one leg.

At the time, I laughed, figuring Q was just putting on a stage play.

No one else laughed. Everyone else thought it was mighty impressive. Q was wearing PEOPLES clothes. Q had now become elevated in the eyes of the Collective.

I should have known better than to hope that it would die that day. I'm convinced there is some entity in the universe that listens to all my secret hopes and dreams, and seems intent on doing the exact opposite.

The next day, half the Collective was wearing some sort of peoples' garment. Mostly, it seemed like they'd just stuck their head through whatever hole they could find, whether it was meant for a head, or a foot, or a leg. Bedecked in their farcical finery, the whole lot of them swaggered around the village like they'd all become peoples themselves.

Needless to say, this did not sit well with the True Dogs, who viewed the whole debacle with their judgy, dogmatic eyes peering over the top of their recently-completed Stick Wall. Which is, in a way, part of the reason I am meeting with Gracie this afternoon.

So now I find myself walking through a wonderland of idiocy—or possibly a wasteland of brains—surrounded by dogs who all think they're the steamiest turd in the pile. And don't think for a second that it stopped with just one garment. Oh, no. Dogs are very simplistic thinkers, so, in their minds, if it's awesome to have one item of peoples' clothing on your body, then it must be awesomer to have two...or three...or four...

Where will it end? With all of the dogs buried in graves of fabrics?

There's shirts, and panties, and sunglasses, and hats—though they're never worn on the head. Hell, half this shit isn't even worn remotely in the right body region. Sunglasses are hooked uselessly into collars. Shirts hang around necks like cumbersome robes. Panties dangle from tails. And hats they just kind of carry around with them in their mouths.

Next thing you know, they're going to be trying to walk on two feet.

I wend my way through the tall weeds between my crash pad and Gracie's, and when I emerge from the newborn jungle at the foot of Gracie's back porch, I find her lounging with Hiro on one side of her, and Longjohn on the other.

Hiro is licking her ears like someone put peanut butter in there, and Longjohn is perched atop her rump, gently kneading it.

Gracie, meanwhile, simply absorbs all of this with her eyes closed and head lifted to the sky, as though in beatific rapture.

Personally, I'm a bit miffed to see my servant being used as a masseuse.

"Analingus!" I growl at him as I mount the steps.

Everyone's attention turns to me, as though I've just stumbled into some private ceremony, but they don't want to be rude and tell me to get lost.

Hiro, at least, is friendly as ever. "Oh, hey, Sweetpea!" he says around a mouthful of ear. "Always good to see our fine feline friend!"

Longjohn, however, after meeting my gaze, doesn't otherwise respond, and just continues to knead away at Gracie's rump, with a bit of a challenge sparking in his eyes.

I prowl up to them and stop before Gracie, whose eyes are half-open, some tension coming back into her otherwise relaxed features. "Analingus," I say again. "Desist!"

He just keeps kneading.

"Gracie!" I raise my voice into regions of holy, righteous fury. "My servant is being disobedient! He requires your discipline!" I lean closer to her and lower my voice. "Try not to damage his legs, though. I need him mobile."

"Actually, Sweetpea," Longjohn utters in that insufferably pompous voice of his. "I'm no longer Analingus, and I'm not your servant."

"You see?" I say to Gracie, indignant. "Complete insubordination!"

"Since we're no longer following the law," Gracie says languidly. "We have no use for you to remember it for us. And since you're no longer His Supreme Masterfulness, then you no longer need Longjohn as your assistant. I've decided to make him my attaché."

I'm floored by this development. No one fucking told ME about it!

My eyes race between Gracie and Longjohn, back and forth, back and forth, trying to spy the joke, but no one is laughing. Though Longjohn looks like he might birth an evil cackle at any moment.

"You're serious about this?" I gasp. "The fuck do you need an attaché for?"

Gracie frowns and looks away from me. "To do attaché stuff, obviously."

I'm not sure she knows what an attaché is.

I consider throwing a tantrum about it, but this is just the way things have been going for me lately. After riding so high in my position of power, I've now been relegated to "Fine Feline Friend," which is basically a nice way of saying "Fucking Nobody." And tantrums only work if you're somebody.

"Alright," I grind out between teeth clenched hard enough to crack bones. "Moving on," I struggle to say with anything close to civility. "We need to talk."

Gracie's eyes swing back to me and become severe. "You're damn right we need to talk! I need you to tell that fat bitch to keep her teeth and claws to herself! Did you hear about poor JuJu Bean?"

Of course I've heard about poor JuJu Bean. She was caught in the woods by a few of the True Dogs that were out for a hunt, and they didn't take kindly to her wearing her peoples' socks on her feet and stilting around in them like a newborn deer. The details are a little hazy, but the facts are this: JuJu got fucked up. Bite marks all over her legs and haunches. And her socks were taken from her.

"I'm positive that it wasn't Banger that did it," I reply as coolly as I can, ever the peacemaker at this point, albeit a failing one.

"It doesn't matter if she did it with her own teeth!" Gracie jerks to her feet, sending Longjohn flying off with an offended yowl. "She encourages the fanaticism that led to it! Such violence! Such hatred!" Gracie growls low in her throat. "And she thinks she's so holy—she thinks the peoples love her so much more than us—" And then, screaming it in the direction of the True Dogs' half of the village: "—BUT THE PEOPLES ALWAYS HATED DOG VIOLENCE!"

"Uh-huh, well, I take your point, but you also have to try to appreciate the fact that they see wearing the peoples' clothes as incredibly sacrilegious."

"Oh, sacrilege smackrilege. Everything's sacred to them. We can't piss on the wrong blade of grass without committing some sort of sacrilege in their eyes."

"It's true, they give new meaning to the word...dogmatic." I wait for delighted laughter at my pun, but everyone just stares. Fine. Whatever. "But all I'm saying is that, if you know that they're going to freak out about you wearing the peoples' clothes, then maybe don't do it right in front of them?"

"We're a free pack!" Gracie declares. "We don't have any rules! We can do whatever we want!"

"Well, sure, but if you do whatever you want right in front of them, then you shouldn't be surprised when there's consequences."

Gracie's eyes narrow at me. "I thought you were a neutral party."

I rapidly backtrack. "Oh, yes, neutral, very neutral. And objective. Highly, highly objective. I really..." another sly glance for whoever might catch it. "...Don't have a DOG in this fight. Huh? Huh?"

Again, nary a chuckle. Philistines.

I sigh. "I'm not taking sides, Gracie. I want the True Dogs and the Collective to be at peace with each other, that's all. I want them to unite again into one pack and stop all this separatist bullshit."

"Well, talk to the bitch with the wall," Gracie snarls. "She's the separatist."

"What would it take for you guys to put all this behind you and become one pack again?"

Gracie considers for long enough that I get my hopes up, thinking she might come back with a reasonable request. She doesn't.

"Banger and her True Dogs are welcome back into the Collective anytime they want to stop being overzealous jerks, forget about their stupid laws, and embrace the freedom of the lawless."

"You know, I'm all for freedom. But I'd be remiss if I didn't point out that lawlessness is giving you a different set of problems."

Gracie looks shocked. "Problems? Like what?"

Has she really not heard? "Your pack is stealing from each other."

"Stealing? What are they stealing?"

"Well, at this point, it's mostly clothes they're stealing from each other. Ever since clothes became a status symbol for the Collective, everyone's been trying to get more and more clothes, but it's a zero-sum game, so the only way to get more is to take it from someone else."

Gracie scoffs. "Please. You're worried about a few swiped shirts?"

"What's next, though? Are they going to start stealing food from each other? I'm just saying, maybe complete lawlessness is just as bad as too many laws."

Gracie leans into me, her voice hardening into stone. "I will NOT allow ANY laws. And the sooner you can convince Banger to drop HER laws, the sooner we can be a united pack again. And not before."

I let out an exhausted huff. "Alright. I'll tell her."

・・・・・・・・・・

"You tell that peoples-hating tramp of a dog that we can reunite the pack as soon as she steps down as their leader, takes a dang bath, pukes up her food, and follows the law!"

"Uh-huh," I say, bored at how things just keep going exactly how I expected them.

What am I even still doing here? In the village, I mean. I could be out doing cat things. Hell, I don't need this village, and I don't need these dumb dogs. I could strike out on my own and be just fine, away from this truculent batch of mad canines.

And yet, here I am.

"What do you mean, 'uh-huh'?" Banger demands.

I drag my attention back to her from where it's listed during her diatribe, taking in the orderly movements of the True Dogs. When I look to Banger, I find her frowning deeply at me.

"What?" I say, innocently.

"Are you bored or something?" she grinds out.

Well, somebody give her a cookie. Oh wait, there aren't anymore.

"Oh, no, Banger. How on earth could I possibly be bored? How could a feline of my prodigious intellect and talent be bored with the task of playing go-between for a pair of dogs with their heads crammed up their asses, bark-farting the same damn nonsense, day in and day out?"

I would never have said that to Gracie. But I don't know Gracie like I know Banger. And though I see Banger's hackles rise, I remain unconcerned.

I press forward. "What're you gonna do, Banger? Bite me?"

"I'm thinking about it," she menaces.

"Go ahead!" I cry, turning my rump around towards her. "Take a big mouthful of my ass—you're obsessed with the smell of it, why don't you see if you like the taste too?!"

Her lips peel back, revealing her teeth.

"Oh!" I say, flicking her face with my tail. "But what would DAD think about that, huh?"

A flash of horror crosses her eyes.

"Yeah! That's what I fucking thought!"

"How dare you use Dad against me!"

"Why not? You use him against everyone else."

"I do not!"

I spin around to face her again. "You do, and you know it! You keep your stupid pack of quote-unquote True Dogs in line with fear!"

"They're not afraid! They just love the peoples!"

"Are they following you because they love the peoples, or because you scared the shit out of them by telling them that if they don't follow your laws they'll be abandoned by the peoples forever?"

Banger looks worried, like this is the first time she's ever really considered the consequences of her actions. "The True Dogs aren't about fear, they're about love of the peoples!"

"Really?" I gape. "You really believe that?"

"I know it!"

"What makes dogs aggressive, Banger?" I push closer to her. "What makes dogs fight and bark and bite at each other?"

Banger seems flustered, like she wants to come up with an answer that I can't use against her, but feels compelled to tell the truth—which she knows I'll use against her. "Aggression comes from fear," she finally spits out.

"Ohhhhh, DOES IT NOW? But it couldn't possibly have been fear that made your dogs chew poor JuJu up? No, they must've done that out of love, right?"

"Love for the peoples—and the SANCTITY of their belongings!"

"Wrong! Fear!" I shout at her. "Fear that little old JuJu with her fucking socks is going to curse your whole pack to eternal abandonment! Fear that YOU put into them!"

Banger's face becomes vicious again. "Oh, I see," she says, as close to a growl as you can get without actually violating their law against growling. "So you're one of them now."

"On the contrary, Banger," I say, suddenly feeling genuinely hurt. "I thought I was one of YOU. I thought that me, you, and Mash were a pack. But then you ran off without us and you won't even be our packmate anymore."

Banger makes a rude, derisive noise. "You never gave a crap about our pack before."

I hiss at her. "Don't mistake my natural aloofness for not caring. Who was willing to remember all your stupid laws in the first place, huh? Who's the one running back and forth between you and Gracie, trying to patch things up?" My ears flatten out. "Who's the one that has to listen to lonely Mash whimper at night because you won't even cross your damn wall to come back home?"

She seems shocked to hear this. And she should be.

"He won't admit as much," I say, still angry, but much quieter. "But he paces back and forth as the sun is going down, looking out the windows and checking the car cave a dozen fucking times to see if you're going to come home. Every night for a month now, Banger. When's the last time you even saw him? You who's so worried about abandonment—did you ever think about how you've abandoned Mash?"

"I didn't abandon Mash," Banger says, sullenly. Guiltily. "He chose to stay with the Collective."

"No," I snap. "He chose not to be a part of your bullshit fight. And you abandoned him for it."

"Those dogs," Banger seethes, though concern has now taken up residence in her eyes. "They're pushing us further away from the peoples!"

"According to what? According to who? You?"

"No!"

"Then who?" I demand. "Who else came up with the idea that the peoples abandoned us because we were Bad Dogs?" I realize too late that I've included myself with the dogs. At the same moment that I'm disappointed with myself—and maybe a tad embarrassed—I also know that it's true. For some ridiculous, brain-washed reason, I'm identifying as one of them. "Who else came up with the idea that the peoples would only come back if all the dogs were Perfect Dogs? Who else came up with the idea that the peoples might come back AT ALL? Because I don't remember Dad saying anything close to that. Was it some other peoples that told you all of this?"

"No..."

"So you just made it up?"

"I didn't make it up!"

"Then where'd it come from?"

"It...it...felt true!"

"Oh, it FELT true," I marvel at her irrationality. "So let me get this straight, Banger. Let me see if I can really nail down the basis of your philosophy here. The idea of the peoples leaving because we were Bad just FELT right to the ONE DOG in the entire Collective that hates all the other dogs? My, my! What a coincidence! The dog that hates all the other dogs FEELS like all the other dogs ruined things with the peoples!"

"I never hated the other dogs!"

"Don't try to sell that shit to me—I'm not buying! You can stretch definitions and redefine terms all you want, but at the end of the day, what else do you call a dog that'd sooner rip another dog's face off than pass the greeting of the day with them?"

Banger is so still and silent, that for a briefly terrifying moment, I think she really is going to lose her shit and lunge at me.

"I don't care if you believe me or not," Banger finally says, in a halting way that makes it sound like she's really struggling not to hurt me. "But I KNOW that those sacrilegious jerks are holding us back with their lawlessness. They're lawless because they have forgotten their love for the peoples, and the peoples will never come back until all the dogs love them, and prove their love by following the law and being Perfect Dogs."

I feel something die and wither inside of myself. I'm pretty sure it was hope.

"You know what's funny?" I say, without a breath of humor. "Right before Dad left, he told me to remember to listen. And I did. I listened. But I don't remember him saying any of that shit."

She doesn't seem to have a response to me. She doesn't seem like she's even heard me. She's built up a wall between me and her, just as sure as the one she built between the Collective and the True Dogs, except that, even though this one is invisible, it's so much harder to cross.

I wince at the realization that we are no longer packmates.

Our pack—the pack that had once been Dad, and Banger, and Mash, and me—has fallen apart.

I turn to walk away, but stop and look back at her once more.

"You think you're pleasing the peoples," I say, my voice heavy with sudden depression. "But do you really think they'd like what you've become? Do you think Dad would?"

She doesn't even look at me. She's staring off like I'm not even there.

Like I mean nothing to her anymore.

And I'm surprised at how much that hurts.

I turn away and only barely manage to croak out my final words to her: "You suck, Banger."

· · · ● · · ● · · · ·

"I don't know what to do with these fuckers," I say to no one in particular. Perhaps the Universe. Perhaps Dad. Perhaps anybody that might be listening.

I've retreated to the woods now. I couldn't even bear the thought of walking back across that stupid wall, or walking through all those stupid dogs with their peoples' clothes draped haphazardly over them. So when I walked away from Banger, I immediately headed for the woods. The only place that isn't rife with idiotic conflict.

I crane my neck, looking up and all around. "Nothing, huh? Nothing to say to that, Dad? Or anybody?"

Nope. Nothing. Just the birds chirping—from a safe distance away. Insects buzzing. Some small woodland mammal—a squirrel or chipmunk, perhaps—rustling through the leaves.

I set my gaze straight ahead and glower at nothing in particular. "I'm trying to work with you here. It sure seems like you want me to do something. Fine. I'm here. I'm ready. I need answers. Or advice. Or...for fuckssake, I need someone to tell me what to do here. What's the right answer? Because right now, I feel like the right answer is to show the village my ass and get gone. Clearly my talents are not appreciated."

I know that a response is finally coming when I feel my tail fluff up. I still don't know whether my often-one-sided conversations with Dad are all in my head. And while most of the time my cries for clarity go unanswered—and even when they are answered, it's often enigmatic—I have had several exchanges with...Dad, or a ghost, or my own subconscious.

I won't tell you that I've grown accustomed to it, but I've started to notice that, just before I hear that voice, my body reacts, and the first thing to react is my tail.

"Oh, you're gonna talk today?" I say to the woods. Tough to restrain your irritation when you're constantly in need of clarification, and it only comes every once in a while, seemingly whenever its convenient for the voice to manifest itself.

The whisper comes, soft as ever: "Sweetpea."

"Yeah, yeah," I gripe. "You know my name. That's me. I'm here. Again."

"Remember..."

"Oh my fuck, this shit again?" I hang my head. "I remember. I really, really do. I remember a shocking amount. Me remembering is not the issue, Dad—if that is even you. It's your stupid, precious dogs that can't remember."

And then, all of the sudden, it's not a whisper anymore. It's a big, strong, very real voice that seems to surround me and penetrate me like I'm lying on a loudspeaker.

"First of all," the voice says, causing me to rocket to my feet, back arched and all my fur standing out. "Don't take that tone with me."

"Holy shit," I mutter, my eyes so wide I feel like they're going to fall out. My pupils have dilated an unhealthy amount—I can tell, because everything has suddenly become overbright. "It really is you!"

Because all the other whispers-on-wind could've been anyone. But this voice is real, and it is a voice that I know. It is unmistakably Dad. That's something I'll ALWAYS remember.

The voice speaks again, with a bit of a longsuffering sigh in it. "It's always been me, Sweetpea. You think it's easy to manifest in your reality?"

"Well..." I consider that for a moment. "You always seemed pretty capable."

"It's not about me, Sweetpea. It requires no effort from ME."

I frown. "Then why can't I always hear you this clearly?"

"I can only be heard by those that want to listen."

"I always want to listen! How many times have I asked for your guidance and you haven't said a word?"

Another sigh. "Now's not really the time to get into this, Sweetpea. When you are capable of hearing me, then you will hear me. Let's leave it at that, because you don't have much time."

"I don't have much time?" That worries me. "Like, I'm gonna die or something?"

"No, I meant that your ability to hear me this clearly is already maxing out. But yes, you will die."

"Whoa!"

"Eventually."

"Oh."

"Now listen..." And as he says those last words, I notice that he already sounds muted again, like I'm hearing him through a door. "You need to speak to them. To the dogs. You need to tell them..."

There are other words, but they're getting too faint to make out completely.

Nonsensically, I incline my ears, as though that'll help anything. "You're fading out!"

Another burst of clarity, still muffled, but now like Dad has pushed his face close to the door and raised his voice. "Tell them to remember!"

"I've BEEN telling them!"

"They need to remember who they were. With us. Together. Tell them. Tell them, and then..."

"Yes? And then?"

An inscrutable murmur.

"No, no! Say it again, I didn't hear you!"
Nothing.
The forest has fallen silent again.
I've lost him.

22

Mash

I LIKE FREEDOM. I really do. I like the freedom to growl and bark when the urge comes over me. I like the freedom to get on the Cloud Throne, because when I'm there, I can close my eyes and pretend that Dad's sitting there with his arm around me, and my head on his lap. And I particularly like the freedom to do those things without having to take a bath and throw up my dinner afterward.

But I really don't know what to do with the clothes thing.

Personally, I don't feel like wearing the peoples' clothes. And I don't like to think of myself as judgy, like the True Dogs are, but I am kind of confused by the whole thing. I'm confused about why they're doing it.

At first, I thought that it was to feel close to the peoples, like I feel when I climb onto Dad's Cloud Throne. And when I thought that, I felt a bit of hope. Because, if the Collective was trying to feel close to the peoples, then maybe they didn't really hate the peoples after all. And if they didn't hate the peoples, then maybe I didn't need to feel so guilty for the things I said at the wall so many days ago that made them all shout those terrible things.

But now I'm not so sure that they're doing it to feel close to the peoples. It doesn't seem like it has anything to do with the peoples.

Maybe that's all Q was doing when she came out with those first pieces of clothing, but now it's become something else.

It's all about the dogs now. Except that it's not about the dogs in the ways that things used to be about the dogs.

This is really hard for me to explain. I have so many feelings right now, and I've never been very good at putting them into words. But I'm going to try.

When dogs do dog things, like passing the greeting of the day, or play fighting, or running around together, it's always about the pack. When I do those things, I'm not thinking about how I look when I do them. I'm just doing them because it feels right to do. It feels healthy. It feels like it's good for the pack. There is a feeling of…Oh, I don't know how to put it. Like all the dogs that make up the pack are actually one single dog. And when the pack moves and plays together, that feeling of all being one is wonderful.

But that's not what's happening with the clothes. It's become something else. Something I don't recognize. Something that isn't normal for dogs.

All of them that are running around wearing peoples' clothe? They're not doing it to feel like they're all part of one pack, and that the pack is a part of them, and that they're all the same animal. No, I've realized they're doing it for the opposite reasons. They're doing it to feel special. To feel unique. To feel…

Better than everyone else.

That's just not something dogs do.

Even when we play fight, we're not really trying to dominate the other dog. I mean, I'm a pretty big dog, as dogs go, and you already know that I'm super-fast. I could dominate some of the smaller dogs when I play with them. But that's not the point. So I run in, and as soon as it seems like they're getting too much of me, then I back off. I let them chase me. And when they're tired of chasing me, I let them catch me, and I roll over onto my back like they've totally won. And then they'll back off so I can get up again, and we just keep doing that.

It's not a competition. It's about having fun and feeling the oneness of the pack.

But these clothes have become a competition. The dogs that are wearing them are trying to be better than the other dogs. They want the other dogs to look at them, and respect and be jealous of them for the quantity of peoples' clothes they have on.

It's the exact opposite of oneness. It's...separateness. It's cutting one pack into a dozen different pieces. And without the oneness, nobody's playing right anymore. When we run, someone's always trying to run faster than everyone else—and not because running fast is fun, but because they actually want to make the other dogs feel bad about not being as fast.

And the play fights! The play fights have been getting...well...rough. Dogs aren't letting other dogs get up when they submit—they're standing over them and growling. They're dominating each other.

Nobody's having fun anymore.

And yet, they're all PRETENDING like they're having the most fun ever.

They keep saying, "Isn't this fun?" Like they're trying to convince themselves.

And others keep responding, "Yes, this is so much fun!"

But in their eyes there's a desperation that reminds me of the mice Sweetpea will capture and torture. Like they know they're not really having fun, but they have to pretend, because the only other option is to admit that they don't know how to get out of the situation they're in.

Heck, I don't know how either.

I just want everyone to be happy again.

I just want everyone to have fun again.

·········

I'm sniffing around a message post, getting the day's news and checking up on everyone's health. But everyone's urine smells off. Every message that has been left in this spot has a tinge of unhappiness to it. It's the smell of a dog that's kept inside while their peoples work long hours away from the home.

I'm pondering what connection there might be between that faint scent of unhappiness, as well as the stink of low-level anxiety that seems to be in everyone's messages, when I hear a commotion down by The Wall.

This particular message spot is on the corner of one of the houses, and I can't see The Wall from where I'm at, so I hurriedly summon as much good-cheer as I can manage and then squeeze out a few happy drops—one desperate little message sent out to whoever follows: "It's not all that bad, guys! Try to have fun!"

Then I turn and scramble out into the street to see what all the ruckus is about.

The second I bound my way out of the overgrown lawn and onto the concrete, I skid to a stop. All sense of happiness that I just tried to convince myself of immediately flies off, like a flock of spring robins spooked out of a field.

This is what I see: Sweetpea's tan-furred body, perched atop The Wall, his voice raised, his tone pleading. And, yeah, maybe a little bit pissed off. But I can't hear what he's saying, because he's surrounded on all sides—the True Dogs on their side, the Collective on ours—and they're all yelling things at him. There's so many dogs shouting that I can't make out what anyone's saying, but it doesn't sound nice.

What's he saying to get them all riled up? And why are BOTH sides mad at him?

I think of JuJu, with all those bite marks all over her shoulders and haunches, and I'm suddenly scared for Sweetpea. Scared for what the True Dogs might do to him if he says anything that offends them—which could literally be ANYTHING. And as unhappy and competitive as the Collective has been, I'm not so sure they wouldn't do the same to him. They say they're all about loving other dogs, but honestly, I haven't sensed much love lately, and he's not a dog.

I break into sprint, racing down the slight hill towards The Wall, not knowing what the heck I'm going to do when I get there, only knowing that I have to keep anything bad from happening to poor Sweetpea. Sure, he can be a bit of a jerk sometimes, but if there's anyone in this place that I still feel a connection to, it's him.

For better or worse, he's my packmate.

As I get closer, I start to hear what everyone is shouting.

"Blasphemy!" the True Dogs are clamoring. "Sacrilege!"

"What do you care?" the Collective are barking and growling at Sweetpea. "You're not a dog!"

Finally, I get close enough to hear Sweetpea, who is sitting there with his head held high, enduring the badgering from both sides, and trying to shout over them: "Don't you remember what it was like when the peoples were still here? Don't you remember the joy and happiness you felt, knowing that everything you needed was provided for you by your peoples?"

"They didn't give us freedom!" It's Gracie that says this, and I see that she's front and center, close enough that she could reach up and snatch Sweetpea down from his perch, and I really hope that she doesn't, but I can feel the tension in the air, and the threat of violence, like the smell of a big storm rolling in. "They never loved us in the first place!"

"They did love you!" Sweetpea replies, looking right at Gracie. "I know that they did!"

"Then why didn't they let us do the things that we wanted?" It looks like it was JuJu Bean that asked that last one. "Why didn't they just let us be dogs?"

Exasperation flashes across Sweetpea's face. "What laws did you really have to follow with the peoples?" he says. "Not the laws that you made up to try to be Perfect—I'm talking about each of you, individually, and your personal relationship with YOUR peoples. They didn't care about all the stuff you turned into laws! And most of the rules they DID make you follow were for your own good!"

"Don't listen to his lies!" Hank bellows from the True Dog side. "He's trying to get you to abandon the law! Stay true, True Dogs!"

Sweetpea spins on him. "How am I lying? Did your peoples make you follow all of the laws you follow now?"

"What's Bad for one dog is Bad for all dogs!"

Anger is clear in Sweetpea's face now. "Don't quote doctrine at me! I was the one that made that shit up in the first place! And it IS made up—do you not remember all the afternoons at the Park, coming up with all this shit that you think is so important? Those weren't peoples' rules! Those were YOUR rules! And they're wrong!"

Boos and jeers follow this, mostly from the True Dog side.

"Look at yourselves, dogs!" Sweetpea pleads desperately, now turning this way and that, yelling to the True Dogs now, and then to the Collective. "Do you think this is what the peoples would have wanted? To see all their beloved dogs divided amongst themselves, fighting and bickering and ATTACKING each other? All over some stupid rules we made up in a time of confusion and desperation to make sense of what was happening?"

"Blasphemy! The peoples want us to be Perfect Dogs by following the law!"

"Oh, shut up!" Gracie yells at the True Dogs. "The peoples aren't coming back anyways! They left because they never loved us in the first place! Only dogs love dogs!"

Sweetpea turns to her again, straining to be heard. "Then why are you divided? Why are you set against yourselves? If you love other dogs so much, why do you hate the True Dogs?"

"Because they're self-righteous butt-holes!" someone else cries out—I can't tell who's talking anymore, they're all pressed so tightly together, squirming and tumbling over one another in their anger and frustration.

"Because they're not really dogs!" another shouts. "Real dogs have fun like us! They're not True Dogs—they're Fake Dogs!"

A chant goes up: "Fake Dogs! Fake Dogs! Fake Dogs!"

"Down with the Fake Dogs!"

I don't actually make a conscious decision to intervene. One moment, I'm standing on the outskirts of the gathered Collective, fear for Sweetpea tightening my heart and my lungs. And the next moment, I'm on The Wall with him.

I don't even know how I got there. I don't remember pushing through the crowd. For a moment, I look all around me and see what Sweetpea has been seeing this whole time: Dozens of enraged faces, and all of their anger directed at...me?

I almost faint and fall off The Wall.

Sweetpea looks shocked to see me there with him. He gives me a worried look. "Mash! What are you...? Hey, are you okay?"

Rather than answer him, I take a big breath to keep from passing out, and turn to the Collective. "He's right! Sweetpea is right! We should listen to him!"

For a tiny slice of time, I think I've broken through to them. But I guess they were just too surprised at my sudden appearance to say anything, because it gets real quiet after I say that, and then it gets real loud again.

"Screw you, Mash!"

"Where's your clothes?"

"Are you too good for clothes?"

"He's a True Dog!"

"No!" I cry out. "I'm not a True Dog! Seriously, you should listen to Sweetpea! You've all changed—you say you're having fun but you're not! I know you've all smelled the message posts. Are you really going to try to tell me that you're having fun?"

"We are having fun! Freedom is fun!"

"But you're not free!" I shout, getting angry right back at them. "Just because you don't follow the laws doesn't make you free! You're all miserable and you know it! You're miserable because you don't really love each other like packmates anymore!"

"Tell that to the True Dogs!" Gracie snarls at me, jutting her face up close and actually snapping her jaws—she pulls her bite, but I see the flash of teeth anyways. "The Collective is all about dog love!"

"Then why are you fighting with each other?" I ask her. "Why are you competing with each other? Why are you stealing from each other?"

It's someone from the True Dogs that I hear next: "The Collective isn't about love! They're about dominating each other! WE'RE the True Dogs, and WE'RE the ones who are all about love!"

It's so ridiculous that I'm almost silenced by it. But the words come pouring out of me anyways. "That's a lie, and you know it! You're the most hateful bunch of dogs I know! Look at what you did to poor JuJu! Look at how you treat each other with your punishments every time one of you messes up! Look at how you treat—AGH!"

Someone just bit my back leg!

I spin around, my tail immediately tucking, but I can't tell who just bit me, or even which side it came from. And then I really am silenced. Because all I see is hate. Hate from all sides. Hate in their eyes. Hate for anything different. Hate for ME. And teeth—everyone's teeth, the True Dogs and the Collective alike—bared and gnashing, clacking and clicking, getting closer and closer as they get bolder and bolder.

They...they actually want to hurt me.

"Mash!" I hear Sweetpea scream out, and when I turn to look, I see a dog that I know I've seen before but somehow don't recognize at all, with Sweetpea's tail in their mouth, dragging him off The Wall. Sweetpea's eyes are wide, claws extended and dug in—he's latched on, and trying desperately not to lose his grip.

Something bursts inside of me. Something I never even knew was there. It's like there's always been this pocket of savagery sitting down deep in my chest, and now it floods my veins, and my eyes can't see anything but what is right in front of me—Sweetpea, and that dog biting him—and everything is sparkling and reddish-black, and my lips curl up and my teeth come out.

Before I even know what's happening I hear a sound like a wild animal's snarl, full of fear and anger. And I realize it's coming from me. I lunge. I lunge for that other dog's face, and just as my jaws are widening, I look into their eyes and realize it's...

Banger?

By the time it even registers with me, I've already bitten down. The flesh of the side of her face, and her ear, in my mouth. The feel of my teeth breaking the skin. The taste of blood and fur. I immediately release, and realize that Banger's already let go of Sweetpea.

For the tiniest second that seems to last for hours, we stare at each other.

Surprise. Shock. Dismay.

Anger.

Hatred.

"Why'd you do this?" I whimper at her.

"Mash!" Sweetpea is clawing at me. "We gotta go!"

Banger's jowls ripple with a growl. "You...are a BAD DOG!"

She snaps at me, no play in her eyes at all, but I've always been faster than her, and manage to jerk my face away while her teeth clack together inches from my hide.

Then I turn, and I run, and Sweetpea is running too, along the top of The Wall, towards the trees in the distance, and we're chased by the sounds of the True Dogs and the Collective alike, screaming for our blood, screaming that we're liars, screaming that we're Bad, Bad, Bad.

23

Mash

(Day 300)

Sweetpea tells me that it's been almost a year since Dad disappeared. I'm kind of surprised that it's only been that long. I mean, I guess you already know that my concept of what makes a year is a bit loose, but I know it's less than a lifetime, and I feel like it's been a few lifetimes since I've seen Dad, or heard his voice, or felt him scratch behind my ears.

I look back, and I think about that day, and the days that followed, and in all of my memories, I don't feel like it's me in them. It feels like all those memories belong to a different dog.

I remember Sweetpea teaching me about October. That has come and gone again. The leaves turned yellow, and then they all fell away, but there were no peoples wearing furry boots, or gaining their winter weight. Now it is cold, cold, cold, and I have no place to call home.

I am a homeless dog. I am a stray.

I never thought this would happen to me. When Dad came and accepted me into his pack, and took me and Banger out of the Place of Judgment, I thought that would be it—I'd be home forever, and nothing would ever break my pack apart. But now

I don't have a pack anymore. I don't have a place inside, on the peoples' Cloud Throne to sleep, warm and comfortable. Dad left, and Banger got weird, and the pack that I thought had replaced them—the Collective—they don't want me either.

Sweetpea tells me I'm being "morose," a word I don't know, but that I think means that I do a lot of thinking. He also says that I'm having a "pity party," which I'm also not familiar with, though I think I can figure it out, and it's a lonely party, and not very fun.

And maybe that's Sweetpea's point. So I try—I swear, I do—I try to be happy, but while I'm trying really hard to be happy, I always think about how I used to be happy without having to try, and that makes me sad.

At least I still have Sweetpea. I remind myself of that all the time. We live out in the woods now, me and him, out of the way of both our old village and Hiro's, so that we don't run into hunters from either pack. Not that they're hunting us. But, you know. It'd be awkward.

So, it's just me and Sweetpea, and Sweetpea spends a lot of time talking to Dad these days. That, or he's totally crazy and talking to himself. I still can't figure out which it is, but I like to think that he really is talking to Dad, because that makes me feel like our pack is ALMOST back together again.

Except for Banger.

And that thought makes me sad again.

One time, Sweetpea tried to explain how his talking with Dad worked.

"It's not always talking," he said, curling up between my legs and against my belly one evening as the sun was setting and the night was getting cold. "In fact, most of the time it's not. When it is talking, it's almost like he can only say what I already know—or ALMOST already know. You know?"

I frowned, confused, and shook my head.

"Ugh, don't do that. You know I hate it."

"Sorry," I said. "Once you start using your head to talk, it's a really hard habit to break. Anyway, no, I don't really know what you're talking about."

Sweetpea sighed in that disgruntled way of his, which I understood meant that he wished I was a bit smarter. "It's like..." He thought for a moment more, looking upwards at the first stars of night. "It's like I have to almost learn the lesson, or at least learn what the lesson is about, and then he shows up and teaches me, but only if I'm most of the way there already. If he had something to say to me that was totally out of my understanding, it'd come through as fuzzy images and half-ideas. Daydreams, almost. Which is mostly what I get from him."

"Oh," I said, a bit disappointed. I thought there'd be more real, hard proof that it wasn't all in Sweetpea's head. "Well, how do you know they're not YOUR daydreams?"

Sweetpea pulled his head back a bit, ears flattening a touch. "Yeah, I dunno, Mash. That's a hard one to answer. Been trying to figure that shit out since the first time."

"And you haven't been able to figure it out?"

"Not really. All I can say is that it seems like...when it's Dad trying to say something to me, there's...I dunno. A different effect, maybe. Like, ultimately, the idea is pointing me towards others, and wanting good for them. Whereas when it's MY daydream, it's generally about things that I want. You know? Small creatures I'd like to kill. Female cats I'd like to rut. All the things I'd like to say to Banger and Gracie, to make them feel like the pieces of shit that they are. Etcetera, etcetera."

I instantly felt guilty. "Is it bad to daydream about killing small animals?"

I asked, because, well…things had changed since we were kicked out of the Collective. We had to do all our own hunting, and I'd become quite good at catching rabbits. And…

Well, I don't know quite how to say this next part, but I'll just be super honest about it: I was starting to enjoy it. Not, like, how Sweetpea enjoys torturing mice. No, please don't think that about me. I make sure that all the rabbits I catch are killed as quick as I can shake them. No, it's more just that I felt very good about being so self-sufficient. And, in a way, it was almost like I was closer to…something. Closer to how I was meant to be?

Oh, I'm bad with words. All I need you to know is that I'm not a complete psychopath, but I DID start to enjoy the process of hunting, and it was making me feel a bit guilty when I realized that I was thinking about the next hunt, and looking forward to it.

"Mash," Sweetpea said, earnestly. "I'm not real sure there is much that is 'Bad.' The best I can piece together from my talks with Dad, there's Good, and then there's not-so-good."

"Doesn't not-so-good just mean Bad?"

"No, it's not quite the same. Not-so-good is like…like you should eat meat, but you decide to eat trash instead. The meat would have been good for you. And it's not that eating the trash is Bad, so to speak, but it's certainly not good for you, and possibly might make you sick."

"Ohhhhhhh," I said, connections being made in my head. "So, it's not like things are Bad-Bad, like we used to think of things as Bad—as in, the-peoples-hate-me-because-of-this Bad. But just that there's things that are helpful to us, and things that are not-so-helpful to us."

"Yes. Exactly." Sweetpea gave me a smile. "Hey, that was pretty good. Look at you, learning how to articulate your thoughts and all."

I preened a bit. "Yes, I'm very morose."

Sweetpea quirked his head. "Maybe you should stay away from the big words, though."

So, that's been our life for a while. Just me and Sweetpea. Hunting in the mornings and evenings. Sometimes we're successful. Sometimes we aren't, and we go to sleep hungry. Mostly, I'm the one that doesn't succeed, but Sweetpea will always share what he has with me, even if it's small. But there was one time that I succeeded and he didn't. That was a pretty awesome day for me. But Sweetpea doesn't like to talk about it.

During the day, when it was warmer and easier to fall asleep, we'd nap in a sunny clearing near to where we had dug ourselves out a little burrow nestled in some big rocks and an overturned tree stump. I'd drowse for a while, and wake up to find Sweetpea had wandered off into the woods. Often, he was just close enough that I could see him through the leafless trees, but not close enough that I could hear him. That's when he would talk to Dad.

It was a tough transition for me. Going from being a very sociable animal with dozens of other dogs to interact with on a daily basis, to living kind of a solitary existence, with only Sweetpea to keep me company.

I was just starting to get used to it, when everything changed again.

The first time we realized we weren't alone, Sweetpea had just come back from a very long afternoon talk with Dad. I'd caught a rabbit that day, and Sweetpea had scored himself a fat mockingbird, so I got to eat the whole rabbit by myself—still feel really weird about saying that, but anyway—and I was dozing with a full belly in the warmest patch of sunlight in the clearing.

I blinked and raised my head with a jaw-crackling yawn, as Sweetpea picked his way across the forest floor towards me. Usually he didn't make a sound, but some sort of noise had woken me up, and as I watched him, I realized that his gait was a bit unsteady, his paws landing on patches of dry leaves and twigs that he would have normally avoided. His eyes were wide, the pupils so constricted that I could barely see them at all. His mouth hung open in that delicate little half-pant that cats will do when they're overheated, even though the day was cool.

My first thought was that my friend was sick.

I stood up, controlling my usual urge to pepper him with questions so I could figure out what was wrong. I'd come to realize that I can be a bit much when I'm like that, and, usually, if I calm down, I'll get the answers in time.

Still, he looked so loopy, that I had to say something. "Hey, Sweetpea. You don't look so hot. Did you swallow too many feathers again?"

He didn't respond, but just kind of staggered up to me and then plopped his rump on the ground, and kept panting, very un-catlike. I sat down next to him, brimming with worry and curiosity, but knowing that it was best not to overwhelm him.

After a while, his breathing calmed. He licked his chops, and his dazed eyes got a little brighter. I knew he'd regained more of himself when his tail started twitching contemplatively from side to side.

"Something you want to talk about?" I prodded, gently.

His ears were all the way forward, as though focusing on something deep within the woods. He looked like he does when he's spotted a mouse moving in the leaves. Except...you know...less murderous.

"The dogs," he finally said, his voice husky and dry. And quiet. Like he was thinking aloud. "They're doing the same exact shit that the peoples did."

"Oh." I was a bit confused, because he'd said it like it was a bad thing, but I thought it sounded good. "But if we do the same stuff as the peoples did, won't we learn how to be awesome and great like they were?"

Sweetpea swiveled his gaze to me, and his eyes got a weird, spooky glow to them, and it seemed almost like he was looking through me. Or INTO me. "I don't know how to tell you this, Mash, but the peoples weren't always so awesome and great."

I recoiled like he'd clawed my face and gasped, "WHAT?!"

"I know, I know," he said. "It's hard to accept. But I think it's true."

"Oh, Sweetpea," I moaned. "How could you say such a thing? You sound like the Collective!"

Sweetpea just looked away from me again. "I saw things today," he said, slowly, cautiously. Like you might search through brush when you know there's a poisonous snake around. "I saw the peoples how they were when we knew them. How kind they were to each other, and all their fellow creatures. How they lived in harmony with the world around them. That's why they lived in the villages, Mash. They didn't used to—they used to live in cities, until they realized they were killing the world. But, that's the thing, Mash. That's what I saw next. I saw how they were BEFORE. A long, long time ago. Long before any of us were alive, and even longer still."

He finally looked at me again, and his voice became haunted. "Mash, they were terrible. They were filled with fear, and there was no love in them. They...they HATED each other."

"No!" I whispered.

"They killed each other."

"They would never!"

"They did. All the time. And they killed everything around them, too. They had no control over themselves, because they hated themselves as much as they hated each other. And they were all sick, and they were all crazy, and they were all angry and terrified, all the time."

"ALL THE TIME?!" I cried in hopelessness.

Sweetpea pulled his head back and squinted upwards. "Well...you know...maybe not ALL the time. Maybe I was seeing more like a highlight reel of peoples' worst moments. But the general gist of it was that they were pretty damn shitty to themselves and each other and everything around them."

"But...but they changed, didn't they? They had to. Because those aren't the peoples I know."

"No, they're not," Sweetpea agreed. "But I don't know how they changed themselves. I didn't get to see that part. Just that they weren't always as good as they were when we knew them."

"So what does that all mean?" I asked. "Why did Dad show you these things?"

"I'm not really sure," Sweetpea admitted, curling his tail around him. "But I think we need to figure out what they did to change, so that the dogs can change too. Because, right now, it sure as shit looks like the dogs are going down the same bad road that the peoples went down."

And that's when we heard it: A rustle in the woods. Too big to be a squirrel or a rabbit. Too clumsy to be a deer.

Sweetpea's ears rocketed all the way forward. "Oh, shit! That's a dog! They found us!" And then, just as quickly, his ears slapped back and his eyes turned to angry little slits. "Alright, you motherfuckers!" he screamed at the woods, claws coming out and impaling the leaves under his paws. "Don't play fucking games! If you wanna fuck around then quit hiding and come face me, if you have the balls for it!"

Then he leaned into me and whispered, "Growl!"

I quickly issued a growl, but it came out playful and maybe a tad confused? Like my growl was a question?

"Not like that, asshole! Growl like you wanna rip their faces off!"

"Oh!" I got into my Big Dog stance and rumbled out a deep, threatening growl, complete with a lip quiver and a flash of my long teeth.

"Yeah!" Sweetpea yelled at the woods again. "You hear that? We are going to FUCK! YOU! UP!"

"Uh," came a scared voice from behind a stand of brush, maybe a dozen loping strides away from us. "Please don't."

I glanced to Sweetpea in question, but he was as taken aback as me. But, quick to recover as ever, he wiped the confusion away and got back to being threatening. "I dunno," he leered at the brush. "Why should I spare your life? What's in it for me?"

"Well, uh..." A shape appeared from behind the brush. Two shapes, actually, one right after the other, slinking out with their tails between their legs and their ears pasted back in supplication. One big, black and tan dog. One small, white and tan dog.

"It's Boozer and Colby," I said to Sweetpea, and I was about to call out a friendly greeting to them when Sweetpea hissed, "Don't be friendly!" So I returned my face to its mean, growling pose, and tried—with only limited success—to keep my tail from wagging.

"First of all," Colby said, stopping when he was still several strides from us. "I'm sorry that I interrupted your teachings, Voice in the Wilderness. It's just that we've been hiding here all day, waiting for you to explain your visions, and my leg cramped up."

Sweetpea blinked a few times. "Wait...um...there's a lot to unpack there."

"How long have you been spying on us?" I asked, more hurt at the implication of distrust than actually being spied on. "And who's the Voice in the Wilderness?"

Colby and Boozer exchanged a glance.

"Well," Colby says. "The Voice in the Wilderness is Sweetpea. And we haven't been spying on you. We've just been sneaking in while you guys were hunting and then waiting to listen to what Sweetpea had to say."

I cocked my head to one side. "Isn't that spying?"

Colby cocked his head as well. "You know, it sounds a lot like it when I say it out loud."

"Wait, wait, wait," Sweetpea snapped, stepping towards them. "You mean to tell me that you guys have been hanging around, listening to what I have to say about stuff?"

Another glance between them. It was Boozer who spoke up that time, in his big, deep voice. "Yes. That is, in fact, what we're telling you."

"After you wouldn't listen to a fucking word and chased us out of the village?"

Boozer looked scared, which is odd for such a big dog. "Oh, crap."

"So," Colby said, slinking a bit, like he couldn't decide whether he wanted to roll over on his back or run. "You know how it is, don't you? Come on, Mash. You can back us up here. The pack gets to barking, and the next thing you know, you're barking too, and you know how hard it is not to chase after something once everyone else is chasing after it—especially if it runs! So I guess what I'm trying to say—what me and Boozer are trying to say—is that…well…I guess…we didn't mean it. And we're sorry. And we've been out here every day for the past week, listening to you, because we think that you do have some important things to say. And because you're the only one we know who can still talk to the peoples."

Sweetpea just stood there for a while, the very end of his tail twitching back and forth, his head swiveling slowly between Colby and Boozer, who had both frozen in place. Then Sweetpea relaxed back into a sitting position.

"Huh," he said. "That is...unexpected."

"Hey," I said, stepping forward to where Sweetpea was. "Colby, aren't you a True Dog?"

Colby looked a bit ashamed. "I am. Or...was...but still kinda am? I mean, I stay on that side of the wall. But...now I'm here. Listening to Sweetpea. So, I guess I have some doubts."

I looked at Boozer. "And aren't you from the Collective?"

Boozer hung his head, and slowly shook it. "I can't hate the peoples, Mash. I just can't do it. I tried. But it just doesn't make sense. I remember my peoples. And I know they weren't like the Collective keeps saying they were like."

"How many more are there like you?" I asked.

Colby scratched behind her ear. "You mean how many other dogs have doubts about what they're being taught, but are too terrified of being kicked out to say anything? I'd guess that there's got to be a lot more, but I don't know who they are, because we're all too terrified of being kicked out to say anything."

Boozer, seeing that their lives were apparently no longer in danger, crept forward a few steps. "Is it true? Is it really the peoples you're speaking to?"

Sweetpea let out a long, hearty guffaw, then abruptly cut it off. "Maybe. Could be I'm talking to my peoples. Could be I'm talking to ALL peoples, but simply personified by the voice of MY peoples. Or I could be bat shit crazy and talking to myself. I mean, I'm pretty sure I'm not crazy, but then again, that's just what a crazy feline would say."

"Is it true what you said?" Colby asked.

Sweetpea blinked. "Er...which part?"

"Is it true that the peoples used to be Bad, and that the Collective and the True Dogs are starting to be Bad, just like the peoples were?"

"Well," Sweetpea said, cautiously. "That is what I perceived, yes."

"What should we do about that?" Boozer asked.

Sweetpea considered him for a long moment before speaking. "I don't know, Boozer. All I can tell you is what I've been told. And I've been told that the dogs need to remember. They need to remember how it was when they loved the peoples and the peoples loved them."

"I remember," Colby said brightly. Then immediately devolved into wails. "I REMEMBERRRRRRR!"

Boozer started howling as well. "Oh, I remember how wonderful it was and how it can never be again!"

"Alright, shut up," Sweetpea warned them. "Can you possibly not try to attract any more attention? If it hadn't occurred to you already by the fact that we're living in the woods in the middle of nowhere, me and Mash are trying NOT to be found!"

Colby and Boozer both tapered off into whimpers.

Sweetpea sighed at them. "Do you think you could get the other dogs to remember?"

"I think they already do," Colby answered. "Some of them, anyways."

"If they do remember," Boozer put in. "Can they come listen to you?"

Sweetpea frowned. "The fuck would they want to do that for?"

"Because they all want to hear from the peoples," Boozer said. "But Gracie won't even let us talk about them anymore."

"And Banger won't listen to anyone that says anything different than her."

"Can we bring them here?"

"Can we please?"

"Ugh, don't beg," Sweetpea sneered. "I'm not passing out treats." He gave them a mean look. "I'm passing out cold, hard truths!" He relaxed a bit. "But...if they can stomach the truth...then, yeah, sure. Why not?"

My tail was suddenly wagging again. "I can have friends again?!"

Sweetpea narrowed his yellow eyes at me. "What? The Voice in the Wilderness isn't good enough for you?"

"Well, you don't really play..."

"Yeah, you got me there," he admitted. Then, quieter: "But don't get your hopes up. They might still try to kill us."

24

Mash

(Day 300...ish)

THE DOGS ARE COMING in droves now to listen to the Voice in the Wilderness, as they call him. And they're from everywhere: The Collective, The True Dogs, and even a few from Hiro's Pack. They come to listen to Sweetpea tell us all what it is he thinks the peoples want us to know.

Some days he doesn't have much for us. But today, he definitely does. Or, at least, I assume he does, since he's been gone all morning, and we've been waiting around for...you know what? I'm not even going to bother with the time. It's after noon some time, because the sun is on the other side of its arc. That's all I know.

Sweetpea didn't even hunt for himself yesterday, or today. And with all the comings and goings, the rabbits have been harder to find. But Boozer was nice enough to bring me a chunk of a deer's foreleg that they caught a few days ago, so at least my stomach isn't growling. Yes, I left a bit for Sweetpea, though it was kind of a challenge. Dogs aren't known for their restraint with food.

Now, Sweetpea is quietly picking his way back toward us, and I can see from his face that he's looking very contemplative about something. Almost stern.

"Here he comes," one of the other dogs mutters, and they all straighten from their laying or curled positions where they've been resting and waiting. There's nearly a dozen of them today. If a dozen means what I think it means. Which is a number somewhere between a few and lots. Right? Anyway, they sit like obedient dogs, and wait patiently, all eyes on Sweetpea.

His gait is a little better this time around, but he doesn't quite have all of his usual grace. Is it wrong that I get excited when I see him stumble a bit? I think it means he's got some really good stuff for us. That, or these visions are damaging his brain.

He reaches the foreleg of the deer, stops, sniffs it, and looks up at me with squinted eyes. "That for me?" he husks.

"Yeah," I answer, warily, because I think he's about to tell me it looks disgusting, seeing as how what's left on it is half-shredded, and covered with my slobber.

I'm sorry, I can't help it. I am not what you'd call a dry-mouthed breed.

"Thank God," Sweetpea mutters. "I'm fucking starving." And then he hunches over the foreleg and begins gnawing, slowly, deliberately. Like he's really hungry, but he's so exhausted that even chewing is tiring.

We all sit there and watch him with ever-increasing expectation. He ignores us completely. We exchange glances that bounce around the circle from dog to dog and back again. Sweetpea lets out a mighty hack, coughs out a bit of gristle, stares at it on the ground for a moment, and only then does he raise his eyes to us.

"Oh," he says. "You're still here."

I glance sidelong at the dogs and murmur in Sweetpea's direction, "They've been waiting for fifty-million hours. Give or take."

"Ah." Sweetpea sits down. There's a speck of deer gristle on his whiskers. He doesn't seem to know it's there. Normally he'd be cleaning himself after that messy eating session, but he doesn't seem terribly inclined towards hygiene at the moment. "Well. Uh..."

"What have you learned from the peoples?" one of the dogs cries out, unable to bear the suspense any longer.

The dam of silence broken, they all begin to chorus: "Speak to us, Voice in the Wilderness!"

"Alright, alright, alright," Sweetpea waves a limp paw at them. "I know it's natural for dogs to be sycophants, but its unhealthy for both of us. For you, because you need to grow a fucking spine and stop worrying about what everyone thinks of you, and for me, because I'm struggling with an addiction to being the object of your sycophancy."

I don't think anyone knows what that means, but they shut up, and that seems to satisfy him.

Sweetpea stares at them all. "Right. Uh. So..." he seems to almost be gnawing on the words, like a tough bit of meat he can't quite get down. He looks like he's struggling for a moment, and then just sort of gives up all at once with a sigh. "Don't...I mean...Stop competing with each other."

"Don't stop competing with each other?" I ask, for clarity's sake, ready to inscribe this lesson into my brain.

"No, no," Sweetpea says. "Just the last part."

"With each other?" I say, my tone going up in confusion, and unable to keep my head from twisting.

"Dear God. Okay. Scratch that. Forget what I said. I'm going to start fresh. Ready?"

"Ready."

"Stop competing with each other."

"So..." I frown at the ground. "Don't compete with each other?"

"No," Sweetpea glowers at me. "I said, 'STOP competing with each other.'"

"Right, so, 'Don't compete with each other.' Isn't that another way to say it?"

"Question!" It's Colby. "What if we never STARTED competing with each other?"

"Then don't start," Sweetpea says.

"That's what I just said," I mumble.

"Oh, for fuckssake," Sweetpea wipes a paw across his face. He happens to clean the gristle from his whisker, but again doesn't seem to notice. "It's Bad, alright? Competing with each other is Bad."

"I thought you said there weren't really Bad-Bad things."

"Right. And this would be one of them."

"So...is competing with each other Bad or not?"

"It is, but not in your warped, sycophantic, dog-version of the word Bad." Sweetpea gazes heavenward. "I was trying to keep it simple, and you're making it sooooooo fucking complicated."

"I think I got it," I say. "You're just saying that...competing with each other, not in, like, a friendly, game-playing way, but more in, like, competing for food or competing for standing in the pack...those things aren't very good for you."

Sweetpea visibly relaxes. "Actually...yes. Yes, that's it."

I'm learning a thing or two.

"Uh, excuse me!"

"There's always one." Sweetpea turns to Gus, who had spoken up, and tries very hard to look friendly, and fails very bad. "Yes, Gus?"

Gus has a heavy-lidded look of misgivings. "What else?"

"What else?" Sweetpea echoes. "As in, don't compete with each other isn't good enough for you?"

"It's just..." Gus glances sheepishly at the others. "You were gone for a long time. And we've all been waiting here for a long time too. And we had kind of hoped...well...that you'd have something more...more..."

"Groundbreaking?" Sweetpea offers. "Inspiring? Revelatory?"

"Yes," Gus agrees with a wag. "Those things."

"Nope," Sweetpea states, flatly. "Just, 'Stop competing with each other.'"

JuJu Bean speaks up now, looking a little flustered. "You talked to the peoples for THAT many hours and all you got was 'stop competing with each other?'"

"No," Sweetpea growls, swinging his head to JuJu. "I saw a very complex vision, and I knew that if I tried to relate it to you, you'd take it completely wrong and wind up doing something stupid, so I decided to bring it wayyyyyy down to your level. Hence: Stop competing with each other."

"But why?" JuJu pleads. "At least tell us that!"

"Tell us the vision!" Gus begs.

"Yes!" Boozer adds. "Tell us what you saw! We can handle it! We won't interpret it wrong and do stupid things!"

Sweetpea sighs laboriously. "Alright, fine! Turning into a fucking pushover for you mutts," he grumbles as he situates himself again, tail curling around him, the very end twitching irritably. "I saw a monkey," he begins.

"He saw a monkey!" someone whispers, overly-loud and overly-excited.

Sweetpea pauses and squints at them. "No. Don't start."

"Sorry," the dog whispers, ducking down behind the others as though to hide.

Sweetpea draws himself back up again. "Anyways. I saw a monkey lose its fur. And when the monkey lost its fur, its hide got sunburned during the day, and it got cold at night. So the monkey took a whole shit ton of big-ass leaves and used them like clothing to cover it from the sun, and to keep it warmer at night. Well, this went on for quite some time, and there were a lot of other monkeys involved. Skipping skipping skipping, now all the monkeys are wearing these leaves, right? And they start to look at each other's leaves, and they start to think. They say, 'this monkey's leaves are nicer than mine, I want what he has, I'm going to take it.' Or the monkey will see other leaves and say, 'Those AREN'T as nice as mine, so I must be a better monkey than this monkey with the shitty leaves.' So they start to hate each other over the differences in the quality of leaves, and they start to fight over certain types of leaves, and steal from each other. Entire wars were fought over fucking leaves, I shit you not. Okay, now I'm gonna jump back a bit and tell you something: The monkeys had their own peoples. Not, like, you know, OUR peoples, but they had a…being…thing…ball of energy…whatever. And it loved them and looked after them. But then it went away for a while. And that was when all the monkeys went literal ape-shit over leaves. And then the…the light ball or whatever, it comes back and it sees what the monkeys have done over the leaves, and the light ball gets kinda pissed and says, 'The fuck are you doing with these leaves? Look at yourselves! You're so worried about the stupid, shitty leaves, that you've started to hate each other and fight each other and kill each other, and I raised you asshats better than that!'"

Sweetpea pauses for a long time, looking thoughtfully skyward. I can't tell whether he's contemplating a mystery of the universe that has just now lodged itself in his brain, or if he totally lost his train of thought and is trying not to show it.

Eventually he blinks and then seems to realize we're all still standing there.

"And that's it," he says.

The dogs are very quiet for a while. I think they're all doing what I'm doing: Trying to parse through what they just heard and pluck some lesson out of it. I feel like there's one there, but it's just right outside of my ability to grasp.

"I think I get it," Boozer says.

All eyes turn to him.

His ears go back and his tail tucks. His eyes are darting all around our woodland environment, growing wider and wider. "The leaves," he whispers in quavering, mounting horror. "The leaves are EVIL!"

Everything in my body spurs me to join the ensuing panic as all the dogs realize that they are, in fact, standing on a bed of dried, dead evil, and are trying desperately to get away from the leaves, which they can't really do, at which point Boozer starts climbing a tree. Or I should say TRYING to climb a tree, which essentially involves a lot of panicked yipping, jumping, and clawing at the trunk of the tree.

I realize, in a way that is somehow outside of myself, that this is incredibly ridiculous. I realize this, even as my body is literally shaking against the restraints of my mind, wanting to join in the group-think of the pack and join their freak out.

"Dear God," I hear Sweetpea mutter.

There is only one dog besides myself that is not freaking out. It is Q, who has clambered her old, spindly legs up onto a stump and suddenly begins savagely barking at the others. "No, you idiots! That's not it at all! Get ahold of yourself! The leaves aren't evil! They're just decaying plant matter!"

A glance in Sweetpea's direction reveals that he's become very interested in what Q has to say on the whole thing. His vibe is somewhere between hope, curiosity, and a breathless cringe.

Boozer, panting, and still quite unwilling to place all four paws on the ground at the same time, at least stops trying to claw his way up the tree, and holds himself in one position, prancing in place.

"What? They're not evil? You're sure that wasn't the meaning of the vision?"

JuJu Bean is beside herself. "It better not be the leaves, because I'm surrounded by them!"

"There's nothing wrong with the leaves," Q snaps at them. "Don't you get it? The leaves are a METAPHOR. The story isn't about leaves, it's about what the leaves REPRESENT."

"Oh." Boozer stops prancing. "Oh, I see."

"What are the leaves supposed to represent?" I ask, feeling like I've almost figured it out myself, but Q seems so confident, I figure she must know what she's talking about.

"Ugh," Q looks disgusted with me, and I guess the others too. "You still don't see it? It's so plain and clear." She shakes her head in exhausted irritation. "It's obvious that the leaves represent the peoples clothes that we've all been wearing..."

Sweetpea visibly brightens.

But then Q shrieks, "...And it's the CLOTHES that are EVIL!"

The dogs immediately fly, not into a panic this time, but a rage. I guess because there's no clothes present with us at that moment to be terrified of. And Sweetpea just closes his eyes like the life has drained out of him.

"DESTROY THE CLOTHES!"

"THE PEOPLES HATE THE CLOTHES!"

"THE PEOPLES HAVE ALWAYS HATED THE CLOTHES, BECAUSE THEY WERE TRAPPED IN THEM THE WHOLE TIME!"

"OH, I WISH I'D KNOWN MY PEOPLES WERE TRAPPED IN THEIR CLOTHES! I WOULD HAVE TORN THEM TO PIECES FOR YOU! I COULD HAVE SAVED YOUUUUUUUU!"

Maybe it's just because I've been out of the pack for so long now, or maybe it's because I've been hanging out with a cat, but I once again resist the urge to panic.

Q's interpretation of the dream doesn't feel the same as the one that's just on the edges of my brain. If I could just be a little smarter for half a second, my brain could jump out and grab it like a rabbit...

I bark loudly to get their attention. In their current state, it's pretty easy to get them to pay attention, because they're primed for some dog to take charge and lead the way forward. We're pack animals, what do you expect?

"Guys!" I shout, then slowly lower my volume as they start to lower theirs. "That's not it either! The story isn't about how the monkeys were EVIL for putting the leaves on. And yes, the leaves are a metaphor, I guess, for the clothes you guys have been wearing, but the leaves in the story aren't EVIL, and neither are the clothes, and neither are the dogs that wear them. No one is EVIL, okay? That's not what this is about!"

"But-but-but," Q stammers breathlessly. "If the peoples didn't like it, then it's EVIL and BAD!"

"No, no, that's the wrong type of thinking that got me and Sweetpea banished in the first place!" Now I am getting a little indignant, because why does it always take these dogs so long to figure things out? Then I wonder if my interpretation is wrong too, so I look to Sweetpea, but he's just gazing on in what I dare to believe is cautious admiration.

And then he nods at me. "Go ahead, Mash. You tell 'em."

Encouraged, I turn back to the others. "We have to stop thinking of the peoples as these angry beings that punish us for doing certain things that THEY don't like. That's not who the peoples were. Don't you remember how kind and loving your peoples were? Sure, they all had a few rules, but most of those rules were for our own good, because we just want to have fun and not worry about the consequences, but we have the tendency to eat stuff we shouldn't eat, and to go places we shouldn't go, and to chew on things we shouldn't chew on, and all kinds of other things. And that doesn't make us EVIL! That makes us fun-loving dogs, which is why the peoples loved us in the first place! But it does mean that we have to learn to listen to our peoples and trust them when they tell us that they can see how something might be bad for us, even when we can't."

"But," Boozer says, looking confused all over again. "The leaves kept the monkeys warm at night, and kept them from being sunburned during the day. How is that bad for them?"

"That's exactly the point!" I say, wagging excitedly, feeling my brain finally get its jaws around that truth rabbit. "There was nothing wrong with the leaves, and there's nothing wrong with the Collective wearing the clothes. What's NOT good for us, and what WASN'T good for the monkeys, was that they started to use the leaves—and the Collective started to use the clothes—as a way to compete with each other. And that's why Sweetpea said the lesson from that vision was 'Don't compete with each other.'"

Slowly, ever so slowly, the darkness of ignorance and confusion fades from their faces. Their body postures relax. Their tails raise. Their eyes lighten up. And then the truth finally beams out of them.

"Ohhhhhhh," the chorus of realization comes from all of them in one gust of breath.

"Okay," Boozer says, with a slight chuckle in his voice. "I get it now. But, honestly, I probably would have worded the lesson differently, Sweetpea."

"Would you have?" Sweetpea asks, boredly.

"I would have said 'STOP competing with each other.'"

25

Mash

(Day 300-ish, Give Or Take A Week...Or Maybe Two)

Sweetpea tells us this:

"I saw a tree. And Dad was standing in front of it. It was a weird looking tree. Actually, I think it was like some sort of hybrid or something. Because it was growing two different types of fruit. And I saw Dad pick one of the types of fruit and eat it. And he said, 'Now I know what is good.' And then he tried the other fruit, and immediately spat it out, and said, 'Now I know what is bad.' Then things really sort of sped up. I think I was watching all of human history. Don't ask me how I know that. I deduced it because there was a lot of peoples killing other peoples, and also a lot of peoples being nice to other peoples. And everywhere the peoples went, sometimes killing, and sometimes being nice to each other, these trees would start to grow. But the trees were more and more different, and the peoples had to keep eating both types of fruit to figure out which was good and which was bad. Then I noticed something. I noticed that the peoples that were killing other peoples, they kept on eating the bad fruits, and wherever they went, those trees would sprout up, and they would have more bad fruit on them than good fruit. But on the other hand, I saw the peoples that were being nice to each other, and they were eating a lot more of the good fruits, and the trees that sprouted up wherever they went had more good fruit on them than bad fruit. Eventually, it seemed like the peoples started to be able to recognize good fruit from bad fruit, and then they only ate the good fruit, and then they were nice to each other, and eventually all the trees with the shitty fruit on them withered and died, and the only trees that were sprouting up were trees full of good fruit. It's not that the good fruit was MAKING them do good things, or that the bad fruit was MAKING them do bad things. Not entirely. But it was more like they kept on choosing the bad fruit, because they were already doing bad things, and eating the bad fruit made them more likely to do bad things, and doing bad things made them more likely to choose that bad fruit. Like a circle. Or a spiral. Same thing with the good fruit. If the person tended to be nice, then they tended to also choose good fruit, which also made them more likely to do more nice stuff.

"And then, in the last part...well, this is kind of hard for me to say. But...uh...I was a dog. In the last part. No, I was just seeing through the eyes of a dog. No, I don't recall seeing my own nose—is that a big thing for y'all? It was just a sense I got, okay? I could tell I was a dog. Just accept that and move on.

"I was a dog, and I was looking up at a peoples, and the peoples' face was smiling down at me, and their hands were on my head, scratching behind my ears, and they were saying 'Good dog! Good dog!' And then immediately after that, I saw the peoples frowning and wagging their finger in my face and saying, 'Bad dog! Bad dog!'

"I'm not perfectly sure what it means. I can only tell you what I understood while I was in the dream, even if it might not make perfect sense to you when I say it now. But what I understood when all this was happening, was that...well...this is the process. Peoples started their journey by learning the difference between good and bad. And now they've completed their journey, and that was why they left us. In fact, they didn't leave us. They just finished their journey. But before they did, before they left, they taught the dogs good and bad, too. Not all of the things that might be good and bad, but they taught us that there IS a good and a bad, and how to tell the difference between them. And that, I think, has started dogs on their own journey."

··········

The very next day, Sweetpea tells us this:

"Alright. So here's the deal. There was this group of peoples, right? Except they didn't really look like peoples, I just knew they were peoples, because sometimes I just know shit, you know? Anyways, they were peoples, but they were made out of...dirt, or mud, or whatever. And, they weren't smart or loving like the peoples we knew. It's like that part of them was missing. And they were on this path that was supposed to lead them to the place where they could find the part of them that was missing, and become whole peoples. So, off down this path these mud-monsters start trudging, and it's a long-ass journey. The path had been put down by someone or something that loved the mud-monsters for whatever reason, and wanted them to be whole. And because the path was so long, and went over some rough terrain, this thing...person...being...that had made the path, had also placed all these little gemstones along the way, so that even though it was a hard journey, it would at least be beautiful. But the mud-monsters, boy, I guess they had a thing for gemstones. At first they just kind of appreciated the gemstones along the way, but then they kind of got obsessed with them, and they started to talk amongst themselves, wondering if the journey was really worth it, when they could just stop where they were and enjoy all these awesome gemstones. And you know what? A lot of them never bothered to go further down the road. And even the ones that did continue on, most of them wound up getting distracted by the gemstones, and forgetting about the journey itself. Some of them were all into rubies, and some of them were really obsessed with sapphires, or emeralds, or whatever. But they all forgot that the gemstones were just there to make the journey itself beautiful, but they could never be as beautiful as the thing those mud-monsters would have gotten for themselves if they'd just kept on going."

··········

One day, this is all Sweetpea has to say:

"I see a starving dog, gnawing at a deer's antlers, while all the meat on it spoils and goes to waste."

··········

Then, another day, Sweetpea lays this one on us:

"So, there's this dog. And he's really fucked up. I'm not sure if he was born fucked up, or somehow wound up that way, but in any case, he can't see. He's blind. And I guess he can't smell either—I know, terrible luck, this guy—because his master has to lead him to his food every day. And every day the master puts the food in the same spot and he gently leads this fucked up dog to his food so he can eat. Makes sure he does it the same way every day, so eventually, the dog kind of learns the path to his food, right? But still, the master stays with him, keeps showing him the way, even though the dog has it memorized. But one day the master comes to the dog and says, 'Yo, I got this thing I gotta take care of, and I'm gonna be gone for a good bit, but I've left plenty of food for you, and I know you know how to get to your food, right?' And the dog's all like, 'Yeah, yeah, I can make it, I've done it a thousand times.' So the master leaves. And, at first, the dog's good to go. He follows the path that the master taught him, goes to his meal, and eats. But eventually, the dog starts to think, 'This path that the master made feels really long, and I'm really hungry. I bet there's a faster way there.' So then he starts trying to find a faster way there. But, remember, he's blind as shit, and can't smell. And, predictably, it doesn't go well for him. And by the time he realizes that he can't find his way to the food, he's so turned around he can't even find his way back to the start of the path that the master had taught him. All he had to do was what the master told him to do, and he would have found his food. But he got it into his head that the master hadn't already laid out the best path to the food, and wound up screwing himself over. You're right, Boozer, that was a pretty fucking dumb thing to do. But that's not the end of the story. Oh no. See, the master comes back and finds his dog starved almost to death. And do you know what he did? No, JuJu, geez. He didn't let the dog starve to death for being Bad. The hell's wrong with you? No, he went to his beloved companion and scooped him up and brought him to his food, and fed him because he was too weak to feed himself, and nursed that blind, scentless—and yes, probably pretty stupid—dog back to health. And once the dog was back to full strength, the master smiled at him and said, 'Why didn't you just follow the path that I taught you? Did you think that I didn't love you enough to already pick the best path? Did you think I would be cruel or play tricks with the dog that I love so much?'"

· · · **· · · ·** · · ·

After that last one, and once the dogs that had come to hear the Voice in the Wilderness had all left, I'm feeling a bit concerned, and I feel like I need to talk to Sweetpea about what he saw.

He's tired from the day's work—hunting in the morning, getting visions from the peoples all day, and then spending the entire afternoon talking to the other dogs about it. He lays with his legs and paws tucked under him in that way that cats do that makes them look like a furry blob with a cat's head. His eyes are half-lidded and he seems to be enjoying a ray of sunshine coming through the trees, bathing his face and making his tan fur flash like gold.

I saunter up to him and plop my butt down. "Hey, Sweetpea?"

"Mm?"

"In that story you told us today," I begin, piecing my thoughts together as I speak them. "Do you think that the path that the master laid out for his dog was...the law?"

Sweetpea's head pulls back a bit and he opens his eyes to look thoughtfully at me. "Well. That's certainly one way someone could interpret it."

I frown at him. "So, if the path was the law, then why aren't we going to join the True Dogs who follow it? According to your vision, the True Dogs would be following the master's path, wouldn't they?"

"Would they?" Sweetpea says.

"Well, if the path that the master made is the law, then..."

"But is the True Dogs' law the MASTER'S law?" Sweetpea presses.

I can tell he thinks I'm missing something. But I don't know what it is. If I knew, I wouldn't be missing it. I try my best to reason it out. "Well, it's the law that we made to try to please the peoples, which is the master, right?"

"Yes, I believe the master represented the peoples. But, Mash, did Dad ever tell you that you couldn't get on his Cloud Throne?"

"Well, in the beginning he did, before he found me worthy."

"Oh, Mash. It's just not that complicated," Sweetpea sighs. "In the beginning, Dad had never had dogs. Not before you and Banger. You were his first dogs. And he just didn't know that being on the Cloud Throne was so important to you. He probably just didn't want you getting dog hair all over his Cloud Throne. But then he realized how important it was for you guys to snuggle up with him. It wasn't that he found you worthy—you were worthy when he chose you out of the Place of Judgment. It was that he realized the joy he was bringing to you by allowing you on the Cloud Throne was more important than keeping the Cloud Throne clean and not smelling like dirty-ass dogs."

"Did he tell you all this?" I ask, surprised, and maybe a bit hopeful.

Sweetpea grooms his chest fur a few times. "It's...an understanding that I have." He looks at me, working his own fur around on his tongue. "But that's not the point, Mash. The point is, at the time that Dad left us, he didn't care about you being on the Cloud Throne, did he?"

"No," I admit. "He didn't."

"And did he tell you that you couldn't bark or growl or whine anymore?"

"No, but I did piss him off a few times doing it."

"I think you pissed everyone off a few times doing it. It's an annoying fucking noise. But he never told you that you couldn't. And did he ever tell you that you couldn't chase squirrels?"

"No."

"And did he ever tell you that you couldn't get wild and crazy when you were play fighting with Banger?"

"No." The tip of my tail gives a few wags, patting the ground at my feet. "He used to laugh about how crazy we'd get when we were play fighting."

"Who was it that gave you all those laws?"

"Well...Banger. And Gracie."

"Mm. So whose law is that law? Is it the master's law, or the dogs' law?"

"I guess...it's the dogs' law."

Sweetpea returns to grooming himself, working down his forelegs. "I guess you're right."

Understanding reaches me like a fresh breeze, blowing away my worries. "So the law that we came up with was never the master's law." Sweetpea gives no reply, so I guess I've figured it out. But that brings up a new thought. "But if that's true, then what IS the master's law? What's the path that we're supposed to be following?"

Sweetpea squints at me, discerningly. "Lemme give you a little piece of advice, Mash."

"Okay," I say, warily.

"If you wanna know what it is that Dad wants, maybe you should stop asking everyone else what THEY think, and start using your own personal knowledge of who Dad is. I think you might find that a bit more fruitful."

26

Mash

(Day 330...Plus A Week, I Think...Plus...More...Carry The One...Wait...Crap...I Forgot Where I Started...)

I HAVE ENCOUNTERED A predator's problem: If you're constantly hunting the same area, then you run out of things to hunt. I haven't caught a rabbit in...several days. Sweetpea has been more successful hunting birds, which is something I'm just not quick or stealthy enough for. He has tried to share his last few birds with me, but there's barely enough on them to feed Sweetpea himself. I lied and told him that I'd been catching plenty of rabbits and I wasn't hungry. I don't think he believed me. Maybe it was my stomach growling that gave me away.

I can't catch birds. Squirrels are too quick to run up trees where I can't get them. Deer are too big for me to catch by myself. And I think the village has been having trouble hunting deer too, because the dogs that show up to listen to Sweetpea haven't been bringing me any meat from their kills.

Man, it's days like today that make me really miss kibble. How good we had it, when the peoples would just pour us our meal, and we didn't have to do anything to earn it except wag our tails and be thankful.

My only option is to hunt a different area than I've been hunting. The woods between my old village and Hiro's is pretty large. Large enough that I haven't encountered any other dogs yet. But I'm venturing into unfamiliar territory today, so I keep my head up and my ears pricked for movement. I don't expect any drama from Hiro's Pack, but who knows what'll happen if I run into the Collective or the True Dogs? Sure, plenty of dogs from both of those sides have been coming to listen to Sweetpea, so I assume they're okay with me. But there's still lots of other dogs that haven't.

I'm way out of my usual area now, and I won't lie to you, I'm a bit nervous about it, but I'm catching little hints of something, a delicate little scent that bursts into my nose when I cross little shallows where the smell has pooled towards the ground.

I sniff my way from scent puddle to scent puddle. It's getting stronger. I'm almost sure it's a rabbit, but I need to get a little closer to what's giving it off. I can already tell that it's a male (sorry, Buddy, but we all gotta eat). I can smell its fur and dander. And I can smell dirt, and the dust of dried forest leaves crumpled underfoot. But that's pretty much what everything that lives in the woods smells like—me and Sweetpea included.

Oh, and it's definitely an herbivore. Sweetpea taught me that word. I'd just been calling them meat-eaters and plant-eaters, but he told me that makes me sound juvenile. And I'm still unsure whether that was a compliment or an insult.

Meat-eaters—carnivores, I believe is the technical term—have a distinct, sour tang to their dander. Whereas herbivores smell more dull and earthy. This one's definitely an herbivore, but I can't really tell which plants it eats...

Oop. There it is.

I catch a big puddle of scent. Fresh, too. And it's definitely a rabbit. I can smell the mild grassy scent of what it's been eating. Smells like clover.

I feel bad admitting this, but I'm trying to make peace with my carnivorousness: My mouth starts to water.

I'm just panning my nose around, trying to get a direction on my new prey, when the sound of dogs barking blasts through my brain and lights off all of my primal instincts.

Obviously, I'm scared. I'm a big enough dog to admit when I'm scared. But what makes it worse is the KIND of barks that I'm hearing.

These barks aren't communicating the usual, "Hey, you over there! Hullooooo!"

No, these barks are communicating danger, and rage, and wildness.

My first instinct is to bark back—because that's just what you do when you hear barking. But I strangle that bark out of my throat with a huge effort of willpower, forcing myself to think about how I'm all alone out here, and I'm hearing SEVERAL dogs that do not sound friendly at all.

My next instinct is to run. Actually, it's a very real thought that I have: Run, Mash! Run before they see you! You're faster than every single dog in the village!

But how pissed are they? And are they pissed at ME? I can outrun them, but where will I run to? And if I run back to Sweetpea, will they track me there? Is this a pack of dogs that Gracie or Banger has sent out to squash the Voice in the Wilderness? I can imagine either one of them being furious that members of their pack are coming out to listen to him.

I can run, I decide, and then double-back on myself, and break the trail. I've tracked enough things at this point to know how a scent trail gets broken.

I'm turning to do just that, when I hear desperate words in amongst the furious barking.

"Stop! Everyone stop!"

I can't tell who it is, but something in that voice pleads to me, and I find my will to flee completely snuffed out. I swing back in the direction of all of those noises, and before I even know what I'm doing, I'm running towards them, instead of away from them.

What am I doing?

WHAT ARE YOU DOING, MASH?

Snarls. The kind dogs make when they're latched onto something.

And squeals. The kind dogs make when they're being latched onto.

Half of me wants to turn tail and escape. The other half of me is apparently stronger, because I go faster, even though I have no idea what I'm running into, or what I'm going to do when I get there.

Yips and yaps.

"You're killing him!"

Oh, no...

And then all the barking and snarling and yipping abruptly ends.

What does that mean? How far away am I?

I try to hear more, but the wind is roaring past my ears, the branches and leaves are lashing at my face, and my pulse and my breath are too loud to hear much else.

The silence seems to last forever, until I detect the faintest whine through all the other noises—high-pitched and miserable.

I rocket over a slight hill and come clawing to a stop, just shy of the edge of a shallow ravine. Immediately, I see them: Five dogs, all from the Collective. I recognize all of them—Boozer, Gus, Willie, and Gracie herself, and in the middle of those four is Gizmo, laying on his side, blood covering his legs and shoulders and neck.

"Gizmo!" I cry, not even thinking about what might have happened and what kind of danger I'm in, especially with Gracie there. But I don't care about all that. Gizmo is my friend, and he's hurt.

When I cry out, all the dogs look up, and my heart bursts with relief when I see Gizmo raise his head—he's still alive! I barely even look at the others, I just start tumbling down the ravine, trying to get to Gizmo.

"Gizmo, what happened?" I say, skidding up to him. He's got bite marks—deep and nasty and entirely unplayful—all over his body. One of his ears is half ripped off. There's a flap of hide hanging from his hindquarters.

Something hits me hard in the side, and I go stumbling off. When I right myself, immediately dropping into an instinctive fighting stance, I blink and see Gracie there, head lowered, paws spread, teeth flashing.

"Did YOU do this to Gizmo?" I gasp.

"What are you doing here?" Gracie snarls.

"I heard the barking and—"

"Are you with Banger?" Gracie gnashes out, teeth clacking just inches from my nose, forcing me back. "Did you have something to do with this?"

"No!" It comes out of me as anger, though all I can feel is fear. I snap back at her and she seems surprised, recoiling. "I'm not with the True Dogs! They kicked me out of the village, remember?!"

"WE kicked you out of the village!" Gracie says.

"You ALL kicked me out of the village!"

"Is that what this is about?" Gracie demands. "Are you trying to get back at us?"

"I didn't do anything! I wasn't a part of whatever happened to Gizmo! I was just out here hunting and I heard the barks and it sounded like someone was hurt!"

Gracie doesn't seem satisfied, and looks like she's about to launch into more angry snarls, when Boozer shoves himself between us, flashing his canines. "Both of you chill out! Gracie, be cool! He's not with them!"

Gracie's eyes snap between me and Boozer. "How do you know that?"

"Because he's been living out in the woods with Sweetpea this whole time!"

Gracie looks shocked, and that pulls her out of her aggression. "How do you know THAT?" she asks Boozer.

Boozer hangs his head a little sheepishly. "I've...gone out to visit him."

Gizmo whimpers again, and my attention swings over to him. He's still got his head up, trying to lick at the open wound on his hindquarters. He's shaking all over.

"Guys, Gizmo's hurt!" I plead.

"We know he's hurt!" Gracie practically howls. "It was the True Dogs that did it!"

"Why on earth would they attack you like this?" I ask.

Gizmo's voice is pained. "We had a deer. Killed it right there where you're standing."

I look down and see what he means: The area around my paws is scratched to the dirt, the leaves matted and shifted as though a struggle occurred, bright red splashes in amongst the brown leaves. Tufts of deer fur. And the scent of it, thick and heavy. But when I look up and around, I don't see a carcass.

"Where's the deer?"

"They stole it," Gizmo breathes. "They said they'd been hunting that deer all morning and it belonged to the True Dogs. I tried to stand over the kill..." he winces and whimpers again.

Gracie is staring at him, eyes filled with horror. "You were very brave." She glances back to me. "There were seven of them. As soon as Gizmo tried to stand over the kill, they all attacked him at once. We tried to break it up, but they'd already injured him so bad, and we were outnumbered, so we backed off."

"Then they stole the deer," Boozer finishes, bitterly.

"First JuJu Bean, and now this," Gracie seethes, the hackles on her back starting to rise again. "Is this what it's come to? Are they going to try to kill us all?"

"Well," I say, instantly panicking at the rage I hear in Gracie's voice. "They didn't kill him—"

"Only because we stopped them before they could!" Gracie screams at me. "And who's next, huh? I tell you what, I've had enough of the True Dogs! This ends now! Today!"

"Wh-wh-what do you mean?" I stammer.

She wheels on me, eyes flashing like fire. "I mean to get that deer back! We hunted it, we killed it, and the Collective is hungry! They stole from us! And they've attacked us twice now! I'm not just going to roll over and give them my belly! They're going to see what happens when they mess with us!"

"Gracie, think about what you're saying," I beg her.

"I know what I'm saying!" she barks. "I don't expect you to understand—you're not a part of our pack, and you're not a part of theirs. You're not a part of ANYBODY'S pack. But that's how the pack works! When you hurt one of us, we hurt one of you!"

"But...but this isn't what the peoples would have wanted!"

A strange silence crashes down on us.

I look desperately to Boozer, hoping that he'll back me up, since he's been out to listen to Sweetpea. He knows that we can't let ourselves go down this path. He's heard all of the warnings that Sweetpea has given us. He knows this isn't what the peoples want for us.

But Boozer won't even look at me.

"The peoples?" Gracie says, suddenly quiet. Then she lets out a mean little laugh. "The PEOPLES, Mash? What makes you think we give a crap what THEY think? Or WOULD think, if they were even here anymore. But they're not! It's just us!"

"I just know that they would have hated for dogs to hurt each other."

"Well, maybe you can tell that to your friend Banger," Gracie menaces. "Because they sure have hurt us. And now we're going to hurt them. Because that's how it works, Mash! Because there is no law, and there's no more peoples, and we're all by ourselves out here, and no one's looking out for us but ourselves! If we want our pack to survive, then we have to fight!"

"But—"

"She's right," Boozer suddenly snarls at me.

I draw back. "Boozer?" I say, alarmed and dismayed.

"Just..." A tiny hint of regret in his eyes. "Just stay out of it, Mash. It's no place for you. Or for your cat."

I stand there in shock as Gracie marches back to Gizmo. "Gizmo, can you walk?"

Gizmo tries mightily to get to his feet, and he does manage it, but he's swaying and shaking and looks like he might fall over at any second.

"Gus. Willie." Gracie points to Gizmo with her nose. "Support him and help him back to the village. Me and Boozer are going to run ahead and warn the others."

Before I have time to think of anything else that might keep this from happening, Gracie and Boozer are off, sprinting through the woods back towards the village, while Gus and Willie both take positions on either side of Gizmo.

Gizmo starts walking, unsteadily. But then he stops. Looks at me.

"Boozer was right," Gizmo says, sadly. "You should stay out of this. For your own sake."

27

Banger

THE FIRST INKLING I have that something is off is when the hunting party completely ignores my tail wagging and congratulations on their successful kill. Brute is leading the pack, not so much because he's fast, but because he's so strong. He's currently latched onto the neck of the deer and is dragging it backwards at an oddly quick pace, the others from his hunting party tugging along at the deer's legs as they drag it into our section of the Village.

I'm still trying to work out why none of them have responded to me when I catch Brute's eyes flashing towards the woodline, as though someone might be pursuing them. He's entirely out of breath. And then I notice that the deer carcass hasn't been eaten at all.

Usually, the hunting party gets first dibs—they did the work, so they deserve to fill their bellies first, plus it lightens the deer up for the haul back to the Village. This deer, though, is intact. They haven't even opened up its belly to pull out the guts yet, which is a good bit of its weight. No wonder they're all exhausted.

"Brute, what's going on?" I demand, shoving my snout in close to his, meaning to help him drag the deer. But as my nose brushes past him, I catch the scent of a dog that is not a part of our pack. And it's not a dander smell, like they've been carousing. It's a blood smell.

Brute's got another dog's blood all over his snout.

"Holy crap," I gasp. "What the heck happened out there? Brute, stop dragging the stupid thing and talk to me!"

Brute growls, but releases his hold on the deer. The carcass flops as the others let go and stand about, heaving for air, their muscles twitching with exhaustion.

"Collective," Brute rasps out. "They tried to steal our kill. We had to fight them off."

I don't know what hits me harder—the sudden rage at what has happened, or the sudden fear of what might happen in a little bit. My eyes shoot up to the woodline that Brute's so preoccupied with. "Are they chasing you?"

"I'm not sure," Brute says, leaning down to seize hold of the deer again. "But Gracie was with them. And she was pissed."

"That stupid, hopped-up crossbreed!" I snarl.

"We need to get the deer behind the wall," Brute says, then sinks his teeth back around the deer's jugular and starts pulling it along again.

I stoop to help him, my body humming with bad feelings, and I almost miss it.

Two shapes come darting out of the woods.

It's Gracie and Boozer, at a full sprint, tongues lolling out of their mouths as they run. They lock eyes with me, and I come upright, barking and snarling an alert. "There they are!" But just as Brute and his hunting party look up to defend themselves, Gracie and Boozer peel off, no longer heading straight at us, but angling for their side of The Wall.

"She's going to get more dogs!" Brute seethes. "Quick! We're not letting them take our kill! It belongs to the True Dogs, and we're just as hungry as they are!"

I look to one of the other dogs in Brute's hunting party. Colby is there, attached to a hind leg, and not looking like he's contributing much. He's entirely too small to be pulling a deer, and he's already exhausted from bringing it this far.

"Colby!" I shout, jumping into his place. "Go gather the True Dogs and tell them we're gonna have trouble with the Collective!"

Colby lets go and pants heavily. But he doesn't run off like I told him to. His eyes meet mine, and I almost snap at him to get moving, but my mouth is full of deer hoof.

"Banger," he whines. "I think we did something Bad!"

"You shut up, Colby!" Brute gnashes out, dropping the deer's neck again.

I have no idea what the issue is, but I know I don't want Colby to shut up. I need to know what happened out there. Especially if my True Dogs did something Bad. "You just keep pulling!" I snap at Brute, then turn back to Colby.

He doesn't even wait for me to prompt him. His ears are back, pasted plaintively to his skull, and his tail is hanging. He looks like a very guilty dog. "It was Gizmo! We attacked Gizmo! And I think we might've hurt him real bad!"

I'm too shocked to move. The deer's hind legs clatter past my paws. I feel like I've become rooted to the ground. Despair begins to leak in past my shock, and that trickle becomes a river that fills up every hollow space inside of me.

What do I do? They've attacked Gizmo. And, judging by the blood-smell on Brute's nose, they did indeed hurt him.

I feel a faint whiff of something like shame, because I realize in that instant that I'm more concerned with Gracie's reprisal than I am that my dogs injured Gizmo. But if Gracie is coming for a fight, I'm not just going to roll over and give her my belly. We're the True Dogs, and we stand with the peoples.

But would the peoples have wanted us to fight?

"Go get the others," I say, hoarsely. "Tell them to get ready for a fight."

28

Sweetpea

I HAVE A CONFESSION to make.

I haven't been entirely honest about all that I've been doing out here in the woods. It hasn't all been hunting and hanging out with Mash and talking to the peoples. Sure, that's been most of it. But there's a reason that I'm wasting away, as I'm sure you've noticed my svelte physique has declined a bit. And it's not because I'm a shitty hunter.

I haven't been sharing all my kills with Mash. I know he's been struggling to catch rabbits, and I've been trying to share a bird a day with him, but it's just not much, even for me. What you might not know is that I've been averaging about THREE birds a day.

What have I been doing with those other birds? Well, I sure as shit haven't been eating them myself, I can tell you that. No, I guess I'll have to go back a bit to make this clear.

See, when I was His Supreme Masterfulness, I got a lot of respect. Maybe not so much from Longjohn, and not even from the other cats. At first. But while Longjohn has remained my bitter enemy, the other cats definitely warmed up to me, due to my position of power.

Then I had all that stripped away from me. But...I'd kinda already maybe sorta made really good friends with another cat that may or may not be a female. And she may or may not have been visiting me out here, on the regular, unbeknownst to Mash. And she may or may not have gone into heat two months ago...

Alright, I'll cut the bullshit. I knocked her up.

What? Voice in the Wilderness or no, I still have needs!

Not, like, emotional need for touch or romance, or any of that horseshit, but the need to make sure there's another generation of cats as awesome as I am. And, apparently, I've succeeded.

I'm not really sure why I kept it from Mash. I guess it's just kind of instinctive. Logically, I know Mash isn't a threat, and yet I'm still possessed by the need to keep the mother of my children in hiding. And Fiona—that's her name, by the way, as long as we're being open about things—feels much the same. She doesn't particularly like staying in the woods while she percolates our litter, and she misses roaming free, and messing with the dogs in the village, but she is also at the mercy of her instincts here.

So I've been supplementing her hunting with my own, because she's eating for a half-dozen or so now. And I've been doing it on the sly, which actually hasn't been all that hard, because, let's face it, Mash just isn't a very perceptive guy.

So there it is, the long and short of it. And I'm just now snapping the neck of a fine, fat cardinal, and weighing whether I'd like to eat those plump little breasts myself or take him to Fiona, when I hear the tumble of dog paws tearing through the woods at me.

Naturally, my Prime Directive is instantly ready to go off like a rat trap.

But when I spin to see what canine is running up on me with such abandon, I see none other than the doofy face of Mash, ears flattened back, and...

Oh, shit. He doesn't look very doofy right now. He looks downright panicked.

"Sweetpea!" he practically shrieks at me. "Sweetpea-Sweetpea-Sweetpea—"

"Oh my fuck, I'm right here!" I snap back, half pissed at having the snot scared out of me, and half worried over why Mash is all in a tizzy.

Mash comes skidding to a stop in a wash of dry leaves and forest dirt, panting hard. He catches sight of the cardinal and, momentarily distracted, says, "Oh, hey, you caught another bird today! Good work!"

"Uh, yeah," I say, trying to figure out how I'm going to simultaneously NOT offer my second bird to Mash, while also NOT giving up my secret. "You know. He was asking for it. Hey, you look super worked up—what's wrong?"

Mash's face immediately goes right back to pure panic. "Dang it! I got distracted again! Sweetpea!"

"Spit it out!"

"The dogs in the village! They're gonna fight each other!" And then there's just a giant slew of communication issued so fast that I barely have time to make sense of it: "I was trying to hunt rabbits, and then I heard dogs barking, and when I got there, the True Dogs had torn Gizmo up real bad, and Gracie was there, and she was super pissed about it, and she said she was going to go get all the Collective together and they were going to go get the deer that the True Dogs stole from them—oh, yeah, there was a deer, and they fought over the deer, and the True Dogs dragged it away after they almost killed Gizmo—and, ohhhhhhhh! Sweetpea! What are we gonna do?!"

"God, dog! Take a breath!"

Mash looks on the verge of passing out, but saves himself with a giant inhale. And then promptly begins freaking out again: "We gotta do something! What are we gonna do? Don't you have a plan for this, Sweetpea? Please tell me we have a plan!"

"Dammit," I say, the bird forgotten at my paws. "I knew this was going to happen. I saw it, Mash. The peoples showed it to me."

"So you've come up with a plan, right?"

"Well...no."

Mash looks rigid. Breath caught in his throat. "Ah...ah..."

I just need to keep him from falling out. Fiona's lunch will have to wait for later. "Well don't just stand there, you idiot!" I snap at him, taking off at a run. "We'll make up a plan on the way!"

・・・・・・・・・・

Plan. Right. A plan. I need to come up with a plan.

God, running sucks.

The heaving breath has already dried my throat to a leathery tube. My depleted muscles are screaming at me to stop and rest, but I can't. My irritation has given way to a deep, undeniable dread.

Please, don't let the dogs be killing each other. Please, just give me a chance to at least TRY to talk some sense into them. Please, don't let this be how everything falls apart.

Please, don't let us go down the road that the peoples went down, because I know how long it took them to crawl their way out of that.

I don't know who I'm begging, but I sure hope they're listening.

Oh, right! A plan.

Shit. A plan.

Isolate and manipulate. Yes. Classic cat stratagem. If I can get Gracie alone, I can talk reason to her. Maybe. And if I can get Banger to forget about her fucking dog-cult for ten seconds and remember that we're packmates, then maybe I can cool her off.

But only if I can get them separated from their packs. I know how this social animal shit works. We cats aren't the poster children for social animals, but we know a thing or two, and being around dogs nonstop has really helped me hone in on how their brains work. It's not too different from how the peoples' brains worked, actually.

If their friends are there, then they'll feel compelled to stand by whatever ridiculous shit they spouted to their friends, so as not to lose face. But if I can get them by themselves, then it'll just be my words, and the truth, and their own conscience. And that's the only chance that I have to get this to stop.

"Mash!" I gasp out, mid-sprint.

"Yeah?"

"Who do you think will listen to you—Banger or Gracie?"

"They both hate me!"

"They both hate me too!"

"Banger might hate me less than Gracie!"

"Alright, you find Banger and try to get her away from the True Dogs! I'm going to find Gracie and do the same!"

Up ahead, daylight twinkles through the trees, and I know that we're reaching the edge of the woods, beyond which we will see the village.

I may just have a chance to stop this from turning into that vision. First off, its daylight, and the vision happened at night. Secondly, I don't smell any smoke, and in the vision, the houses were all burning. So maybe, just maybe, things aren't as bad as they were in the vision...

Mash and I burst through the tree line, and immediately come skidding to a horrified stop.

This is my nightmare. What lies before me is my vision made manifest. It's happening in broad daylight, and there's no fires burning, but the carnage is just as bad, and just as soul-rending.

The second that I'm not drenched in the sounds of my own running through the woods, I'm inundated with the hellish noises coming from the village. It is the sound of primal instincts—kill, or be killed—tearing out of dozens of canine throats, all at once. Yips and yowls of pain are the only sounds that punctuate the nonstop cacophony of snarling and barking and snapping.

Dogs are running amok everywhere within the Village. The barrier of The Wall has been entirely dismissed—True Dogs are vaulting over it to attack the Collective on their side, and dogs from the Collective are doing the same. Other Collective dogs have set upon the barrier, tearing the sticks and branches out of it with wild abandon.

Swirls of furry bodies create tiny tornadoes all throughout both sides of the village. Flashes of tensed haunches and white teeth. Ripping and tearing at each other. Whirling dervishes of instinctive rage.

"We're too late!" Mash groans.

"The fuck we are," I growl at him. "The plan hasn't changed! Go find Banger and get her the hell out of there!"

I don't wait for him to respond. I tear off down the slight slope towards the village, weaving in and out of the tall weeds and racing through the trails that have been scraped through the overgrown lawns by thousands of passing paws.

I need to find a vantage point from which I can spot Gracie in all the tumult. The weeds are too high for me to even see the dogs anymore, but I'm terrified of running out in the street in the middle of them—at this moment right now, I don't trust any of the dogs from either side, whether they've been coming to listen to me or not. Their brains have completely left them, and all they are is sacks of instinct with claws and teeth and big old chips on their shoulders that they might just decide to take out on me.

Two houses loom up in front of me, and I'm angling for the space between. The furious sounds of the massive dog fight blast through the weeds and surround me, getting thicker with every stride I take towards their melee.

Then I spot it, on the side of the house to my left: The very top of an air-conditioner unit. It's ringed in tall weeds, but just above that is a window, and on that window there is a flower box filled with the dried remnants of long-forgotten plants.

I bound towards the air-conditioning unit and make the double leap from air conditioner to flower box like a fucking champ, despite my weakened state. It's like the Prime Directive is driving me, but not for my own preservation. Somehow, my instincts have been switched over to include these stupid mutts as something worth saving.

The flower box shifts treacherously beneath me and I hear things popping that shouldn't be popping. Shit! I thought I was starved to feather-weight!

Delicately balancing on my perch, and trying desperately not to make anything else pop, I crane my head out as far as I can. I have a good view of the street, except...no dogs. I can hear them, but they must be further down the street, and the house is blocking my view.

Dammit, dammit, dammit...

I'm just about to bound down from the flower box when I spot something else, coming down the street towards the fight: Hiro, along with five of his packmates.

Coming to join in the fight? Or coming to try to break it up?

I have an idea, but it pretty much hinges on Hiro not turning psychotic on me in the next minute or so. I'm putting a lot of faith in my impression of him as a very zen dog that PROBABLY doesn't want to kill anything today.

"Hiro!" I scream at the top of my lungs.

He's still a good ways off, but he stops when he hears me and scans around, his ears pricked up. He spots me on the flower box, and I yell at him again. I see his eyes get focused. And I take a gamble that what he's seeing isn't something he wants to rip apart. I'm pretty sure I see some kindness there, or at least that's what I'm telling myself I saw.

From fifty fucking strides off. God, I hope my binocular vision is as good as I think it is.

You know, it's not always curiosity that kills the cat. Sometimes it's misplaced hope.

I'm down in the weeds again before I can think better of it, and I'm running in the direction of Hiro and his dogs, and either I'm going to burst out of these weeds and find a friend, or that Prime Directive is just gonna have to switch right on back to focusing on old Numero Uno.

Somehow, I'm still surprised when I crash out of the overgrown lawn and find Hiro and his dogs right there on the sidewalk, waiting for me. A burst of panic screams at me that this looks a helluva lot like an ambush, and my tail fluffs up and my claws come out, but I manage to keep myself from bolting.

"Hiro!" I gasp, cringing, clinging to that little hope like a kitten holding onto curtains by a single claw.

Relief floods me when I see genuine concern in Hiro's eyes.

Fuck yeah, binocular vision!

"Sweetpea! What on earth is going on around here?"

I suck wind for two big lungfuls, then stammer out, "Way too complicated to explain right now! I need you to help me find Gracie!"

Hiro lifts his noble head, looking like a movie poster for some epic hero dog. "Not a problem at all! I can see her now—oh, holy crap. She's tearing that little dog apart! Gracie! Stop that!"

"Hiro, I have to get Gracie alone and talk to her!" I plead. "And I need you and your dogs to keep me from being mauled on the way!"

"Right!" Hiro says, his voice taking on the timbre of The Pack Leader Of The Fucking World. He spins to his dogs. "Protect The Pup! You know the drill! Form up!"

In a few breathless seconds, I'm fully surrounded by a wall of dog bodies.

"Wait, you've practiced this before?"

Hiro gives me a roguish wag of his tail. "A dog of peace must always be prepared to defend his loved ones from other, less-evolved animals." He lifts his stern countenance to the others. "Pack! Forward at a canter!"

As one, the circle of dogs begins to move forward at an easy, loping stride, with me scrambling along in the center of them.

"Angle towards Gracie!" Hiro commands.

And all of the sudden we're in the thick of it. One, strangely calm little bubble in the midst of chaos. Beyond the evenly-paced legs of Hiro's pack, I can see dogs spinning and crashing into each other and yanking each other down and going for the jugular. They're not just fighting to prove a point, or to get the other side to back off. They're fighting the worst kind of dog fight. They're fighting to the death.

And yet, weirdly, none of them seem to even notice Hiro's pack. They just flow heedlessly around him, as the circle of dogs plows ever onward.

"Gracie!" Hiro belts out, with a tone that sounds shockingly like Dad's Voice of Thunder.

Just in front of us, between the two lead dogs' flanks, I see Gracie whirl about with a bit of Q's white fluff still stuck to her jaw, and she freezes at the sound of her name being shouted with such remonstration.

"Hiro?" she gawks, absently tonguing the fluff away. Her eyes flash with something like guilt, like she's been caught chewing the Special Poofs. Except she really should feel worse about chewing poor Q—who, by the way, has managed to get to her feet and take off like a rocket, yipping the whole way, so I guess she's not dead.

Rather than respond to Gracie, Hiro hollers at his dogs: "Pack! Encircle! Go!"

And just like that, the two lead dogs split, and kind of absorb Gracie into their circle.

"What's going on here?" Gracie rages, apparently completely missing my presence.

"Pack! About face and exfiltrate!"

All the dogs spin so that Hiro is now in the lead, and they take off again at the same pace, me and Gracie forced to roll with them. Well—she's forced, but I'm all too willing to get the hell out of there.

"Hiro! Stop this right now!" Gracie snarls at him.

Hiro cocks his head at her. "What in the world do you think you're doing, Gracie?"

"The True Dogs! They attacked Gizmo and stole our deer!"

"And your answer to this is to cause more hurt and destruction?"

"Don't you judge me! You have no idea what it's like to live with these religious zealots!"

"I'm bitterly disappointed by this!"

"Would you have rather me let my pack starve?!"

"I would have rather you came to me for help! We've got plenty of hunting land! Instead, you choose to fight other dogs?"

"I'm not just going to let them dominate me! I'm not just going to roll over and show my belly!"

We're clear of the fight now, and Hiro's pack pulls to a sudden stop by some unspoken command—or, hell, maybe Hiro's telepathic. I wouldn't put anything past him at this point.

With the circle of dogs stationary, and now free of the carnage, Hiro's pack faces outwards in a protective perimeter, while Hiro whirls on Gracie.

"Take your pride out of it, Gracie!" Hiro says, his voice pleading, but firm. "Sometimes it's better to show your belly than to shed blood for your pride!"

"Didn't you always say that even Good Dogs have to know how to defend themselves? Isn't that why you hated those rules against play-fighting? BANGER'S rules against play-fighting?"

"That," Hiro says, pointing to the fight with his muzzle. "Is not defense, Gracie. That is aggression, plain as the daylight I stand in."

"Hiro," Gracie snarls, her feet spreading into a low, aggressive stance, her teeth showing behind pulled-back lips. "You get the heck out of my village, or there's going to be bloodshed right here."

Hiro's ears pull back a bit, but he doesn't rise to her aggression. "You will not listen to reason then?"

In response, Gracie only peels her lips back further and growls deep in her chest.

Hiro's head briefly sags under the weight of disappointment. But then he straightens again. "Pack, we're going home." He backs away from Gracie, unwilling to show his tail to her, and I don't blame him. "This is no place for us anymore. These are..." he looks pained as he says it. "Wild dogs."

And then he turns, and he and his dogs trot off, never even looking back.

That's about the time that I realize I'm now alone with a panting, growling, teeth-bared Gracie, who is not at all in what I would call a headspace amenable to diplomacy.

"Soooooo, Gracie," I say, trying hard to sound friendly. Anything short of friendly is liable to get me killed. The Prime Directive is entirely confused as fuck now. Split completely in half. Pulling me in two directions—self-preservation, or dog-preservation? I can't believe that's even a question in my mind. "How are things?"

She snaps around to face me. "You!"

I glance for an avenue of escape, but I'm completely exposed right now. Hiro's pack deposited us in the middle of the damn street, and I'm at least ten strides from the cover of the nearest overgrown lawn. And Gracie is fast. About as fast as Mash.

"I've heard about what you've been doing," she menaces, edging closer to me.

I back up a step. "Now, hang on a minute, Gracie, I'm just here to talk."

"Talk, talk, talk. You're the Voice in the Wilderness, yeah? That's all you do is talk. Filling my pack's heads with nonsense about the peoples and what they want."

"But it's true, Gracie! I swear, it's true! I wouldn't make this shit up. What on earth would I get out of it?"

"An inflated sense of self-importance?"

"Okay. That's fair. It's a personality weakness of mine, but I've been working on that. And we all have personality quirks, don't we? I mean, you, for instance, can get so mad that you might hurt a cat that's just trying to talk to you, and I think you'd feel bad about that in the future, don't you? Like, looking back on it, you'd be all, 'Aw, poor Sweetpea, I really shouldn't have snapped his neck. He was a good cat and he only wanted what was best for the dogs.'"

"What's best for the dogs?" she snaps. "What's best...FOR THE DOGS? I'll tell you what's best for the dogs—freedom! We don't need the collar of the peoples strapped around our necks anymore! We don't need their rules! We don't need their laws! We don't need them to take care of us! We don't need their LOVE!"

"And yet, they love you anyways."

Shit. It just kind of came out. I had not intended to say anything challenging. But it comes out of me like a hairball anyways—words that seem to have been placed in my throat, and I can't swallow them back, I have to spit them out, no matter the consequences.

I'm pretty fucking smart, so I piece it together quickly: It's not me that's talking. Those aren't my words. It's like Dad is with me right now, putting the words in my chest, and all I have to do is speak them.

I don't know if that's comforting or extra-terrifying.

I stop backing up. I stare right into Gracie's menacing face.

"Your peoples loved you, and they still love you, and there's nothing you can do to change that."

"You don't know when to shut up, do you? You're just so used to running your mouth and getting away with it."

Boy, this isn't going great. I really thought some peoples-inspired words would do the trick. I always thought that when I spoke with the voice of the peoples, the dogs would just shut the hell up and fall in line. But these words are falling amazingly flat.

Frankly, I feel a little betrayed.

"Dad," I hiss under my breath. "You're kinda hanging me out to dry here!"

The response I get is more words tumbling out of my mouth, against my will:

"Gracie, the peoples are appalled by this violence. Dogs fighting dogs? You don't need a set of rules to know that's wrong! You can feel it in your bones right now!" Wow, Dad. Are we really doing this right now? "And yet, they still love you, Gracie. Even this fight isn't enough to stop them from loving you. Just end it. It's not helpful for you, or them, or anyone."

Gracie takes a step back from me like I've given her a shock to the nose. She looks stricken. The words have found their mark.

Yes! I've got her. All I've gotta do is deliver the final blow. What do I say, Dad? Tell me what to...

It's like I've been passed from Dad's hands into someone else's. It's an unfamiliar presence, and yet it's familiar all the same, because it is a peoples. Two peoples. It is Gracie's peoples, speaking through me. And they want me to say...

"Seriously?" I mutter. "THAT'S what I'm supposed to say?"

Gracie's eyes narrow at me. "Are you...?" she trails off.

Shit, I'm losing her.

I sigh and gather myself for the indignity of it. "Alright. Fine." I peer at Gracie, half-cringing, and, with a weird, sing-songy voice, I utter these words: "Gracie, Gracie, bo-bacy, banana-fana fo-facy, me my mo-macy, Gracie!"

Gracie's eyes go wide. Her ears flatten back. Something in her spine seems to melt a bit, the aggression coming out of her posture in one swooping breath. "My...my peoples use to sing that to me."

"Yeah, well—"

And that's when a whirlwind of snarling, barking, clawing, biting dogs slams into me.

The last thing I see before I'm buried in fur and teeth and pain is Gracie, screaming my name.

29

Mash

Speed is my only friend, because it's obvious I don't have any friends around here.

I bound across the tattered border of The Wall, and find myself in the thick of it on the True Dog's side. I see dogs that have been out to listen to Sweetpea nearly every day, and when they see me there is no love of a pack member in their eyes. They've lost their dogness. They've become something terrible that dogs were never meant to be.

They see me running through their midst, and it's like their hatred lunges out and absorbs me into it, for reasons that I can't even begin to figure out. I dance away from their snapping jaws, horrified that they would want to hurt me, and thankful that I'm so quick on my feet.

"Banger!" I shout, hurtling through the midst of all that chaos, dodging scrums of dogs from both sides that seem bent on no purpose whatsoever outside of causing pain to others. "Banger!"

It's no use. In all the running and jumping and juking, I don't have a single second to raise my head above the swirling fight and try to get my eyes on Banger. I can't trust her to respond to my shouts, and chances are, she can't hear me anyways—it's too loud, and she's half deaf as it is.

I need to get free of the fighting so I can take a second to spot her.

I'm close to The Wall, and I glance at it, hoping that if I jump on top of it, I'll have a good view of the dogs below, but I see other dogs jumping on top of it, and every time they do, another dog comes flying out of nowhere and tackles them off, like the most mean-spirited game of King of the Hill I've ever seen.

My attention careens around just in time for me to pull my face back from a pair of snapping jaws that I swear pluck one of my whiskers out.

"Holy crap!" I exclaim, jumping back, and realize that I'm face to face with Boozer. "What the heck's wrong with you, Boozer? It's me! It's Mash!"

Boozer's eyes flicker with recognition, but his teeth stay bared and his hackles are still up. He seems to struggle with something inside of himself, and his voice comes out strained, like he's being choked. "I'm sorry, Mash! I have to defend my pack!"

"I'm not attacking your pack!" I plead with him. "I swear, I'm just looking for—"

"If you're not with us, you're against us!"

The statement is so incredibly stupid that, for a moment, I think maybe I'M incredibly stupid for not getting it, but then realize, no, it's actually just a super dumb thing to say. I quirk my head. "Boozer, that makes no sense at all. Just because I don't agree, doesn't mean I'm against—"

He launches himself at me, and I leap back, but my hind-end hits The Wall and my paws go squirrelling out from under me.

Boozer's jaws are shooting towards my neck, and there's nothing I can do about it—no way that I can wriggle my body out of the way in time.

But just before he slams his fangs into my throat, something hurtles out of nowhere and crashes into Boozer's side.

I scramble to my feet, and I'm about to take off running and not waste the time to see who saved me, but just as I'm gearing up to sprint, I hear a familiar voice, shouted with complete desperation and panic: "Mash!"

I whirl and find that it's Gracie, extricating herself from a dazed Boozer. She jumps away from him, but he looks like his paw has got twisted and he doesn't go after her.

Wait. Gracie saved me?

Did Sweetpea convince her?

"Mash!" she shouts again, bounding up to me, and not stopping. She shoulders me hard to get me moving, and hollers, "It's Sweetpea! He's been hurt—bad!"

All of the sudden, I'm running with Gracie. She angles for The Wall, and being cross-bred with the very nimble poodle, she vaults over it, not even touching the top. I have no clue what I'm cross-bred with, but whatever it is, it's just as good at hurdling The Wall as a poodle, and I clear it in a single bound.

Gracie lands gracefully, like a deer.

Me, not so much. I crash into her on the other side and gasp breathlessly as I come to my feet again, any pain I might have felt completely washed out by sudden fear, as what she said finally makes it into my brain. "Who hurt Sweetpea? Did YOU hurt him?"

"No!" Gracie cries, taking off running again.

I realize that if Gracie is talking to me, Sweetpea must have convinced her to chill out, but if that's the case, why the heck is everyone still fighting?

"Gracie! Tell the Collective to stop fighting!"

"I can't!" she wails. "They're not listening to me anymore! I tried to stop the dogs that attacked Sweetpea, but they just wouldn't listen! I had to fight them off of him—my own packmates!"

"Oh, no! Oh, no!" I pant, as, just ahead, I can see a tawny shape lying in the middle of the street.

Just before I reach him, I realize that I've become distracted again. I was supposed to find Banger! That was Sweetpea's plan! Oh, he's going to be so pissed if he realizes I forgot what I was supposed to be doing...

I scrape to a stop, just shy of Sweetpea, my chest already bucking and issuing whimpering noises with all the worry that's flooding me for my friend. But I can't go to him just yet—not when I haven't done what I was supposed to do.

"Gracie," I pant, and it comes out with a whine of fear. "You have to find Banger!"

Gracie looks like I've just asked her to stick her head in a beehive.

And that, for some reason, makes me pretty mad. My face gets all scrunched and serious, no longer begging, but TELLING. "Gracie!" I bark at her. "You have to find Banger and put an end to this! That's the only reason Sweetpea came here in the first place! And now look at him! He did that for YOU! Now go do something for him and end this!"

Gracie's ears pull back and her head lowers, but she nods. "I'll go."

I don't wait to see, but I hear her go bounding off as I turn to my wounded friend. His tan fur is matted with dog slobber and blood. A vicious bite mark his neck and shoulders, and his right paw is mangled and hanging at a weird angle. Half of his tail has had all the fur ripped out of it, and his pink skin beneath is flushed and raw. "Oh, Sweetpea! Are you alive? Come on, buddy! Talk to me!"

His hairless little tail does a flop, and a shiver works its way through him.

"That's it, buddy! It's me! It's your old friend, Mash!"

Sweetpea raises his head, straining with the effort. "Oh, hey there, Mash," he says, his voice thin and dreamy, and somehow still filled with that wry amusement of his, like this has all turned out to be quite a joke. "I, uh...I got sucked into a dog-nado."

"You're gonna be okay," I pant, half trying to convince myself, even as I refuse to look at his wounds again for fear that they will tell me that I'm lying.

But Sweetpea knows. He lets out a breathy gasp that I think was supposed to be a laugh. "I doubt that. I can't even move my back legs. Ah, hell, look what they did to me, Mash."

"I don't wanna look at it."

"Ugh. My beautiful body never even had a chance to come back to its full physique. A tragedy for the world." He grumbles something I can't hear and his head sinks back. "Didn't think it was gonna go this way."

"Tell me what I can do to help you," I whimper. "Can I lick it? Do you need me to lick it?"

Sweetpea rasps out another dry chortle. "No. I...uh...don't think I could stand the indignity in my weakened state." He turns his head, but it looks like he can't quite do it all the way, like something in his neck has been cranked around and he can't get past it. He looks at me sidelong. "Hey, do you remember what Dad told you that day? The day that the peoples disappeared?"

"Yes," I say, some strange mix of feelings making my chest and throat all tight, like they're trying to pull away from each other. "He said to remember that I was loved. And he said to remember to love others."

"Hey," Sweetpea says with something like a feline smile. "That's pretty good remembering for a doofy dog."

I hang my head. "But sometimes I forgot, Sweetpea. He told me to remember that I was loved, but sometimes it was really hard to feel that. And sometimes other dogs really pissed me off. And it was even harder to remember THAT part."

"Oh, don't wilt like a guilty pup, Mash. You're forgetting it right now."

I quirk my head to him. "I am?"

"Why wallow in guilt?" Sweetpea says. "Note how you fucked up and move on. But all of you dogs just keep mentally punishing yourselves because you didn't remember the most important part of what Dad said."

"What'd I forget?" I say, and honestly, feel even guiltier...which then makes me feel even guiltier for not remembering to not feel guilty. Dang, this is hard.

Sweetpea's eyes flutter closed, and he sighs, softly. "I swear. The cat has to do all the remembering around here." With obvious effort, he forces his eyes open again. "But I suppose I wouldn't be a very good friend if I didn't tell you the one, most important thing."

A whimper shudders in my throat, and my tail gives a low wag. "So...so..."

"Yes, yes. We're friends. It's official. You may rejoice."

I sit down beside him, my tail lightly batting the concrete, as my jowls hang loose on my face, staring down at him. "Okay, friend. Tell me."

"Wow. You're really doofy when you're tragically happy-sad."

"I don't know what that means, but I know I'm doofy. It's my face."

"Listen," Sweetpea says, his voice suddenly much weaker. "Whoo, boy. It's coming on strong now. Shit-fuck. Alright, are you paying attention?"

I close my eyes because I can't bear to look at him. "I'm paying attention."

His voice is soft, like a breeze in the trees. "Dad said to remember that you were loved—NO MATTER WHAT. And to remember to love others—NO MATTER WHAT. That's the part that everyone forgot. Even you, Mash. That means you can't do anything to earn it. And you can't do anything to have it taken away. It just...is."

What does an epiphany feel like?

It feels like finding that toy you'd lost, half-buried in the lawn. It feels like running full tilt down a hill, with the sun in your face and the wind in your ears, and not knowing how in the heck you're making your body do this wonderful thing, you just...are.

It just...is.

I lurch to all fours again. "Sweetpea, just hang on for a little longer. I just had an epiphany. And if a doofy dog like me can have an epiphany, then so can Banger. Gracie's going to find her. And then you're going to tell her what you just told me. And then they're going to stop all this fighting. Can you do that for me, friend? Can you hang on?"

"I feel like you're...taking advantage of my friendship. But fine. You only have...a little while longer...to luxuriate in my presence. I can wait."

30

Banger

Brute and I have been guarding the deer carcass, but no one is trying to take it from us. There was a brief, desperate attempt by a trio of dogs at the very outset, but they were too small to drag it, and once Brute and I started after them, they broke off. Since then, everything has devolved into chaos.

The Collective doesn't seem to even remember that this was about the deer carcass to begin with, and set themselves to tearing apart The Wall instead, but it seems even that has been forgotten in favor of simply fighting each other.

I don't think anyone remembers what this was about.

I don't know if I remember either.

"Screw this," Brute growls. "We've got them pushed back to The Wall. I say we take it over to their side and finish it. Rout them out of the village and chase them over to Hiro's. The lawless idiots deserve each other."

Right. Yes. Because that's what this was really about, right? Those lawless, people-hating dogs on the other side of The Wall, polluting our village, and destroying our chances to be Perfect Dogs.

Because, just the fact that they're in the village with us, makes us a part of each other. Even though we think of ourselves as separate packs, maybe the peoples still see us as one pack. One pack, divided against itself. Maybe the only way for the whole pack to be Perfect is to purge it of every dog not willing to follow the law.

It makes perfect sense.

So why am I still standing here?

This is our moment to make a clean sweep of things.

And yet, instead of the uplifting thrill of winning, I feel something heavy deadening my chest. Pulling me down.

"Banger, you hear me?" Brute asks.

"Yeah, I hear you," I answer, not liking how lost my voice sounds. I'm the leader of the True Dogs. I should be more confident in myself. I should be surer of my cause. I should have more faith in the law.

Oh, why does everything feel so rickety?

"Soooo..." Brute presses.

I begin moving forward, which takes a shocking amount of effort. "So let's go."

Brute flashes his teeth and lowers his head, and charges into the fray without hesitation. I don't. I hang back, still moving into it, still moving through it, but where Brute immediately finds a scuffle to throw himself into, I only see pathetic dogs yipping and snapping. Those few of the Collective still on our side of the wall are small, and desperate, and looking for a way out.

I almost want to give it to them.

Something in me just wants to leave this whole thing behind me and wander back to my old house and curl up in the corner of the Cloud Throne. I wish I could go back to when none of this was a thing, and there was no Collective, and no True Dogs, and it was just me, and Mash, and Sweetpea, lying on the Cloud Throne together.

Of course I'd love Dad to be there. But that just seems so far away and impossible.

But isn't it ALL impossible? I ran Sweetpea and Mash off, didn't I? I hedged my bets on the law, and the True Dogs. I hedged my bets on my love of the peoples.

I should be right. I should FEEL right.

But I don't. I feel wrong.

I feel...Bad.

I'm nearly to The Wall when a flash of brown fur comes flying over it and lands right in front of me. I'm so surprised that I pull up short and even back up a single step, alarm causing all my concerns to disappear under a wash of fear and aggression.

"Banger!" the dog barks at me.

My lips are pulled back, a growl working its way up from my chest, and I realize that the dog in front of me is not attacking, or even holding their body in an attack position, and only after that do I realize who it is.

"Gracie!" the growl comes out of me, low and hateful. "You backstabbing, scheming, food-stealer!"

Gracie draws her head back. "You're calling ME a food-stealer?!"

I advance a step, my legs rigid, hackles risen, tail stiff and level. I notice that some of the dogs around us—both Collective and True Dogs—have stopped fighting to watch. "That's what this is about, isn't it?" I hurl at Gracie. "The Collective can't hunt for themselves, so they steal from the True Dogs?"

Gracie bristles, her face indignant. "We killed that deer fair and square! It was OUR deer! YOUR dogs are the ones that stole OUR kill!"

"That's not how I heard it from Brute."

"Brute was the one that nearly killed Gizmo!"

"Gizmo shouldn't have tried to steal our kill!"

"Are you not listening?" Gracie yowls, so frustrated she sounds like a cat. And maybe that weird noise she just heard herself make rattles something loose in her brain, because all at once, her eyes completely lose any aggression they had.

"You getting scared, Gracie?" I ask, moving forward again.

The dogs all around us press in, closing ranks, intensely focused on me and Gracie.

"No, it's not..." Gracie glances about and seems to see that she's entirely surrounded—but not just by the True Dogs. Her own Collective is there a well, watching her, panting, waiting to see what she does. Waiting to see if their leader is as tough as she acts.

But she's just a house dog. She hasn't been where I've been. She hasn't learned the hard lessons that I have. She's never had to fight other dogs just to survive. She was never in the Place of Judgment. She doesn't know what I'm capable of. She doesn't know the hate in my heart that I can unleash at a moment's notice.

Gracie looks me dead in the face. "Banger, it's Sweetpea. He's been badly hurt. I don't think he's going to make it. He wants to talk to you."

Something freezes inside of me. A sudden, icy dread, gripping my heart.

But it's like my heart is on fire, and immediately thaws it. I laugh right in Gracie's face, and bite it off with a snarl. "Sweetpea's out in the woods, Gracie. Everyone knows he and Mash were banished from the village. Stop trying to stall, and let's solve this problem right here and now, just you and me."

"Tear her up!" one of the Collective barks out from behind Gracie.

Gracie shakes her head as though to clear it. "Banger, I'm serious! Sweetpea came back! He got caught up in the fighting and—"

"Lies!" I realize that it's Brute, who's just off to my side, one of the many dogs forming the circle around me and Gracie. "Don't listen to her lies, Banger!"

"You're the liar, Brute!" Gracie yammers back. "You know that was our kill! You know you stole it from us!"

"Enough of that!" I snap, my teeth clacking in the air in front of Gracie's muzzle. "It's just you and me now, Gracie. Let's finish this. Just the two of us. Whoever wins, their pack gets the village."

"Banger, I'm serious!" Gracie bawls at me. "Sweetpea's about to die and—"

I launch myself at her.

But just as I'm about to slam my jaws into her neck, I see a little white shape come hurtling to the top of The Wall, screaming breathlessly, "Wait! Waaaaiiiiit!"

I don't know why I stop, but I do. Maybe I've been looking for an excuse to stop this entire time.

I look up at the shape, and recognize Q, one of my most loyal True Dogs. Her fur is standing out at all angles, matted down with blood from a dozen bite marks, and missing in torn-out patches. Her legs are trembling and she barely looks able to stand there—I have no idea how she had the strength to jump up onto The Wall.

"What do you want, Q?" I bark at her, though I'm filled with a confusing mix of relief and frustration. Relief, because there is a part of me that doesn't want to fight anymore. Frustration, because I feel that it is inevitable.

But Q doesn't answer me. She just hobbles out of the way and looks down at something on the other side of The Wall. I hear a grunt of effort, and the shifting of loose sticks, and then a familiar shape crests the wall.

It's Mash.

Something in my heart lets out a tiny little ray of joy that makes my tail wag.

Just once. Because then I see what Mash has, gently held in his mouth.

A furry, tan shape, all speckled and splashed with blood.

"Oh no," I whisper, all the fight, and all the aggression, and all the hatred, just draining out of me, like someone's opened a hole in my paw and let it all flow out.

The circle of dogs around me and Gracie has stilled. A silence has fallen over the entire village. The sounds of fighting and snarling and yipping and yowling are all gone now. Even the panting has quieted.

Someone whispers, "Is that His Masterfulness?"

Another answers, just as quietly: "It's the Voice in the Wilderness."

Mash slowly and carefully picks his way down from The Wall, cradling Sweetpea's limp form in his mouth with all the gentle care of a mother carrying her pup. His head hangs as he reaches the bottom and approaches me, his eyes locked on mine, filled not with accusation, but only with sorrow. I can hear the thin whine escaping him with each of his breaths.

"Oh no," I whisper again, as Mash tenderly lays the body on the ground in front of me.

For a moment, as Mash removes his mouth from Sweetpea's body, I think that I see the cat stir, and something leaps inside of me—he's not dead! But then the body is still, and does not move again, and I realize that it was only the shifting of the body as Mash pulled his jaws from it.

He's dead. He's actually...dead.

It doesn't seem possible. Sweetpea? He was practically invincible. And so smart. How could he have been dumb enough to let himself get caught up in all of this?

I realize I'm whimpering right along with Mash. "Why'd he do this? Why'd he come here? Why'd he have to be so STUPID?"

"It wasn't stupid," Mash says, softly, looking down at the body. "He knew that he might get hurt. And he came anyways."

"Why?" I groan, as I hang my head over Sweetpea, absently snuffling his fur and finding it devoid of the scent of life. Only a thing now. An empty shell.

"Because he loved you," Mash says. And then he turns to Gracie. "And you." He looks at all of the dogs around us. "He just...loved all of you. Of course, he wouldn't ever admit that. But he came here to try to help you, knowing that you might kill him. And I don't know what else to call that but love."

"Who hurt him?" A voice demands.

With weary, sorrowful eyes, I lift my attention and see Boozer standing there, slightly forward of the circle, glaring around at the other dogs.

"Who did this to the Voice in the Wilderness?" Boozer growls, menacingly.

"Why does it matter?" Mash suddenly cries. "So you can fight them, too? So you can hurt them for hurting Sweetpea? And what does that solve, Boozer? Sweetpea came here to try to get you dogs to STOP fighting each other."

Mash spins in a circle, meeting gaze after gaze, which fall away from his in shame. "Stop," he says, his voice full of a command that I've never heard in him before. "Everyone stop. Please. Just...stop."

With all eyes lowered, and no one else to look at, Mash returns to Sweetpea's body and looks at it instead. "This isn't His Masterfulness. This isn't the Voice in the Wilderness. This isn't any of the things we tried to make him into. This is Sweetpea. He was a Good Cat. And he was my packmate."

Mash sits on his rump with a tired huff. "There was a time when I looked at my pack—Banger, and Sweetpea, and our peoples, Dad. And I remember thinking that nothing could come between us. But then something did come between us." He raises his mournful head and looks around him. "Fear came between us.

Fear that we were alone in the world since the peoples left. Fear that we would never see them again. Fear that they had left because we were Bad Dogs." And then his gaze lands on me. "Fear that the peoples' love for us had terms and conditions that we had to meet." And then he looks at Gracie. "Fear that the peoples' love for us was tainted and selfish."

Mash shakes his head from side to side. "But none of that was real. None of that was true. All of our fears were made up. We were never alone in the world. The peoples have been right here with us the whole time. Sweetpea could talk to them, and he would tell us how they were watching over us, and how they didn't leave because we were Bad Dogs, and how they have always loved us just for being us. Just for being dogs. And there's nothing we can do to have that love taken away from us."

Mash looks at the ground in front of him. "If we'd just have remembered it, ALL of it, we would have never believed that they abandoned us because we were Bad. We would have never seen this as some sort of punishment. And that...that would have changed EVERYTHING." He raised his eyes to the dogs around him. His pack. Our pack. THE pack. "And it still could."

31

Sweetpea

I HATE TO SOUND trite, but I'm watching this all go down from a position somewhere in the air above my mangled body. It's a very surreal experience, to see the thing that I considered to be ME, no longer me at all. Like a snake that's just sloughed off its skin.

I still feel like me, but I don't feel my body at all. I don't have legs, or a tail. I'm surprised to find that I don't feel hampered by this at all. I feel like I can finally move for the first time in my existence.

But I don't move. I stay right where I am, staring down at my old, dead self, and at the dogs surrounding me. I see the pain and anguish in them, and, I'll be honest...It's very flattering.

"Hey, assholes," I call to them. "What are you doing staring at that thing? I'm up here!"

None of them seem to respond.

"Uh. Guys?" I call to them, trying to be louder: "Hey! Banger! Mash! My old packmates! I'm fine! That's just a bit of dead fluff! It never really was me to begin with. I'm me, and I'm up here!"

Still, I see not a twitch of an ear, nor the glance of an eye.

And then I hear that voice again, that voice that called to me so many times, that I'd thought I'd heard with my cat ears, but I now realize I'd heard with something that was never a part of my body. And I realize that my cat ears were the things that got in the damn way. Who'd've thought such finally tuned audible receptors would be the thing to INHIBIT communication?

"Sweetpea." The voice is stronger now than it was when I was in my body. Not sterner, or shouting or anything like that. It's actually quite a nice sound, very gentle, like the master is calling me for neck rubs. But it's clearer now. No mistaking it.

I think it's coming from my old house. I decide to move towards the sound of the voice, and when I decide it, I'm just speeding along, skimming above the overgrown lawns, houses flashing by my side until I reach the one that I used to stay in. The one that I used to call my crash pad. But that's not what it was. It was my home.

"Sweetpea," the voice comes again, from around the side of the house. Inviting. Joyous. Peaceful.

Laughing in spite of myself, I float over the grass and realize that it's not overgrown anymore. Someone must have finally fixed the mower bot. The back lawn is a perfect carpet of green, blazing in a cool sunlight that feels like the first day of spring. The trees are filled with flowers, and I realize that I can see things I never was able to see before—colors that I only knew as gradations of gray and yellow and blue, suddenly explode into existence.

Nothing is how I remember seeing it. Everything has taken on a new life, filled to the brim with a beauty and a potential that had always been there, but that I'd never been able to perceive.

I don't have paws to feel, and yet when I lower myself to the grass, I can feel its cool tickle. And I can feel the breeze, every swirl and eddy of it, caressing me in a way my hide had never been able to feel. And the smells! Oh, the smells of everything—the flowers, and the grass, and the dirt, and the animals in the dirt—they all smell amazing, and their smells are all the colors that I've never seen, all distinct, and yet flowing around each other.

I find myself at the foot of my old porch, but the wood is bright and brand new and it smells alive, like it's not made of planks taken from a tree at all, but that it IS a tree, growing out of the ground, and forming the shape of the porch.

I float up the stairs, feeling, smelling, even tasting the treads, even though no part of me is touching them.

At the top of the steps, there is Dad's Outside Throne, and upon it sits something that I know instantly is Dad, and yet it doesn't look like him at all. It doesn't look like anything, really. Or, better put, it looks like everything? Or everyone?

Oh my. For the first time I can ever recall, I'm finding words a bit of a struggle.

The thing I see is not frightening in any way, though it is strange and unfamiliar. But not unfamiliar in the way of Stranger Danger, or anything like that. Unfamiliar in the way of stumbling across that perfect, sunlit clearing you've never discovered before, right there in the middle of the woods. Unfamiliar, but wonderful, and welcoming.

"Hey, Sweetpea," Dad-that-is-more-than-Dad says, the voice warm and kind. There's no hand to pat at its lap, but I feel that same beckoning friendliness that I would feel when Dad would pat his lap, inviting me up. I want to purr, but I don't have the throat to do it anymore, so I don't make a sound, but I'm still purring...in spirit.

I glide up onto what I guess is the lap. It is the perfect temperature. The perfect softness. The perfect firmness. I feel instantly enveloped by it. Calm, and wonderful, and...home.

"Well," I sigh, contentedly. "It took long enough, but I found you again."

"You did," the presence confirms, with the distinct sense of a smile. "But this isn't where you stay."

"It's not?" I ask, curious, but untroubled.

"No. You have to go talk to the bush."

I peer out at the woods with all of its dazzling colors. "Which one?"

"Your Safe House. Remember that one?"

"Hey. How do you know about my Safe House?"

Something like a chuckle comes from Dad-Everyone-Thing. A chuckle that I can feel all across me like lightly dancing fingers. And I can smell it, and it reminds me of honey, and its color is a warm, golden yellow.

"I know all kinds of things. Not to worry. I won't tell anyone."

"Oh, okay." I guess I don't really care either way. The Safe House doesn't seem all that important to me anymore. However, the fact that I need to talk to it seems a bit odd. "Should I go now?"

"You can go whenever you want. It doesn't really matter."

"Well. This is very nice. And, really, I don't want to leave you..."

"But..."

"But I'm hella curious about that bush now."

"I figured you would be."

I turn. Or, at least, I put my attention back on Dad. "Will you be here when I get back?"

"Well, I'll always be here, yes."

A wry chuckle escapes me. "But?"

"But you might not come back my way."

"Ah. Well. I best get to it then."

"If you want."

I consider it for a while, bathing in the calm of the moment. Yes, I would like to stay here with Dad-Everyone-Thing. And I think I realize what he's telling me. But I'm not afraid. I don't think I'm capable of being afraid.

I am simply possessed of a surety of purpose, and I know that it leads to the bush, and so I must go.

"I think I do want to get to it," I finally decide. "But it was very good to see you again. I hope that it won't be long before...well, you know."

"I know."

A feeling like the best cat masseuse stroking the tension out of me cascades over every inch of my being. Not that there was much tension to stroke out of me.

I drift down off the warm, perfect lap, and float across the lawn in the direction of the woods, not entirely sure which bush used to be my Safe House, and finding myself somewhat amused that I obsessively needed to maintain such things—boy, was I a ball of anxiety and didn't even know it.

Turns out, finding the right bush isn't hard at all, because it's beaming with a golden light that I don't think is natural to any bush I'm familiar with. All the leaves and branches are just how I remember them, but the center of it is just light. And in that light, all things good exist, and nothing bad. And I am loved.

"I'm here to speak with you, bush," I declare.

The golden light pulses out and seems to take on the form of a mist, a mist made of light, and it seeks me out like warm fingers, and tangles itself pleasantly all through me and around me, and it smells like oranges and cinnamon and bright, bright sunshine on a field of freshly bloomed flowers.

I hear something like a voice, but it is so quiet and gentle that I only just make out the words. They're as faint as the first time I heard Dad speak, when there was still a veil of reality between us. Strange that I would hear Dad's voice so clearly in this place, but not the voice of the bush.

"Sweetpea," the light whispers to me. "I guess you can't hear me all that well, can you?"

I strain to hear with ears that aren't there. "Well, I can kinda make you out. Why can't I hear you as clear as I heard the Dad-Everyone-Thing?"

"There was a space between you and Dad before, and now that has been removed. But there is still a space between where you are now, and where I am."

"Oh, okay. I guess that makes sense. Kinda like, I started at the basement level, and now I'm on the ground floor, but I'm not on the second story yet."

"Yes. Something like that."

"Okay, I'm with you. I guess that means you'll have to speak to me in visions?"

"You're a delightfully quick study."

And without waiting for a response, I'm transported somewhere else.

Oh, I know where I am. I'm back looking over my dead body again.

"Okay, so my body is dead," I muse. "What next?"

Then I plummet into myself. Sorry—this is gonna be another words-are-hard part. It's like I zoom in, straight into the fur in my chest, and I become tiny, and I am the fur, and then I'm the hide that it grows out of, and then I'm all the little cells that make up the hide, and in each of those cells, there is an entire universe, and in that universe, there are worlds, and in those worlds, there are cats, and one of those cats is me, not the body-me, but the me-me, the REAL me, and it is alive, and seeking an expression. Seeking a way to make itself known. Seeking a way to become real and experience the universe again.

"I'm still in it," I realize. "I'm still a part of this."

And then I see life forces, like swirling galaxies of light, and they create a funnel in all their swirling, and at the end of the funnel, as they swirl and swirl and swirl, tighter and tighter and tighter, they close in on themselves, and they stop being a swirl, and they start being a circle, complete, and without end. And that's when they reach the end of the funnel and join into one big light that has been waiting for them. Endlessly, joyfully, expectantly waiting for them.

Each life force is not an individual, but an entire race—whole species of beings. And each of these collective life forces is driving the one ahead of them onwards through the funnel, towards their ultimate destiny. Sometimes these collisions are violent, but often they are just a gentle pressing, and no matter whether they are violent or gentle, they're all helping push, push, push all of those life forces through the funnel towards their completion.

And then I zoom in again, to one life force in particular, and I know that it is the life force to which I belong, and it is still swirling, not yet a complete circle. It hasn't reached the narrowest part of the funnel, and it's not even next in line. In front of it, there is another life force, and it is this life force that my life force is pressing against, pushing them onwards to their final stage in the funnel.

"I'm still inside the cycle," I realize. "My loop hasn't been closed yet."

Then I zoom in once again, straight into the life force that I belong to, flying into it until I see that the swirl of light is actually billions of individual lights, each an individual energy. Then I focus on one of those individual energies, and I feel that it is a her, because these energies have not had their life forces close the loop, so they are still polarized and opposite, and I also feel that I know her...

I get closer and closer to that singular energy, until I realize that it isn't one energy at all. It's one larger energy, with seven tiny, embryonic energies attached to it. Even as I watch, I see that each of these tiny energies is bursting with a fresh light—all but one. And that one, I realize, is where I'm heading.

"Oh shit!" I exclaim, as joy and awe and an inexplicable sense of velocity overtakes me. I can feel the light of the bush pushing me, catapulting me on. And just as I'm being thrust into that one, tiny, waiting ball of energy, I realize what's happening. "You're gonna reincarn—?"

32

BANGER

My body feels so heavy. My legs ache under the weight of it. Part of that is because they're tiny. But mostly it's because of the shame I feel. Every part of me is drooping. I feel like I'm melting, but not from heat. I'm melting from cold, if such a thing were possible.

My head is hanging so low that I don't realize that Mash is approaching until I see his paws right there at my nose.

"Why are you hanging your head in shame?" Mash asks me, gently.

"Because I forgot what Dad told me," I whimper. "I couldn't...I just couldn't remember to love other dogs. It was the one thing I just couldn't bring myself to do."

Mash nuzzles my face, and forces me to lift it with his own. I stand there, staring into his eyes, and I see the sorrow in them, but also a...joy. A freedom. A...dogness that's been missing from us. I didn't even realize that dogness was gone from us until I see it right here, right in front of me. And I know that it is something I've lost, because I see it here before me, and I know that I don't have it.

"You remember the time I chewed the Special Poofs?" Mash asks me.

"Uh…" I tilt my head, recalling that day. Watching from the Cloud Throne as Mash started chewing at the corner of one of the Special Poofs, almost like he didn't realize he was doing it. "I remember I kept telling you that you were going to be in trouble if you kept going."

Mash's tail wags lightly. "I kept saying I just needed to get one more bit of fluff out."

I laugh, despite myself. "You were in quite a state."

"And do you remember when Dad came home and I got in trouble?"

My shoulders wilt just at the memory of it. "I remember his Thunder Voice I remember you running and cowering, and I remember him pulling you by your collar back to the Special Poofs so he could point to them and say 'NO.' We were both so scared."

"And do you remember what happened next?"

I frown over that one. "I…I only remember his Thunder Voice and being scared and feeling like he might kick us out of his pack. I don't remember what happened afterwards. Did he beat us and I just blocked the memory?"

Mash laughs. "No, he didn't beat us, Banger. He took us outside to play fetch with the gray ball."

"He did?"

"And when he opened the door, we were both still too scared to get close enough to him to go through the door. And do you remember what he said?"

"I don't remember, Mash."

Mash nuzzles me again, pushing my head up even further. "He said, 'Oh, stop cowering. You've been corrected. You learned your lesson. Now let's move on and have some fun.'" Mash comes upright as he says this last part, his tail thumping against the ground. "Dad doesn't want your shame, Banger. He doesn't want your cowering. He doesn't want your sacrifices. He just wants you to learn what you need to learn, and then get back to having fun. Get back to being a dog."

I look hopefully at Mash, something hard and callused cracking into a thousand pieces in my chest and something like warm, golden light pouring into it, scouring those hardened bits away. "Are you able to talk to the peoples like Sweetpea was?"

"Well, I don't know," Mash admits. "But I don't think I could have remembered all of that on my own."

I feel like I've been carrying something around with me that suddenly just falls off. My undersized legs now feel positively energetic, able to carry me anywhere I wish. My thick body feels as light as dandelion fluff.

And I remember.

I remember love. Not just my love for the peoples, but their love for ME. For US. For DOGS. And when I remember that, when I really recall what it felt like—so strongly that I feel its presence around me now, as sure as if I'd been on the Cloud Throne with Dad's arms wrapped around me—that's when I find it impossible NOT to love these other dogs.

I am a dog. They are dogs. We are all dogs. We are all part of the same whole, and that whole is loved by the peoples. It is not just Dad's love for ME, or MY love for Dad, but all peoples' love for all dogs, and all dogs' love for all peoples. They seem to swirl around each other, tighter and tighter, until there's very little difference between them, and I cannot see the start of the peoples' love for dogs, nor the end of my love for both them AND dogs. It's all a part of the same thing. It extends to me, and through me, and from me, into others, like a river I have no hope of diverting.

"I remember," I say, my tail beginning to wag as I look at Mash and all of his beaming dogness, and I feel that same dogness welling up inside of me from a place where I had pressed it down for so long. But you can never really get rid of your true nature, can you? It's a part of who you are. Denying it only brings misery. And now, as I accept it, as I accept myself, and all of these other dogs, just as Dad accepted me, just as the peoples accepted dogs, it becomes more than just a memory.

It becomes reality.

All of the sudden, I am not a dog that has been abandoned by its peoples. I am not a dog that is alone, or set apart. The peoples' bodies might be gone, but their love still surrounds me, as real a thing as the sunshine warming my fur. I am a part of them, and a part of this dog pack. And it is not just these dogs that I am a part of, but all dogs.

I am a dog.

And not only that...

I am a Very Good Dog. And I know that I am a Very Good Dog, because Dad told me so, and he knows things.

Everything else vanishes—all of my fears, and worries, and angers, and loneliness. It doesn't just melt away, but disappears all in an instant, like it was never there to begin with. And before I even know what I'm doing, I've dropped my front legs to the ground, my hind end sticking up, staring at Mash with my tail wagging.

Mash looks shocked, even as his tail responds in kind. "Banger. Are you...in the play position?"

My response is to rush him, boundless energy pushing through my body from some place I'd lost touch with a long, long time ago. Mash is too quick, of course, and feints back. I jolt to the side, then retreat, beckoning him to chase me. And chase me he does.

I bolt away from him, zig-zagging between dogs that stare at me like they don't know what the heck is happening. But their tails are wagging. Mash catches up to me and tackles my hind quarters, bowling me over. I scramble to my feet, panting and wagging.

Mash drops into play position himself now, any sense of propriety gone. Because everyone knows dogs don't have a sense of propriety. We tried to learn it, but that was a disaster. It's just something that we're not meant to worry about.

"What is happening right now?" I hear Gracie stammer out.

"I don't know!" Mash cries, joyfully. "But we're playing!"

I'm still standing there, waiting for Mash to make his move, when out of nowhere, Q charges me, yipping gleefully like she can't contain herself. I juke out of the way and Q goes flying past me, blood-matted fur and all.

She skids to a stop and finds herself nose to nose with Gracie.

Gracie, who still has a bit of Q's blood on her muzzle.

A tense, cringing silence suddenly blankets the gathering of dogs. Panting breaths are held in chests. Hesitantly-wagging tails are stilled.

Gracie's head dips a bit. "Q...I...I..."

"You got a little something on your muzzle," Q says, craning forward, and upwards—because Gracie is so much bigger than her. Gracie doesn't shy away from the contact, but goes very still. And then Q gently licks her own blood from Gracie's muzzle, until it is clean.

"There you go," Q says, leaning back, satisfied. "Like it never happened."

A brightness comes back to Gracie that I haven't seen in her eyes since the peoples disappeared. Her tail comes up and begins to wag solidly back and forth.

Q drops into a play position.

Everyone breathlessly waits.

And when Gracie bounds playfully at Q, and Q leaps back, it is like something bursts out of the chest of every dog in the village. Something that has been held back, just like I held back my own dogness because of my fears and worries and angers.

"PLAY DATE!" someone yells.

And suddenly everyone is running. Everyone is barking, and growling—but not like they'd been before. In these barks and growls, there is not a hint of menace. There is only goodwill and playfulness.

Boozer bolts for The Wall and rips out a giant stick from the center of it, causing a whole section of The Wall to collapse, which no one seems to care about. Then, with the branch hanging out of his mouth, Boozer begins to race through the teeming crowd, shouting, "You can't get my stick! You can't get my stick!"

Dogs begin to chase him, and latch onto whatever twig of the stick they can, trying to wrestle it away from him. Other dogs run to the wall to find their own sticks to play Keep-Away and Tug-of-War. And others simply chase each other. And I am one of them. And so is Mash. And so is Gracie.

I am a dog.

They are dogs.

We are all dogs.

And it is a wonderful thing to be what we are.

33

Mash

(Some Time After That)

WE PLACED SWEETPEA'S BODY in the woods, in the clearing with the full morning sun that he used to love so much. When I came to it again, gently holding Sweetpea's body in my jaws, I almost wanted to cry out, so strong was the sense of sadness that came over me. I could almost see him there, in that bright splash of sunlight, his arms and legs tucked under him in his cat-blob form, eyes closed as he faced the sun, a feline smile of contentment on his mouth.

There has been much joy for us in the days since Sweetpea died. That feels strange to say, but I'm not saying that we found joy BECAUSE of his death. If anything, I found joy IN SPITE of his death. All of the dogs found joy. And they found it, because of the things that Sweetpea did in his life. Because Sweetpea risked everything to show us what we needed to see.

So, while my heart was heavy for the loss of my friend, it was also overjoyed, and filled with gratitude for the gift of that moment. And in that moment, looking at that sunny clearing, I felt the joy of that gratitude, because even though I was there to place my friend's body to rest, it was a beautiful place to rest, and the sun was shining, and the day was warm, and the birds were chirping, and everything around me was filled with life.

But that is part of our gift as dogs: That no matter what, no matter our circumstances, we live in the moment, not fearing what comes next, or worrying about what might happen tomorrow, but simply seeing life as it is in that moment, and being grateful to be a part of something so immensely beautiful.

We did not bury Sweetpea, because that is not our way. We left his body, curled up as though he were in a deep sleep, right there in that patch of sunshine. We left it exposed, because we—cats and dogs alike—are a part of this world, and we do not begrudge it. It is all a part of the cycle that we are in.

In a few days, there will not be much left of Sweetpea. The creatures of the forest will have eaten what there is to eat, and the insects and the birds will pick away at what is left, until there is only bones, scattered about in the leaves.

That seems grim, but you have to see it from the eyes of an animal: This is our world now. It was left to us when the peoples disappeared. And we are wound around the processes of this world, as tightly as vines wind around the trunks of trees. To us, it is not a terrible thing for our lifeless bodies to contribute to that world in one final way—the last bits of our life energy given as a gift, rather than hidden jealously away in the dirt.

I think Sweetpea would have been pleased.

Maybe not the Sweetpea that was His Masterfulness, because that guy was all about being better than everyone else. But the other Sweetpea—the one that he became after we'd been banished from the village, and he'd become the Voice in the Wilderness.

As for the village, things have been going wonderfully. The Wall has been torn down, not out of spite or anger for what it represented, but because it was made of sticks, and if there's anything dogs like to play with, it's sticks.

The village is very different than it was. Now it reminds me more of Hiro's Pack, with dogs running joyously about, lost in each moment, experiencing it in its fullness. Chasing, and play fighting, and running, and barking, and sniffing, and yes, humping. But not, like, dominance humping, which we still try to shy away from, knowing that it comes from a part of us that is maybe not so kind and gentle. But I'll just tell it like this: There are a few litters of puppies on the way.

Hiro's Pack, for their part, made good on their word to stay away from us. That is, until me and a few other dogs ventured over and told them everything that had happened in the village. Hiro was grieved to hear about Sweetpea's death, but he pranced with joy when he learned that there was no more True Dogs, and no more Collective. There was simply the pack, and it was not the pack of the village, but something that we've come to call the All-Pack. Because we are all dogs, and we are all in the same pack together, even if we've never seen each other or passed the greeting of the day. We are all a part of the same life energy, and that makes us a part of the All-Pack.

Nowadays, the woods between Hiro's village and ours is filled with dogs, and there is little difference in our minds between us and them. In fact, I'd say there is actually NO us and them. There is only us. Every dog is a part of the us.

Hiro and the dogs from his village regularly come to visit us. They spend more and more time in our village, and we spend more and more time over there. Eventually, Hiro stopped going back to his village, and chose to stay with us.

Well, not specifically with US. It's no secret that Hiro and Gracie have always had a thing for each other, and, as I said, there are some litters on the way. I'm positively breathless with anticipation to meet them. Will they be curly-haired and brown like Gracie? Or will they be tan and fluffy like Hiro? Or some weird combination of the two?

All I know is that they're going to be awesome. Because Hiro has always been awesome, and, except for a slight wandering from her true self—which lasted a year, but who's counting? —Gracie is back to being awesome.

Longjohn, who still stays in Gracie's house, has become quite fat. When I find him on the porch, on those occasions when I go to visit Gracie or Hiro, he is always staring off into the woods with a quiet sort of longing in his eyes.

I asked him once what was wrong—why wasn't he the hellish, bombastic feline that I knew from times before?

He sighed, long-sufferingly, and turned his golden eyes on me. "A cat is only great when he has a great enemy. Mine has left me. Now I have nothing to do. I don't know who I am without my old nemesis."

"Well. At least those bird hunting grounds aren't contested anymore. Is that why you got so fat?"

His ears flattened. "No. I got fat because there's rarely a reason for me to leave the porch anymore." He sneered in disgust. "Bird hunting grounds. Mash, let me explain something to you—I can kill any small animal I wish. And I do, when the mood strikes me. But the bird hunting grounds? Pfff. What fun could it be to pilfer those birds if it's not pissing off my enemy?"

Well, I didn't quite understand that, but I left it as it was.

This particular evening, I am on my own porch, and I can see Longjohn on his from across the lawn, only just visible over the tops of the weeds, which aren't just weeds anymore, but small sapling trees now too. Just as he was when I talked to him a while back, he is staring off into the woods, just looking as wistful as a cat can look.

The evening is warm. It was a hot day, and everything is swallowed up in green. I believe that this is called Summer. It's hard to keep track of the time without Sweetpea around to explain it to me.

Banger is inside the house, on the Cloud Throne, probably napping. Getting in touch with her inner playful puppy hasn't made her any younger, and all the running and playing wipes her out pretty quick. She spends most of her days either on the Cloud Throne or sunbathing in whatever spot she's decided to plop herself down on, which really varies. Sometimes she'll just up and crash out on the sidewalk for an afternoon bake session. Sometimes she'll be in the Park. And every once in a while, she'll come hang out on the porch with me.

But the porch has become something of my domain. Not that I would begrudge her if she came to the porch. It's just that we each have our places where we feel closest to the memories of Dad. For Banger, it is on the Cloud Throne, where Dad would sit with her in the evening and stroke her fur. For me, it is on the porch, where Dad would throw the gray ball for me. Which, by the way, has become lost somewhere out there in the weeds. I search for it regularly, but so far, no luck.

This particular evening, the sun has settled below the tops of the trees, and the porch is in dappled sunlight. Beams of it brighten my eyes, and I blink against them, relaxed and filled with joy. Remembering, but not just that—experiencing. As though Dad is there with me, right at this moment.

It is in this quiet moment that I hear something.

My ears prick up and I turn my head, trying to figure out the source of the noise, but it seems to be coming from all around me. It is an oddly familiar noise, but one that I haven't heard since…

Oh my goodness. It's purring.

Without thinking, I'm on my feet, looking all around me, and yes, up into the air. "Sweetpea? Is that you? Are you a ghost? Again?"

Standing stock-still, I wait for a response, my tail held stiffly out behind me, ready to wag at the slightest hint of my old friend's presence.

But instead of a response, I hear a new noise: A tiny little mewling.

I cock my head to the side. "Sweetpea? Are you making kitten noises at me? What's that supposed to mean?"

Then a third sound, this one definitely not a kitten: It's a low yowl, like the exaggerated MROWR noise Sweetpea used to make when he was wandering around, looking for comfort from Dad, though he would never admit that's what he was doing.

And with that sound, I suddenly realize where its coming from.

Hesitantly, almost a little nervously, I creep down the steps of the porch until I can just crane my head down and see underneath it, which used to be one of Sweetpea's favorite places to hide, particularly on a warm day.

I see a pair of feline eyes staring right back at me. My whole body explodes with sensations of warmth and excitement, but they're instantly stilled by the fact that...I do not recognize this cat.

It is definitely not Sweetpea. Now that I have my nose down low, I catch the scent of the cat, and I know that it is a female. Besides that, she's not tawny-colored like Sweetpea was, but jet black, save for a little white blaze on her chin.

I blink a few times, my muscles rigid. "Who the heck are you?" I stammer out, not trying to be unfriendly, but just so surprised to see a strange cat right there under my feet.

The cat is laying on her side, and in the shade, and with all of her black fur, I can't really see much except the general shape of her, and her eyes, and the little patch of white on her chin.

As my eyes adjust from blinking sleepily into the sunlight, to staring intensely into the shadows under the porch, I see something moving around her belly. Several somethings.

Before I can think twice about it, I've leapt off of the porch and land, just a stride shy of where the female cat is laying, my tail wagging furiously. "Are those KITTENS?!" I practically shriek in a paroxysm of joy.

Now, I probably should have thought better about all of that. Because now that I'm thinking about it, you have one female cat that has clearly just delivered an entire litter of kittens, and one large, over-excited dog that's blathering at them from close enough to smell my breath.

Predictably, the cat rears back, ears flattening, and growls out that nasty, feline, come-no-closer noise.

"Oh no! Sorry!" I gasp, not knowing what the heck to do now except the only thing I know to do when my size has made someone else afraid: I drop into the deepest play position my body is capable of, my head practically resting in the dirt between my two front paws. "I'm sorry," I repeat, my jowls all mushed against the ground. "I'm not going to hurt you, I promise. I'm a Very Good Dog. And Good Dogs don't hurt cats.... Intentionally."

The female cat doesn't quite relax, but her alarm at my presence settles a bit—just enough for her exhaustion to take back over—and she wilts back on herself, panting. "Are you..." she says, her voice thin and hesitant. "Are you Mash?"

My tail wags so hard that it hits my sides. "It is! My name's Mash! That's me!" Then I quirk my head to one side. "Hey, wait. How do you know that? Because I don't think I know you."

She eyes me for another moment, her gaze ranging all over my face, probably thinking how doofy it is. "I didn't mean to intrude on your territory," she says. "I was told that this was a safe place for me to have my kittens when the time came."

"Oh, yes. It's super-safe. I mean, I'm usually on the porch, and I'm, like, a really good watch dog." I pull my head back and glance behind me. "Why? Is there something out there I should worry about?"

"Well, you know cats," she replies. "We like to worry first and think about it later." Then she cocks her head to one side. "You DO know cats, don't you? Aren't you Sweetpea's Mash?"

Just to hear it said like that: Sweetpea's Mash! Mash, the friend of Sweetpea! Enough of a friend that Sweetpea must have actually admitted it to another cat.

"Yes!" I say. "I know cats! And yes! I knew Sweetpea! Sweetpea was my friend! We were friends—the BEST of friends!"

"Well..." her eyes frown at me a bit. "That's...unusual. But I'm glad you are who you say you are. Sweetpea told me I could trust you."

"Oh, you can totally trust me. I'm, like, the most trustworthy dog ever. Unless you're talking about keeping time, or counting. Or remembering very specific things. Then I'm not so great. But in all the other stuff, I'm pretty awesome."

Something like a smile comes over her face. "My name's Fiona."

"My name's Mash!"

"Yes, we've already covered that."

"Oh. Right."

Then, all at once, it hits me. I can't really describe what happens to my body. It's an insane rush of feelings, like running the fastest you've ever run through the best smelling field of flowers you've ever smelled, on the sunniest day you've ever seen.

"OHMIGOSH—ARE THOSE SWEETPEA'S KITTENS?!"

"Yes, in fact—"

"OHMIGOSH! OHMIGOSH! OHMIGOSH!" I spin myself in circles until I'm dizzy. I really can't help myself. "He never told me he had a mate! He never told me he had kittens on the way! Holy cow! This is the greatest day of my life!"

"Uh..."

"Do you need anything? Do you need some food? Do you need some water? Do you need me to curl up around you and keep you warm? No, of course not, it's way too hot as it is. That's probably why you're in the shade. Do you need me to groom you? Ohhhhhhhh—do you need me to groom THE KITTENS? I can groom the kittens! I promise, I have a very gentle tongue!"

Fiona looks slightly alarmed, but she doesn't get defensive like she did when I poked my head under the porch. "No, I'm fine, thank you. I just...need a place to rest. And a place where my kittens can stay while I'm hunting."

"Of course!" I cry, prancing despite trying so hard to control myself. "You can stay here as long as you want! I'll watch the kittens while you're hunting! I'll be the best kitten-watcher you've ever seen, and—"

I trail off, my exuberance coming to an exultant peak and hovering there, washing me through and through with excitement and joy, as I see one little head poke up, it's eyes still squinted shut like it can't handle the brightness of this world, its stubby little ears facing me. None of the other kittens look up or respond to my voice, but this one does.

This one does. And it is the only tan kitten in the litter.

Hesitantly, almost awestruck, I ease a little bit closer. I can barely tear my eyes away from the kitten, but I force myself to glance at Fiona. She looks wary, but not full-on Prime Directive just yet. I want nothing more than to slobber her and her brood with sloppy kisses, but I restrain myself long enough to ask, in a slightly quavering voice, "Can I come closer?"

Fiona visibly relaxes. "I guess you should meet them."

And I do want to meet them. I want to meet all of them.

But I want to meet THIS one most of all. While the others are wrestling around each other, searching for their mother's milk, this one just stays right where it is, swaying unsteadily in place, but still "looking" at me, though it can't quite open its eyes yet. Like it somehow recognizes my voice.

I slink closer. I don't want to crowd Fiona, so I stop when I'm just close enough that my big old muzzle, easily twice as big as the tan kitten, is nose-to-nose with it.

I take a big, lusty inhale. The scent of the mother and her afterbirth fills my nose, but there is something else there, something in this little kitten's fur that tickles my memory. I'm immediately thrown back to that clearing, to a time when it was just me and Sweetpea, sleeping away the night, curled around each other for warmth and comfort.

My voice comes out as a whisper: "He smells…just like Sweetpea!"

"Actually," Fiona says. "It's a she."

I gasp in delight. "Ohhhhhh! It's Sweetpea's daughter! Sweetpea has a daughter!" My tail is lashing back and forth, sweeping through the cool dirt of the under porch. "Have you named any of them?"

"We cats don't name our kittens until they're weaned."

"Well…can I…" Maybe I'm asking too much.

"You want to name her?"

"Um…yes?"

"What would you name her?"

"Well…" I consider my options, but I'll admit, my knowledge of naming conventions is extremely limited by my experience. All I can think about is Dad's favorite food, which he named us after. I stare at the scrunched kitten face before me. She's so wonderful. She completes me. She makes me feel just like when Dad would smother us with his love. The one part of the dish that brings it all together.

"How about Gravy?"

34

Mash

(Many Summers After That)

WELL, IT'S BEEN A long time, and a lot has changed.

I barely even recognize the world around me anymore, but I suppose that's what all old dogs say. Yes, yes, it happened to me too. I got old. I wake up stiff and I walk like Banger used to walk, and I sleep about as often as she did, too.

It's strange. I still feel like my old self, like I could just up and run and chase and play, but I get tired so quick. But I will tell you this: I can still be super-fast when I want to be. Just not for very long.

You know how I am with time, and dogs aren't in the habit of keeping track of their birthdays, so I really don't know how old I am. Gravy tells me that she's five years old, because cats keep track of things like that. And I'm a few years older than her.

So I guess my age is...

...Carry the two...

I think I'm ninety-four. Give or take a few decades.

All the dogs I knew since the beginning are growing old too. Some of them have already passed on.

Q got arthritic and couldn't get around much anymore. We brought her food and water for a while, but one day we couldn't find her. After searching around high and low, we found her in the woods. She'd used her last bit of energy to walk herself out there, to make her final contribution to the world.

Gracie got sick with something that made her belly hurt a lot. She left the village when she was still pretty strong. She said goodbye to all her children, and to Hiro, and marched off into the woods to be one with nature. I guess she did it, because she never came back.

And Banger. Yes, my dear, old, sweet Banger. She went just the way she would have wanted—napping on the Cloud Throne, curled up in the corner that she liked best, with her head resting on one of the Special Poofs, as though it were Dad's lap.

I miss them all, but I miss Banger and Sweetpea the most. They were the last members of my original pack, the pack I was welcomed into when Dad took me from the Place of Judgment.

But my pack hasn't shrunk. Oh no! It's grown huge!

Nowadays, the village looks very different. The dogs have boomed, and the things of the peoples' world have slowly crumbled away.

The houses still stand, of course, though parts of them are falling apart because we don't have those dang opposable thumbs to fix them. Greenery of all kinds now grows freely over everything. Ivy and vines cover the sides of the houses. The lawns have morphed into young forests. The streets have crumbled and cracked, and have shrunken over the years, as the earth slowly swallows them from either side, so that there is only a narrow, patchy strip of concrete where the road through the village used to be.

But in amongst all those rundown memories of before, there is new life. Litters were born, and puppies grew into dogs, and those dogs had more litters, and many of those dogs have gone out into the world, to form new villages in other places. But many others have stayed, and made our little village a busy, bustling place.

There are over twenty generations of dogs here! I didn't know what a generation was, but Gravy explained it to me. Every time a puppy grows up and has puppies of its own, it's making a new generation. But also, all the litters born around a certain time are considered a generation too. So...

Yeah, I still don't get it. But there's over twenty of those things. According to Gravy.

And as for the cats? Oh, well, the cats have had some generations of their own too. Gravy, for instance, has already had two litters. Most of her children have gone off, but you know what's interesting? They've gone off to live with other dogs. Turns out, cats and dogs can be the best of friends. Just like me and Sweetpea.

The cats are really good at keeping us dogs on task, organizing logical responses to problems, and remembering details. Because, apparently, if you don't remember the mistakes you made in the past, you'll probably keep making them.

Isn't that wild?

Anyway, the cats have been an awesome addition to every dog family.

There was, of course, the problem of their incessant murder of all things smaller than them. A while back, we realized that the cats, as great as they were for us, were absolutely destroying the wildlife, and wellllll...we kind of freaked out a little bit.

There was, unfortunately, a small period of unrest during that time, where there were some dogs trying to make a set of rules for the cats to follow. Luckily, the cats reminded us of the lessons we learned the LAST time we did that, and helped us find a more reasonable compromise.

Cats have to be allowed to be cats. But a single cat can kill a lot of mice, rabbits, birds, and squirrels. Which would be fine if they needed to do it for food, but let's just be honest...mostly they did it for funsies.

It's kind of how dogs and peoples had to figure out how to live in harmony with each other. Inter-species packs can be a bit of a challenge, and it requires a lot of compromise. Both the peoples and the dogs had to do some things that were counter to their nature in order to get along with each other. But we loved each other enough to make it work.

We dogs certainly love our cats. And I...think...they love us?

You never can tell with cats.

But we've made compromises to coexist together: Cats now run our hunting parties as scouts. They spot the prey, organize the hunt, and then we dogs make the kill. And I gotta say, since cats started running our hunts, our success rate has gone through the roof.

The cats get to take their fair share of the kill, and they get to hunt. Everybody wins.

Also, cats are really good at pest control, so any time they can explain a need for a certain population of small critters to be culled—they've started to call it culling, which I think is supposed to make us feel like it's not murder, but it still sounds a lot like "killing"—then they have free rein to hunt all the mice, voles, moles or whatever else is causing the ecosystem to tilt out of balance.

The cats make a lot of requests for culling. Like...a shocking amount. Like, "So-and-so saw a mouse. That probably means there's an infestation. We suggest that one-thousand mice be culled, effective immediately."

Luckily, we dogs retain the right to say "no," and some smaller, rather harmless populations of critters continue to live in ignorance of how close they came to extinction.

If there's one thing that cats and dogs still disagree on, it's the amount of cullings necessary to keep the ecosystem balanced. But despite all that, we still live mostly in harmony together. Every house in the village is filled with dogs, and usually a few cats, who tend to develop a bit of a bond of loyalty to the dogs in their house, though they refuse to call it that. They prefer to call it a "mutually beneficial relationship," whatever that means.

Yes, many things have changed. Sometimes it's uncomfortable for me and the other old dogs to see how different things are now from what we remember. But today, and really for the last several days that I can recall, I find myself strangely at peace with it all. More confident than ever that the dogs as a species are heading in the right direction.

I'll tell you one thing that HASN'T changed: My evening routine still consists of parking my butt on the back porch and staring off at the sun setting behind the trees. Which happens to be what I'm doing right now. Sure, the porch has changed a bit. It's begun to warp and rot in places. And all around it the young trees have grown up, so that it's in shade nearly the whole day.

It is still the place that I feel closest to Dad.

And, in a way, closest to Sweetpea. Because Gravy has now made it a part of her evening routine as well, to join me on the porch. And even though she—much like her father—talks entirely too much, for now, she is lying in cat-blob form and her eyes are closed against the dappled rays of sunshine, and there is that slight feline smile of contentedness on her lips. And she looks just like Sweetpea.

Some cat-sense must have told her that she was being watched, because her ears twitch in my direction and she blinks her eyes open, fixing me with her amber gaze.

"Why are you staring at me?" she says, her ears half-cocked between relaxation and irritation.

I just smile at her. "Oh, just looking at you. You look so much like your father right now."

She preens a bit. Sweetpea's life has become much honored after he left us. She is proud of who she came from, and she likes it when I tell her how similar she is.

She begins grooming her wicked little claws. "You seem unusually mellow today." A sidelong look, with maybe just a breath of concern in it. "The last few days, actually. Everything okay?"

I turn my head to the sun and close my eyes again. "Of course, of course. Everything is...spectacular."

Gravy looks out into the sunset-drenched woods, as though trying to see what I see, and perhaps not succeeding. But she concedes with a pert little, "Yes, it's quite nice."

"You're kinda quiet yourself this evening."

"Am I?" she says, mildly. "Aren't I always quietly introspective?"

"No, most of the time you talk nonstop."

"Well." She stretches her front paws out in front of her. "There's a lot I have to keep telling you, on account of you being old and forgetful."

"Haven't I always been forgetful?"

"Shh," she says, closing her eyes. "You're interrupting my quiet introspection, chatterbox."

A warmth of love cascades down my spine and makes my tail wag, just two little thumps against the deck. The puppy that still lives deep down inside has an urge to play—mostly to get Gravy riled up, since she's so primly trying to be meditative. But I am old, and the puppy doesn't have quite as much sway as it once did. I am content to lay here in her company. Though I still imagine making her tail all fluffed up and it gives me a chuckle so quiet I don't think she hears me.

Who am I kidding? Of course she heard me. She's just ignoring me.

When I gaze back out into the young stands of saplings and brush that used to be my back yard, my eyes catch onto something. If the light hadn't been beaming through the trees in just the right spot, I would have missed it.

Way out there, towards where the Invisible Boundary used to be, there is a small red object at the base of a young pine tree.

I squint at it. "Hey. You see that red thing?"

Gravy sighs and lazily pries her eyes open. She scans the woods and then glances at me. "You know I can't see red, right? And also, you know you can't see red either, right?"

I quirk my head to one side. I hadn't even realized it until she said it, but she's right. I'm staring at something that is a color I've never actually perceived before. I don't know how I know that it's red. I just know.

"Um," I say, hesitantly. "Yeah, that's really odd. But I swear I'm looking at a red thing. Do you see it?"

"I don't see anything."

Something inside me suddenly feels compelled to go to that red thing. It is an odd sensation. It's almost like I know I need to go to the red thing, but also that I have all the time of eternity to do it. It's not going anywhere. It has always been there, and always will be there.

But now is the time.

Something almost like a shiver goes through me, if a shiver can be warm and pleasant. I feel so suddenly light all over my body, that I don't even realize I've risen to my paws until I see that I'm padding down the steps. My joints feel smooth and painless, my movements as effortless as if I were floating.

"Mash," I hear Gravy's voice behind me, playfully weary of my old dog antics. "What are you doing?"

What exactly AM I doing? Well, I suppose I'm going to see what the red thing is, but something else keeps circling in my brain, and that's what I end up saying: "Now is the time."

"Time for what?" Her voice sounds oddly faint behind me.

I float smoothly overs the pine needles and leaves, eyes fixed on the red thing. "I'm not really sure," I say. "It's just...it's time."

"Mash, you're kind of freaking me out."

I laugh again, but don't reply. I wonder why she sounds so quiet? But I'm unworried about it. Nothing in the world could make me worried now. I'm not sure how I came to be in this place of peace, but that's where I am, and I'm content to stay there.

I think I knew what it was the second I first caught sight of it. What else could it be? But still, when I finally reach it, a fresh wave of joy rolls over me and my tail begins to wag. I feel like a puppy again.

Half-buried in the dirt at the base of that pine tree lays my old gray ball that I lost. Except it's not gray anymore. It's red. And I realize that it was ALWAYS red. I just couldn't perceive it, because I couldn't see red before. I don't really know how it is that I can suddenly see a color that I was blind to for all the previous years of my life. But I'm not really worried about it, because I'm just so overjoyed to have found it.

I paw at it until it comes free of the dirt. Half of it is dark and dirty from being buried, the other half washed out a bit, I guess from laying in the sun. It must have laid here the whole time since I lost it, so many years ago.

Still wagging, I take it in my mouth and give it a few squeezes between my teeth, feeling that soft squelch that I remember so well. The strange, rubbery taste of it, seasoned liberally with dirt and wood and pine. Gosh, I forgot how amazing my ball was.

"Hey, Gravy," I call, turning back to the house. "Check out what I..."

I trail off.

Well...This is very odd.

I can see Gravy, still on the porch, though now she's standing at full cat-alert, as though something has gotten her spooked. But that's not the odd part. The odd part is that the young forest that has overtaken my old back yard has completely disappeared. I have no idea where it went, but now I'm standing in perfectly trimmed, lush, green grass.

For a moment, I don't believe it. How could I? Forests don't just randomly turn into perfect lawns. At least, I don't think they do.

I can smell the grass—that rich, perfect, green scent, as though it's just been trimmed.

I should also point out that the deck has entirely changed. Gone are the old, weathered and rotted boards, replaced with something that I'm kind of struggling to put into words for you. It's like the deck isn't a deck anymore at all. Not a collection of old dead things, cut from dead trees. Now it's alive. As though a tree grew where our deck should be, and formed itself into the shape of the deck.

In the midst of all this weirdness, my chief concern is that Gravy looks like she's about to activate her Prime Directive. I'm not entirely sure what's got her riled up—possibly the sudden change in the landscape? I guess that would freak anyone out. For whatever reason, I'm entirely okay with it.

"Gravy," I say around the ball in my mouth as I start moving back towards the deck. "You okay?"

"Uhhhh," she says, her eyes stretched wide, pupils fully dilated, and, yes, tail maximally fluffed. "What the fuck is happening right now?"

"I found my red ball," I announce with some significant satisfaction. After all, how can you not be satisfied when you've been searching for something for so long and you finally find it? "But you're probably more worried about the trees disappearing and the deck turning into a live tree."

Gravy's eyes dart around, confused. "What are you talking about?"

I reach the bottom of the steps and cock my head to the side, wondering why she's so confused. I mean, sure, a random sudden change to the landscape SHOULD be a bit confusing for anyone, but the way she said it, it's like she doesn't even see what I'm seeing.

"Gravy, don't you see how the lawn has come back?" I look back over my shoulder, curious if perhaps the whole thing was just a momentary daydream on my part, but no, it's still freshly cut, lush green grass where the young forest used to be.

"I don't know what the fuck you're talking about!"

"Well, if it's not the fact that the forest has turned into a lawn," I mount the steps. "Then why are you freaking out?"

Gravy's back arches and she takes a few fearful steps away from me. "I'm freaking the fuck out because you don't have any legs!"

I laugh hysterically. "Of course I have legs, you silly..." I look down.

Oh my. It appears that I don't have legs anymore.

"Mash!" Gravy cries out. "What's happening to you?"

Strange, but even though I'm standing right there in front of her—or, floating, I guess—her voice still sounds distant.

And all at once, I know.

What do I know? Well, quite suddenly, I know a lot of things. But the big one is this: It's time.

Looking at Gravy, I'm suddenly overwhelmed with compassion for her. Something has come between us. It's like I've crossed just to the other side of some thin veil, and I can see and feel and hear and smell and know things that I'd been blind to my whole life. I wish that I could pull her across that veil with me, but I realize that it's not possible. It's time for me, but it's not yet time for her.

I've been where she is right now. I remember it with perfect clarity. I remember the fear that took hold of me—the fear that took hold of ALL the dogs—when our peoples disappeared. But now I see that there never was anything to fear at all. And I wish I could impart that knowledge to Gravy, but it's just not possible.

She is as blind as I once was. I wish I could make her see, but that is not how these things work, is it? No. Everyone has to see in their own time. Everyone has their own journey to make.

I am reaching the end of mine.

She is only just beginning hers.

"Mash."

It is not Gravy that spoke. It is a different voice that comes to me, not muffled or distant at all. It is a voice that is perfectly familiar, and completely strange, all at once.

I turn my head in the direction of the voice, and find a small, glowing shape curled up on Dad's old Outside Throne. And my heart leaps with joy.

"Hey, Sweetpea!"

35

Mash

So, I said that the glowing shape on the Outside Throne was Sweetpea. But there's a lot more to it. The shape of it is feline, but there's also a fluidity to it that makes me feel like it might change at any moment—that it COULD change, and that it only appeared the way it was now for my sake.

"Actually," the glowing cat-shape says. "I'm technically not Sweetpea, although, if we're getting into technicalities, all individuation is misinterpretation."

I peer at the shape, trying to see something different than a cat. And for a moment, it seems to flicker, like it's on the verge of becoming something else. "You sure there's no Sweetpea in there?" I ask.

There is a soft chuckle from the shape, and something about it tickles pleasantly at my brain. "If you're talking about the unique consciousness that you knew as Sweetpea, that little spark of life energy is standing right behind you and looking pretty Prime Directive-y."

I turn to look at Gravy. She is staring me right in the eyes, kind of creepily unblinking, with her mouth half open like she's in the middle of one of those warning caterwauls. And from my new vantage point, I realize that I'd always known she was my best friend. I'd always known she was Sweetpea.

"It's you," I say to her...him...it. "You've been here the whole time."

Gravy...literally hasn't moved. Like, at all.

I don't even see her breathing.

"Hey, wait a minute," I say, eyes fixed on Gravy, but throwing the comment behind me to the glowing shape in the Outside Throne. "Why's she frozen? Did we break her?"

"No," the voice says—the same voice, and yet different now. And so familiar. "What you're seeing is just an instant. Kind of like the after image in your eyes after you look at the sun. To her, no time has passed since you started talking to me. But that's because you transcended. You're outside of time now."

I breathe a sigh of relief. "Oh, fantastic. I always hated that time stuff anyway."

Then it strikes me.

I know that voice!

I spin and see that it is no longer a cat-shaped glowing thing in Dad's old Outside Throne. It is Dad himself. He is sitting there just as he always would in the evenings, relaxed, smiling at me, and holding the red ball.

I don't even care about how he got it out of my mouth. I run to him on legs made of nothing. Or maybe air. Or spirit.

Yeah. Spirit legs. And they're super-fast.

I crash into him, and I am wagging—not with a tail, because I don't think I have one anymore, but with my whole soul—and he is laughing, and I feel how we are twining around each other, scratches and pets and belly rubs, all rolled into a single wave of sensation that fills me up to overflowing.

I'm back. He's back. We're back together. Just like I always knew we would be. Because we are a pack, and nothing can ever come between us. Even when it sometimes felt like there were whole universes between us, we were never really apart from each other.

As we roll around each other, it's like he is explaining everything to me without words. The understanding of it all just comes to me, effortlessly. It's the easiest that I've ever managed to comprehend...well, anything. I see all the things in my life that I never understood in the moment, but which now, somehow, make perfect sense.

I see myself, with a belly full of the Sacred Brown Stuff, and Dad squirting the bubbly liquid down my throat. Except it's totally different from my new perspective. I realize it wasn't anger and wrath at all. I realize that the Sacred Brown Stuff was something called chocolate, and it could have killed me. And the bubbly stuff wasn't Dad's vengeance, it was simply hydrogen peroxide that would make me puke up the chocolate before it stopped my heart.

Wow. I really interpreted that completely wrong.

I see the time that Dad was cooking and that little piece of food dropped to the floor, and I lunged for it, but Dad spoke in his Thunder Voice and kneed me in the head to keep me from eating it. At the time I thought I must have done something terrible. Now, I realize that it was eggplant, which I probably would have hated, and, being fresh out of the frying pan, would have burned my mouth.

I see Dad scolding me for ripping open a trash bag and gorging myself on spoiled scraps. At the time I couldn't understand why the simple joy of rummaging through the trash could be so bad. But then I see myself later that same day, my stomach all in knots as things try to exit my body from both ends.

Dang. I never made the connection there between rotten food and an upset stomach.

Some terrible little things called bacteria had wrecked my system. Who knew?

"Huh," I say. "We really couldn't grasp that you actually wanted what was best for us."

"Hey, no judgment here, Mash. Humans had the same problem. Accepting true benevolence is kind of hard when you're taught from birth that everything's out to get you. That type of thinking goes straight to the root of the animal, and that type of hardwired instinct is not so easy to correct."

"So," I say, looking around at my strange new environment. "How did I get here? And where exactly are we?"

"Oh, that's easy," Dad says. "Just look."

And then, again, my brain is blasted through time and space, which sounds really scary, but if you're relaxed like I am right now, you just accept it and realize that learning new things isn't scary at all.

I see how we dogs are not individuals, but parts of a whole that is the dog life energy, and that whole is also just a part of a bigger whole that is the universe and all the life and light in it. The peoples were never really different peoples either—they were always a part of the whole that was the peoples' life energy.

I see those energies now as spirals. The life energy of the peoples has closed its loop. And the life energy of the dogs is doing the same, right at that moment. What was a spiral has closed in on itself. The cycle is now a circle. The journey is complete.

Or...ALMOST complete.

"Wow!" I say, exhilarated and peaceful and fulfilled. "What a head rush! That was a lot of information!"

I feel love and affection and deep pride emanating from Dad. It is the spiritual equivalent of being curled up on the Cloud Throne and having your belly rubbed and your ears scratched at the same time, while the peoples whisper sweet nothings to you.

"And you did it in record time!" Dad exclaims. "I wasn't sure how it would pan out at the start, but seriously! It took humans over fifteen millennia to figure it out, and it only took you dogs eight years!"

"Eight years," I marvel. "Back when I didn't understand time, it felt like a lot longer."

"I always knew you'd do it. I just didn't know how FAST you'd do it."

"Well, you know. I've always been super-fast."

Dad leans in close, and spiritually mushes his face against mine. "You are, and have always been, a Very Good Dog."

I wag my spirit-tail so hard that my whole spirit-butt is moving, and I may have spiritually piddled a tiny bit in all the excitement.

I realize in that timeless moment, that Dad is all the peoples, rolled into one. He is the people's life energy. And me? I am all the dogs. I can feel them, every dog that ever was, dancing and prancing and swirling around each other, beaming with joy and that inherent, unstoppable playfulness that is our unique contribution to the universe.

And then I hear the call: "PLAYDATE!"

I can't even describe it. All I can tell you is that it's beautiful. And they are all there. WE are all there. Together. As one. Animosities forgotten as though they never existed, fears and needs and misunderstandings banished and scoured away with the dissolution of the fleshly vessels we once inhabited, leaving only our true selves.

We are all, collectively, true dogs.

I am in them, and they are in me, and we are one, and the whole universe is just one big, warm, puppy pile.

Kind of like when I first tasted the Meat Turds of Ecstasy, and the Root Paste of Mystery, and the Gravy of Transcendence. And I guess the Sweetpeas too. Because it wouldn't be the same without them.

And that makes me think...

"But, wait," I say, pulling back from that amazing moment. "What about Gravy? What about the cats? Are they going to transcend too?"

"Everyone has their own journey to make," Dad says. "Obviously, humans took a long time to complete theirs—we made a lot of detours, but we got there eventually. And, of course, our best friends—the dogs—came along right behind us. And now it is the cats' turn to make their journey."

"Soooooo..."

"Well, they've just now started."

"Started what?" I ask. "How does this all work? What's the journey about?"

Dad kneels down and we are face to face and he gently rubs my neck, but he's looking past me as he says, "It's about learning how to love. And it starts with knowing that YOU are loved, and loved unconditionally. Only by knowing it and accepting it can you reflect it to others."

I frown. "I think we had a bit of a problem with that."

"Well, everyone does, in their own ways. Humans certainly did. It's a challenging thing to believe in, when you're stuck in a physical reality. Physical reality requires beings to be self-centered for survival. And love is a hard thing to learn when you're in that state."

"Oh dear," I say. "The cats are super good at being self-centered for survival. Does that mean they don't know how to love?"

"These things take time. They're figuring it out as we speak. Look!" He nods to where he's been looking behind me, and I turn to see Gravy, still crouching there, mid-caterwaul with her hair all standing on end.

"Yeah, I'm looking. She just looks terrified."

"Look...CLOSER."

And as he says that last word, it's like my mind bolts forward, zooming dizzyingly close to Gravy. But it's not like when you look real close at something and can only focus on a tiny bit of it. No, as I zoom in close, I can see ALL of her, right down to her soul.

Dancing swirls of light in so many different colors that I don't even know their names. And the light seems to have substance, like a mist, or a cloud, and there are tendrils of it that extend out from Gravy, as though pulling her in different directions.

I see two of these tendrils distinctly. One is a deeply orange tendril shooting off, seeming to try to PULL Gravy away from me, and I know that it is her Prime Directive. Her inborn, innate, primal fear of pain and death, telling her to flee. To survive.

But...she hasn't fled yet.

And I see why.

Because that other tendril, which is as blue and radiant as a clear spring sky...it's attached to ME. It's been attached to me since the day that she heard my voice as a squinty-eyed little newborn kitten. And she came by that attachment honestly. She inherited it from her father's soul.

My heart beams out of my chest—or maybe it's my spirit. I feel like I'm going to explode, but in a really good way. "OHMIGOSH," I exclaim breathlessly. "Gravy...really does...LOVE me!"

"Just like Sweetpea loved you. So you see? The cats have already started their journey."

I swing around to look at Dad. "So, what's next? How do we help them get over here with us?"

"Well, that remains to be seen. Who knows what challenges they will face? All that matters is that you're there for them, just like we were there for you, as you were figuring it out. That is the process, Mash. Once a life energy is fully transcended, they have to turn around and help the next one through. Luckily for you, cats are very sensitive to spiritual things, which is why we went through Sweetpea to help you guys."

"Can I still talk to Gravy?"

"You're not fully crossed over yet," Dad answers. "But soon, you won't be able to affect their reality anymore. You only have one chance to say what you need to say to Gravy. Once you're removed from their reality, you'll only be able to whisper, and suggest, and hint, and lead—if you can find a cat that's willing to listen."

I stare at Gravy, mulling things over. "What should I tell her?"

"Whatever you think the cats need to know for their journey."

I take a deep breath. By which I mean that I kind of spiritually pull myself together. "Okay. I think I'm ready." I glance back at Dad. "How long will I have?"

Dad's shoulders just bob in a shrug. "I don't know. But you'll feel it."

"Soooo..." I cock my head to one side. "How do I do this? Is there like a secret passcode to get to the other side of the veil?"

Dad chuckles softly and I feel the warmth of his touch on my flanks, firm, but gentle. "The barrier is still passable, but only for a bit. All you have to do is...push."

And as he says it, I feel myself propelled forward, though I don't actually move. All at once, Gravy churns into motion in front of me, as though suddenly unfrozen, and I'm back in her reality.

"Oh shit!" She caterwauls, sidestepping away from me. "Why is your head hanging in the middle of the air? What happened to the rest of you?!"

"Gravy," I say, trying to break through her panic. "Gravy, listen to me."

She's still inching away from me, and I can tell she's on the verge of breaking into a run, and probably heading for one of her Safe

Houses, just like Sweetpea did when this happened so many years ago. "Nope! Big nope! Way too freaky! Can't handle it!"

"Be calm, Gravy," I soothe. "Everything is going to be okay, but I don't have much time, and I need you to listen to me." Already, I can feel myself being sucked back across the veil, like being caught in the current of a river that's pulling me away from her.

"Aah!" she wails. "I don't know if I can do that! My brain is on fire!"

"Your brain's not on fire, Gravy, that's just your Prime Directive. And it's not necessary. There's nothing to be afraid of."

"The fuck there's not! You're a floating head!"

I sigh. "Geez, you sound just like your father. Gravy, come on. Can't you just be chill for one minute? I have something REALLY important to say." Inspiration strikes me. Because if there's anything I know about cats, it's that just about the only way they'll overcome their Prime Directive is if their curiosity is strong enough. "It's a really important secret that you have to know and make sure all the other cats know."

Gravy blinks a few times. But she's stopped backing up. "A...secret, you say?"

Got her.

I lower my voice to a mysterious whisper. "Yes. A great, cosmic secret. Super important. And you have to hear it right now, or you'll never know what it is."

Her fluffy tail lashes from side to side a few times. She glances around, her ears twitching. "Alright. Fine. I'm listening."

"Are you sure? I don't want you to forget this."

Her ears flatten. "Yes, dammit, I'm sure! Spit it out!"

I almost laugh, but that would have ruined the mysterious vibe I have going. And there isn't much time left—I can feel myself fading from her reality. So I tell her the thing that every life energy needs to know to complete its journey.

"Remember that you are loved—no matter what. And remember to love others—no matter what." And then, just as an afterthought, right before I'm sucked back across the barrier, I add: "And, you know, maybe try not to murder things just for funsies, you know?"

Just before I fully cross over, I see her ears flatten and I hear her say, "What? Are you serious? Did I hear that last part right? I really need you to say that last part again, if you really meant it. But, you know, if you didn't mean it, then don't say anything at all..."

On the other side of the veil, I look at my friend, filled with love for her, and for all cats. And compassion for them, knowing the hard road they are about to go down. And maybe a little bit of good-humored exasperation.

I laugh, because that's really all you can do. And Dad and the peoples laugh with me.

"Cats," I say, still chuckling. "Whoo-boy. This one might take a while."

The End

About The Author

D.J. Molles became a New York Times and USA today bestselling author while working full time as a police officer. He's since traded his badge for a keyboard to produce over 20 titles. When he's not writing, he's taking steps to make his North Carolina property self-sustainable, and training to be at least half as hard to kill as Lee Harden (his most popular protagonist). Molles also enjoys playing his guitar and drums, drawing, cooking, and "shredding that green pow" on his Onewheel.

Most nights you can find him sitting on the couch surrounded by his family and three dogs, two of which are the inspirations behind Banger and Mash. The third came later, but is still special since she is named after Rony, the brave heroine in *A Harvest of Ash and Blood*. However, she is definitely *not* brave and prefers to take a back seat to the action. So she won't be saving the world anytime soon.

Roxy (Banger)

Cheeto (Sweetpea)

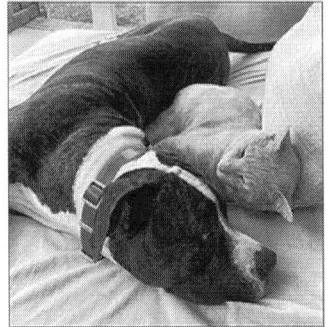

Blitzen (Mash)

Also by D.J. Molles

A Harvest of Ash and Blood
The Valley: A Lee Harden Novel
The Santas
Wolves
The Remaining Series
Lee Harden Series
Godbreaker Trilogy
A Grower's War Series
...and more at **djmolles.com!**

Printed in Great Britain
by Amazon